Reading Geoffrey (

CW01621326

Reading Geoffrey Chaucer: An Introduction offers students, general readers, and teachers an accessible series of essays on select works by Chaucer that emphasizes how those works' deepest concerns and most fraught complexities remain urgently relevant in our present day. Each chapter connects Chaucer's world with particular problems of our own, such as autocratic patriarchal social orders and geopolitical religious/racial conflict. Introducing modern critical approaches to those problems – gender studies and postcolonial theory, for example – each chapter provides in-depth discussion of how Chaucer explores their nature, implications, and consequences by way of his distinctive literary idiom. Texts covered include the General Prologue of the *Canterbury Tales* and the tales told by the Knight, Miller, Man of Law, Wife of Bath, Pardoner, and Prioress and the *House of Fame*, *Legend of Good Women*, and *Troilus and Criseyde*. Each chapter is self-contained, supplying essential backgrounds along with full summaries of the works under discussion. But the book is also criss-crossed with recurrent inquiries, which collectively trace some of the most characteristic qualities of Chaucer's writing. With its unusual combination of breadth and depth, this introduction to Chaucer helps readers at all levels of familiarity appreciate why his work continues to matter.

Robert J. Meyer-Lee (PhD Yale, English) is Professor of English at Agnes Scott College. He is author of *The Problem of Literary Value* (2023), *Literary Value and Social Identity in the Canterbury Tales* (2019), and *Poets and Power from Chaucer to Wyatt* (2007); editor (with Catherine Sanok) of *The Medieval Literary: Beyond Form* (2018); and author of numerous articles on Chaucer, fifteenth-century poetry, and literary value. He was an editor of *JEGP* and a trustee of the New Chaucer Society and is a recipient of the Medieval Academy Van Courtlandt Elliott Prize.

Reading Literature Today

Reading James Joyce
An Introduction
A. Nicholas Fargnoli and Michael Patrick Gillespie

Reading John Milton
An Introduction
David Currell

Reading Oscar Wilde
An Introduction
Michael Patrick Gillespie

Reading Geoffrey Chaucer
An Introduction
Robert J. Meyer-Lee

For more information on this series, please visit https://www.routledge.com/Reading-Literature/book-series/RLT

Reading Geoffrey Chaucer
An Introduction

Robert J. Meyer-Lee

Routledge
Taylor & Francis Group
NEW YORK AND LONDON

Designed cover image: Getty Images

First published 2025
by Routledge
605 Third Avenue, New York, NY 10158

and by Routledge
4 Park Square, Milton Park, Abingdon, Oxon, OX14 4RN

Routledge is an imprint of the Taylor & Francis Group, an informa business

© 2025 Robert J. Meyer-Lee

The right of Robert J. Meyer-Lee to be identified as author of this work has been asserted in accordance with sections 77 and 78 of the Copyright, Designs and Patents Act 1988.

All rights reserved. No part of this book may be reprinted or reproduced or utilised in any form or by any electronic, mechanical, or other means, now known or hereafter invented, including photocopying and recording, or in any information storage or retrieval system, without permission in writing from the publishers.

Trademark notice: Product or corporate names may be trademarks or registered trademarks, and are used only for identification and explanation without intent to infringe.

ISBN: 978-1-032-22613-2 (hbk)
ISBN: 978-1-032-22577-7 (pbk)
ISBN: 978-1-003-27331-8 (ebk)

DOI: 10.4324/9781003273318

Typeset in Sabon
by SPi Technologies India Pvt Ltd (Straive)

Contents

Preface: User Manual for This Book

To students and general readers (and everyone else)

What does this book have to offer that the many existing Chaucer handbooks, companions, and introductions do not? That's ultimately for you to answer. But I can state my basic aim, which is to provide a set of explorative inquiries into select works by Chaucer, accessible to those at any level of familiarity with the poet, that seek to discover how some of those works' deepest concerns and most fraught complexities remain urgently relevant in our present day.

Toward this end, I have emphasized depth over breadth. While many Chaucer auxiliaries supply brief coverage of all or most of Chaucer's writings and/or a broad range of background information or critical approaches, this book is more selective in those respects. My decisions about which writings to cover have been guided by my sense of which set would both represent the variety of Chaucer's work and best convey his bearing on an array of present-day concerns. Consequently, while there are chapters on several of his greatest hits, like the Wife of Bath's Prologue and Tale, others of his most celebrated works do not make an appearance, their place taken instead by some of his most notorious, such as the Prioress's Tale. In turn, the same present-day concerns that have determined my choice of works have dictated the background information that I include and critical approaches that I take. In each chapter, I supply only the background information required to connect the specific present-day concerns at issue with Chaucer's fourteenth-century world. And I take critical approaches that have proven fruitful for understanding the underlying complexities of those concerns (such as women's, gender, and sexuality studies; critical race and postcolonial studies; and poststructuralism).

I have sought to make each chapter self-contained. The book's introduction places the rationale for this project under some necessary self-scrutiny and defines key ideas and questions that inform the chapters that follow. But it need not be read beforehand. At the cost of some repetition, each chapter incorporates whatever it needs from the introduction, leaving you the choice to take up the introduction's more expansive treatments of those matters. Likewise, each chapter provides germane background information and explanations of its critical approaches regardless of how much of that may appear in other chapters. I've also sought, however, to make this book something more than the sum of its parts. By regularly returning to some topics even while considering different ones across the chapters, I've tried to convey the nature and significance of some of Chaucer's characteristic creative habits, thematic obsessions, and manners of engaging with his world as well as their bearing on our present. Nonetheless, each chapter has its own, independent takeaway. Each contributes to that overall picture but does not require it.

Except for the first, each chapter has the same basic structure. Its initial sections identify the present-day concerns at issue and indicate their connection with Chaucer's world. A full summary of the work under focus follows, along with the information about its genre and sources that is important for the ensuing discussion. The aim of these sections is to be inclusive of readers at all levels of Chaucer familiarity, serving to put us all on the same page, so to speak. The remainder of each chapter explores the work's bearing on the present-day concerns raised at its outset, introducing critical approaches and applying them to an examination of Chaucer's text, considering related issues where relevant, and tracing their past and present ramifications. (This sequence is repeated in those chapters that consider two works.) The point of all this is not, however, to arrive at a definite interpretation. Although I haven't been shy about presenting my views, I've tried to resist the temptation to urge you to see the text exactly as I see it. Instead, my aim has been to lead you into a particular interpretive arena and show you where the cruxes, ambiguities, and other challenges lie, in order to suggest how your own interpretation has substantial stakes for the present-day concerns at issue.

To Chaucer scholars and teachers (and everyone else)

There may be moments of interpretive originality in this book, but that, to paraphrase the Pardoner, has not been my intent. The approaches that I've foregrounded all have significant precedents in Chaucer studies, ones that I expect scholarly readers will readily recognize. These precedents inform the focus, critical methods and theories, and even specific readings of each chapter. As I've not aimed to make original arguments, and as I've sought to make this book accessible even to beginning students, I've not supplied the sort of critical apparatus that an audience of professional Chaucerians would expect. Instead, I've limited my explicit acknowledgements mostly to those occasions when I've been aware of a very specific debt. This awareness has certainly been imperfect. Please accept my apologies for the inevitable, inadvertent oversights.

My primary objective has been to make this book useful to teachers of Chaucer: as a means for generating students' excitement about a poet toward whom they might be predisposed to feel hesitation or hostility, as a prompt for classroom discussion that facilitates the depth and complexity for which teachers strive, and – in its form as a set of accessible interpretive essays that may be partnered with scholarly studies proper – as a resource for student papers and other projects. As you may have noticed, this objective does not include an attempt to supply a representative survey of critical opinions about the works and issues covered. Most likely, therefore, you'll find some of the views that I've chosen to highlight wrongheaded or even just wrong. My hope is that you'll nonetheless appreciate how those views may be fruitfully provocative. Regardless of whether a classroom discussion determines that this book is totally off base or that it may have a point, my basic aim – to make Chaucer interesting to those students – will be met.

A note on quotations

All my quotations of Chaucer come from *The Norton Chaucer*, edited by David Lawton, W. W. Norton (2019), and are cited by line numbers and, where necessary, book or fragment. This student edition provides a helpfully normalized version of Chaucer's text, along with a cogent tutorial on his language and a generous amount of background information, with even more available online. There are many excellent resources available for additional assistance with Chaucer's language as well as for more extensive background on him and his world. Some of these are on the list of essential resources that follows the final chapter. Throughout, I gloss quotations of Chaucer in a way that's intended to make them accessible to all readers, albeit at the cost of some intrusiveness. My glosses often repeat Lawton's, although in some cases I've chosen alternative senses.

Acknowledgements

Initial thanks must go to Michelle Salyga, senior editor at Routledge, for reaching out to me for this project and for her subsequent enthusiasm and confidence. Agnes Scott College provided essential financial support in the form of two Holder Fund for Faculty Innovation Grants.

My completion of the book has rested on three foundations. First are the three decades of conversations that I've had with dozens of generous colleagues. I cannot hope to provide here the recognition that these many individuals deserve, so I'll limit myself to just four: Frank Grady, whose assistance on the idea of this book, as well as several of its details, has been indispensable, and Charlotte Artese, Lisa Lampert-Weissig, and Catherine Sanok, whose conversations at crucial junctures supplied much needed encouragement. The second foundation is perhaps self-evident: most of this book's motivation and much of its content owe a profound debt to the students in my Chaucer courses at several institutions and especially to those in Agnes Scott's "Gender, Sexuality, and the *Canterbury Tales*." Finally, I owe thanks to Lucas, Jackson, and Gabriel Meyer-Lee, who have graciously served as guinea pig students for the book and the ideas that no doubt trickled down into too many dinner-table conversations, and to Elaine Meyer-Lee, who, despite the burden of her overwhelming, much more important work, supplied unwavering support in all the ways that matter most.

Introduction

Why Read Chaucer Now?

Chances are that you, the readers of this sentence, may readily answer the above question with some variation of the response, "Because I'm required to." As much as I hope that some of you have voluntarily looked into a Chaucer edition out of some interest of your own – whether artistic, intellectual, recreational, etc. – I must acknowledge that most of you have likely encountered Chaucer in some sort of mandated academic context, as with most of the other canonical, dead white male literary authors. The more accurate if less graceful form of this Introduction's question would therefore be: why are you still being asked to read Chaucer in today's academic context?

There is much to unpack in that question, and indeed this book as a whole represents my attempt to perform that unpacking in light of present-day concerns. One simple answer, however, would cite the inertia of an institutionalized literary status quo: you're obliged to read Chaucer because those so requiring you were themselves so obliged, and so forth down many generations of students and teachers, always on the underlying if not always articulated pretext that "we must continue to study the great authors because they are great." For those past generations, that circular reasoning may have provided enough impetus to lead eventually to less mindless rationales. But today we are rightly more skeptical of such knee-jerk perpetuations of the status quo. In particular, noticing that what has constituted the authoritative set of "great authors" has been mostly the aforementioned dead white males, we have with good reason dissected the adjective "great," exposing its assumptions, prejudices, and oppressive impacts. Without question, the presumed importance of Chaucer's writings should not escape that dissection.

This topic – the ideological complicity of Chaucer's writings – is one that I'll return to at the end of this Introduction. For now, I'll assume that those asking you to read Chaucer are fully aware of that complicity and that at the very least they do not wish to perpetuate its deleterious effects. Their (and my) argument must be, then, that something about Chaucer's writings

DOI: 10.4324/9781003273318-1

justifies their continued allotment of space within the ever-more-crowded syllabus of Anglophone literary academia, despite their ideological baggage. In what follows, I'll seek to answer the question of what that something might be and along the way establish some of this book's defining ideas.

The value of literature: a proposal

In addressing the question of what justifies the continued presence of Chaucer in university curricula, some of his apologists may cite Chaucer's self-evident foundational position within the tradition of Anglophone literature. Certainly, for over six hundred years, his writings have been acknowledged as crucially generative by an unbroken line of other authors, from his fourteenth-century friend and literary competitor John Gower up through twenty-first-century novelist, playwright, and essayist Zadie Smith. If we care about writers such as Smith, this reasoning goes, we must also care about Chaucer. Yet, while there's an undeniable facticity to this sort of literary historical justification, it prompts the more basic question of what it is that other authors find so generative in Chaucer's writings and whether that in turn really justifies their continued study – for surely Smith may be amply appreciated without recourse to Chaucer. This book as a whole represents an inquiry into this "what" (although I can't, of course, speak for Smith or any other author).

Such an enterprise cannot proceed without some larger assumptions about the purpose or usefulness of any literary work whatsoever.[1] We might query, for example, whether it's more important that a literary work entertain or enlighten us or whether it must do both simultaneously, as in the formula for judging the stories told by the pilgrims in the *Canterbury Tales*: "Tales of best sentence [wisdom] and most solas [pleasure]" (1.798). In turn, we might wonder about the criteria that define those options. So, for entertainment value, we might weigh the relative merits of, say, laughter or weeping, and for enlightenment, of political impact or spiritual revitalization. Plainly, these matters quickly and exponentially ramify in scope and complexity, and so they may easily by themselves serve as the topic of a much longer book than this one. To stay on course, then, I offer the following proposition, which I hope is common enough to be granted the benefit of doubt.

When in the process of reading we activate the words of a literary work, we beckon into our minds sentences that we did not ourselves compose. We further take these sentences as cues for imagining something more than precisely those words themselves (say, the landscape of medieval England that they describe), and, in following those cues, we necessarily add something of ourselves (say, the exact sound the described wind makes, for which we draw on our own experience). In this way, the reading of a literary work involves a creative interaction of some intimacy with...whom or what? Not exactly another person, as anyone who's written a story that others go on to interpret in rather unexpected ways will readily acknowledge. More precisely, then, through the mediation of language, genre, literary devices, etc., in reading literature we interweave portions of ourselves with *otherness* generally – another time, place, culture, way of speaking, consciousness, etc. We are, moreover, able to recognize each dimension of this potentially vast array of otherness as such because we necessarily situate it within a larger context of *sameness* (for example, the culture that differs from our own but is nonetheless recognizable to us as a culture). By way of this often intricate, deeply internalized play of similarity and difference, literary works hold enormous potential for casting into clarifying relief myriad aspects of ourselves and our situations while conveying almost experiential awareness – practical, emotional, ethical, intellectual, etc. – of that which is alien to our experience.

If this proposition is acceptable (and for a full-length account of a similar view, see Attridge 2015), then it follows that *for any given reader, situated within a specific context*, some literary works tap this potential more than others. The italicized qualification here is crucial. On the one hand, that qualification sweeps away the supposition that a particular literary work may intrinsically or universally better facilitate a reader's dance with otherness. That supposition would quickly restore the mystifications of canonicity that, as recent decades have confirmed, we are better off without. On the other hand, while the qualification registers the inevitable idiosyncrasies of the situation of reading and aesthetic preference (as evidenced by, say, readers' comments on Amazon), it leaves room for common experiences. In particular, it recognizes the many, various, and intersecting contingencies that shape our distinct experiences of ourselves and our surroundings (time, place, motivation, gender, race, class, ability, sexuality, etc.). While those contingences are perhaps unique in their exact constellations, each of us necessarily shares them in some combination and to some degree with some number of others. The premise of this book is that for a substantial number of individuals living within the contingencies that shape our experience of the world today, the self/other energies that an encounter with Chaucer's works may unleash remain considerable.

Relatability and alterity: the General Prologue's portrait of the Sergeant of Law

One explanation for why Chaucer's works continue to have this potential is suggested by the fact that ever since something like "the medieval" has been distinguishable from "the modern," numerous readers have remarked upon how Chaucer's writings seem uncannily to partake of both. For these readers, Chaucer's works feel linguistically, artistically, and culturally alien to their respective presents but at the same time possess a generous quantity of what many students today term *relatability*. Although where and how this bidirectional pull occurs in Chaucer's writings vary from reader to reader, the general experience remains widespread.

A very brief example that strikes me in this fashion occurs within the description of the "Sergeant of the Lawe" (1.306), one of the storytelling pilgrims on the journey to Canterbury, about whom the narrator remarks, "Nowher so bisy a man as he ther nas; / And yet he semed bisier than he was" (1.321–22). Obviously, this sentence's spelling and obsolete constructions such as "nas" ("was not") will feel alien to modern readers, as will have the preceding lines' detail regarding the Sergeant's professional qualities and activities, which is filled with references to now obscure legal institutions and practices. But once we capture the gist of the sentence – that this exceptionally busy, high-status lawyer may not in fact be as busy as he appears – we may recall similar vague suspicions about socially prominent professionals that we in our modern experiences have harbored: for example, that their apparent competence, industry, and importance may be, to some uncertain degree, a self-promotional pose. For lawyers specifically, we may recollect our nagging unease with the fact that we are paying them to be on our side, and hence their presenting the appearance of being an effective advocate is a necessary aspect of their job. The stereotype of the ambulance-chasing lawyer and a series of bad lawyer jokes are only a few steps away.

I'm perhaps giving away my own feelings about lawyers here (for which I apologize to all the many hardworking, genuinely caring legal professionals upon whom we all depend). But that is the point of the illustration. The sentence triggers a pronounced recognition of an element of my own experience, but it does so only once I have waded through the alien quality – the *alterity* – of some of the details of Chaucer's language and society. I see my own ambivalences toward lawyers, ambivalences that I perhaps had not before fully appreciated, suddenly reflected back at me, but only once I've constructed that mirror out of the late medieval materials of the text. Indeed, the impact of the self-recognition may be propelled by the very effort put into that construction, since the ease of familiarity when no such effort is required may smooth over the provocation. In this way, the dance with otherness enabled by Chaucer's writings can be especially intense, as deep alterity continually ricochets into correspondingly deep relatability. The primary aim of the following chapters is to initiate this sort of dance in respect to particular works, to provoke reverberations between various dimensions of alterity – Chaucer's late medieval artistry, society, culture, language, etc. – and present-day concerns (of rather more weight than my feelings about lawyers).

Chauceer's laconic profundity

Exactly how it is that Chaucer's works can seem so relatable notwithstanding their unfamiliarity is another topic to which an entire book could be devoted. Surely, Chaucer's shrewd manipulations of voice, skill at characterization, and deployment of irony encourage this perception. This book will also often notice a less easy-to-name technique, which I'll term *laconic profundity*. This label denotes the way in which Chaucer's writings so often invoke very weighty, even fraught questions with very little fuss or difficulty. Such questions seem to arise as a sort of side effect of, rather than the underlying motivation behind, a particular moment of narration or dialogue, a moment that may in some cases seem lighthearted or whimsical. For example, the sentence from the Sergeant's description initially comes across as a winking, enigmatic, witty aside – a throwaway remark of the narrator's merely intended to elicit a chuckle. But the comment's more profound recognitions of the legal system's potential for corruption and of the ethical challenges involved in practicing law readily bubble to the surface. And they do so – once we've traversed the alterities of Chaucer's language and society – almost effortlessly, in our enjoyment of the remark's humor. (In this respect, a point of contrast is the pervasive profundities of John Milton's *Paradise Lost*, which often demand maximum readerly effort.)

This technique typically involves evoking questions of some depth, usually implicitly, without subsequently providing definitive answers, leaving open not only the presumed proper responses but also the precise nature and reach of the questions themselves. In the sentence from the Sergeant's description, while there's a clear insinuation of something amiss about the Sergeant's activities, precisely what that is, how far it extends beyond the specific individual to entire institutions, and how or even whether we ought to respond are left unstated. In my particular response, I've filled in some of these gaps, as all readers necessarily will do out of their own experiences. But in that very process of filling-in, we register on some level the fact that all we really know for certain is that one observer, the narrator, believes the Sergeant is not as busy as he seems to be. Any more definitive implications rest upon shaky ground, and yet the sentence plainly seems to beckon us to some such implications. For reasons such as these, this technique of Chaucer's has often been described as *ambiguity*, although it does not so much involve, say, ambiguity of character or plot as the ambiguity of the larger implications that we are to take from plot, character, imagery, genre, etc., even as the presence of such larger implications seems unmistakably signaled.

This book provides several opportunities to engage with more capacious, extended, complex, and weightier instances of this technique in Chaucer's writings. But already my response to the sentence in the Sergeant's description illustrates how this sort of ambiguity – this laconic profundity – enables Chaucer's weighty questions to coincide with twenty-first-century readers' weighty questions. The unobtrusiveness and ambiguity of Chaucer's questions give the text a sponge-like quality, enabling it readily to absorb corresponding questions of our own. In this way, Chaucer continues to matter because many of the concerns that mattered to him also become concerns that matter to us.

This is not to say, however, that Chaucer's texts have any special claim on laconic profundity or, even more so, alterity/relatability. It would not be difficult to find similar features across a range of narrative works past and present. Various forms of laconic profundity are, for example, ubiquitous in film and television, where the technique is evident in how, say, a particular *mise-en-scène* or moment of dialogue easily suggests depths of meaning of ambiguous nature (as instanced *ad nauseam*, for example, in the 1979 film *Apocalypse Now*). And fans of Shakespeare will certainly recognize the powerful coincidence of alterity and relatability in their experiences of his plays. But to acknowledge Chaucer's lack of uniqueness in these respects is also to recognize those features of his works that readers today continue to appreciate in general. Not surprisingly, I find these features to evoke effects of great nuance more often in Chaucer's works than in most other narrative works from his day to ours. But in this, as in all such judgments, you must be the final arbiter.

The "meaning of life" and *The Hunger Games*

The list of weighty questions that Chaucer's writings invoke by way of laconic profundity and through other means is long and diverse. Many of its weightiest entries, however, may be collected under the rubric "the meaning of life." Although that phrase is surely among the wooliest of clichés, it nonetheless supplies focus to a broad set of urgent concerns if we add a dose of specificity to the designations of "meaning" and "life." Let us take "life" to denote no more and no less than our physical, corporeal existence, the material realities of birth, hunger, pleasure, suffering, sensation, death, etc. – what contemporary Italian philosopher Giorgio Agamben has termed "bare life." Let us take "meaning," then, to denote the incorporeal or, more generally, nonmaterial ideas, ideals, and values (for example, the idea of race, the ideal of equity, the value of integrity) that we cannot touch and yet which altogether seem comprehensively to shape our experience of "life." Although this definition is perhaps more accurately termed the nature, significance, value, or purpose of life, I will stick to "meaning" for the sake of familiarity and also to emphasize the way in which we often strive to articulate life's meaning in the form of some overarching organizing principles, as in the "do unto others" golden rule. The phrase "the meaning of life" then specifically designates the *relations* between our material existence and nonmaterial ideas, ideals, and values, relations which, obviously, are enormously complex, ever evolving, and of the highest stakes there are.

The challenges that these relations may present are perhaps most keenly felt when the perceived demands or attractions of life seem in some conflict with the key ideas, ideals, or values that one perceives, however cogently, as constituting life's significance and purpose. Literature, or art more generally, has long meditated upon, staged, and provoked exactly this conflict, which appears everywhere in artistic productions as far back as we have records of them (as with, say, the ancient Mesopotamian epic *Gilgamesh*). Chaucer was intensely interested in this conflict in its many and diverse manifestations, and the rest of this book will regularly work through examples of his engagements with it. For purposes of initial elaboration, however, let's consider a relatively straightforward instance from twenty-first-century American popular culture. Suzanne Collins's *Hunger Games*, obviously, is wholly premised on the conflict, depicting with its titular Games a situation in which children are seemingly constrained to prioritize life – specifically, physical survival – above all other principles, even if this entails killing all twenty-three of the other child participants, including the other participant from one's own home district.

To choose just one of the novel's many succinct stagings of this conflict, we may recall the conversation between Katniss and Peeta, the main protagonists, on the rooftop of the training center on the night before they are to enter the arena. Peeta attempts to express to Katniss his struggle with identity and principle in the face of the imminent death match. "I don't want them to change me in there," he insists. Katniss, neither sharing nor understanding what she silently conceives of as his concern with "purity of self," eventually tells him to "care about…staying alive" (141–42). Her remark triggers an abrupt emotional break between the two, shattering whatever (seemingly hopeless) solidarity they had achieved. Peeta appeared desperately to want his soon-to-be terminated life (as he believes) to amount to more than just life, and he turned to Katniss for some clarity about what that intangible something might be. But she sees such longing for meaning as a dangerous distraction from the physical reality of the imperative of survival.

This passage illustrates several aspects of the conflict latent in the phrase "the meaning of life." First, the conflict seems to pivot on the question of whether nonmaterial ideas, ideals, and values (Peeta: "I want to die as myself") or material existence (Katniss: "but who cares, Peeta?") is the more foundational truth (141–42). Second, for the nonmaterial to take priority, some sort of persuasive discourse with which individuals may articulate their inner truths appears to be required, a discourse that Peeta here, as is often the case in general, struggles to formulate. Third, and in contrast, the priority of material existence not only does not seem to demand such a discourse but rather appears actively hostile to it, insisting on its status as self-evident reality. Finally, despite the apparently two-sided nature of this conflict as so far described, a moment's consideration discloses that it's not really one between the nonmaterial and material, between meaning and life, but rather between different ways of conceiving of each side in relation to the other within a particular socio-political context. Peeta, Katniss, and all those under the rule of the Capitol live within a system in which, officially, the sovereign authority of the state is the master value to which all things material are subject, as signified most definitively through its power to destroy the bodies of twenty-three children each year. Peeta seems to be proposing competing sources of abstract authority over corporeal life, that of the state versus that of personal authenticity, and wants his death to be meaningful in respect to the latter rather than the former. Katniss, in contrast, sees no authority but that of the state, within which system of ideas, ideals, and values she wishes to preserve life by both strategic adaptation to and resistance of that authority.

Ideology

At this juncture, I should acknowledge more explicitly some of the theoretical resources that I've been drawing upon and which will inform, often silently, the discussions of Chaucer that follow. There is, of course, a very long intellectual tradition that considers the nature of the relations between what I've been designating the material and nonmaterial, which more or less corresponds to the philosophical distinction between the *physical* and *metaphysical* or between the *sensible* and *intelligible*. The ancient Greek philosopher Plato represents the fountainhead of one line of thought privileging the latter elements of the pairs, whereas his student Aristotle supplied seminal recalibrations of his views. My discussion has incorporated strands of the critical recrafting of this tradition performed by various twentieth-century thinkers, many of them French. These include Jacques Derrida, who among other interventions critiques the binary, categorical distinction between the material and nonmaterial, and Michel Foucault, whose notions of discourse, authority, and biopower are evident in my comments on *The Hunger Games* (and who is a key influence on Agamben).

Most directly, I have drawn on Louis Althusser (one of Foucault's teachers). My gloss of the phrase "the meaning of life" as "the relations between our material existence and nonmaterial ideas, ideals, and values" is a simplified version of Althusser's famous definition of *ideology* as the "representation of the imaginary relationship of individuals to their real conditions of existence" (Althusser 2001, 109).

Cued by Althusser, we may name views about the meaning of life, whether tacitly assumed or explicitly argued, as *ideological positions*. And we may understand reflective considerations of such positions – which I am proposing that Chaucer's writings offer, as does much other literature, such as *The Hunger Games* – as meditations, perhaps critical ones, upon ideologies within which their authors are in some way enmeshed. Importantly, therefore, the term *ideology* as I use it in this book denotes not only its narrow political senses (as in "left-wing ideology" or "white supremacist ideology") but also its broadest ones, which include, say, the ideas, ideals, and values of a religion, of so-called common sense, and of general perceptions of what's normal, natural, expected, desirable, ordinary, etc. Thus construed, ideology suffuses not just our explicit assertions of value but also our most mundane, everyday actions, since from the moment that we decide each day to get out of bed (or not) we are attributing meaning – significance, value, and purpose – to our material existence. Each of us is hence inescapably ideological, and no more so than in those instances when we believe that we are not – as when we think, for example, "That's nature, not ideology." In the passage from *The Hunger Games*, Peeta is struggling to articulate a counter-ideology that is worth dying for, in confrontation with the official state ideology that demands that he fight for his life. In contrast, Katniss, in her very focus on survival, is perpetuating that state ideology, and over the course of the trilogy her growing awareness of competing ideologies becomes one of the main drivers of the plot.

In sum: what this book does

In one form or another, each of the chapters that follow explores some of the *ideological fault lines* that Chaucer evokes, sometimes by way of laconic profundity. These are those places where a dominant ideological system's underlying incoherencies make themselves felt, often in a way with material, physical consequences for those identities that the ideology does not favor. And they are those places where competing ideologies collide, with likewise material consequences. While countless works of literature meditate upon such fault lines, Chaucer is obsessively drawn to them as a source of inspiration. Through the play of alterity and relatability, we will work through the continuities and discontinuities between what was ideologically broken for him and what remains broken for us.[2]

In a nutshell, this book proposes that one reason to continue to read Chaucer today is that his writings offer complex, multifarious, ideologically reflective meditations upon somehow fractured meanings of life, that is, upon the vexed relations between material existence and nonmaterial ideas, ideals, and values. The book suggests that these meditations continue to resonate with urgent concerns of the present, because of both the nature of the issues that Chaucer raises and the characteristic manners in which he explores them. Not everyone, of course, will find Chaucer's writings valuable for these reasons or accessible in these ways. Some may discover different appeals in them, and others, I must admit, will put them aside as soon as they can. My aim is to open up enough possibilities for connecting to Chaucer's writings for you to find them at least worth the time and effort they require.

P.S.: Chaucer's complicity and how it figures in this book

As I recalled at the outset of this Introduction, for as long as there has been a Eurocentric canon of dead white male literary authors, Chaucer has featured prominently among them (or, more accurately, among a vaguely defined, shifting set of authors that has functioned as a canon, as there has never been an official canon as such). And for authors writing in English, he has been among the most prominent, the one who has indeed most often been celebrated as the fountainhead of the English tradition of canonical literature. By itself, therefore, Chaucer's status in this respect makes him complicit in those ideologies that have been transmitted by this canon. We recognize now that the appreciation of these writers' artistic achievements was never wholly separable from assumptions about the superiority of the sex, race, and class that (until recently) the vast majority of the writers shared, assumptions that determined which writers were likely to gain an audience, or even be allowed to write, in the first place. Accordingly, accounts of literary history that have privileged authors such as Chaucer cannot be separated from the oppressive material history of the accompanying social orders that have granted privileges to some classes of humans at the expense of others.

This ideological function provides ample reason to challenge the cultural hegemony of the Eurocentric dead white male literary canon, a task that many have taken up in a range of ways with varying aims and success. (See, for example, Gates 1992, Mukherjee 2014, and, for Chaucer specifically, Miles and Watt 2020.) Yet obviously that reason alone doesn't provide a compelling rationale to stop reading any particular canonical author, at least no more so than the ideologies of male and white supremacy provide a reason not to be friends with any particular white male. One might query, then, whether a particular author's complicity amounts to something more than just guilt by association. In the case of Chaucer's writings, a clear-eyed assessment, even from the most avid of fans such as myself, must acknowledge that that charge has some merit. Chaucer's works, for all their considerable ambiguity and uncanny relatability, nonetheless transmit no small number of the prejudices that a prosperous, white, non-disabled (as far as we know) English Christian cis man in the fourteenth century would predictably possess. Those works therefore not only have been *used* for ideologically oppressive purposes but also – insofar as the twenty-first-century descendants of those fourteenth-century prejudices continue to justify today's systems of inequity – *participate* in those ideologies' perpetuation.

Whether Chaucer's writings are more or less detrimental in this respect than those of other dead white canonical male authors is surely a question generative of heated debate. Yet that question prompts the more general, fundamental, and difficult one of the nature of the demands to be placed on literature – or art more generally – in respect to politics, morality, social justice, etc. Should we teach and preserve only those works of literature that most align with the ideologies that we hold to be true and right? If so, who is this "we" – that is, who gets to choose those ideologies? (At the time of this Introduction's initial drafting, one such "we" wished to give academic priority to works of literature that reflect the insights of critical race theory, while another "we" actively sought to ban such works from school curricula.) Howsoever those ideologies are chosen, how should alignment with them be measured? And how ought we to respond to the inevitable presence of some degree of complicity within even the most aligned literary works, especially given the inevitable evolution of our ideological commitments over time? Or, if ideological alignment should not be the sole determiner of our literary choices, then what more limited role should it play (as it inescapably plays *some* role, especially when we believe it doesn't)? And what other criteria should we draw upon? For anyone who cares about both literature and justice, these are questions of the utmost concern. They're also ones that raise issues well beyond what I can hope to address adequately in this book.[3] Instead, then, to close this Introduction, I'll offer the following proposition for why Chaucer remains worth reading despite his complicity – and indeed because of it – and then describe the method of reading that this proposition entails.

As mentioned above, Chaucer very often finds inspiration in ideological fault lines, those places where a dominant ideology discloses its contradictions, repressions, or doublespeak or where different ideologies collide. Such fault lines frequently constitute the most potent source for the nuance and complexity of Chaucer's plots, characterizations, imagery, and themes, which in many instances otherwise just reflect the conventional literary repertoire of his day. We'll see, for example, that what animates a medieval romance of two noble kinsmen contending for the love of a princess (the Knight's Tale) is Chaucer's reflection upon the nature of patriarchal political authority, which the tale shows to rest upon the subjection of women. And we'll find at the center of a pious story about a miracle wrought by devotion to the Virgin Mary (the Prioress's Tale) a combustible conjunction between that devotion and brazenly brutal antisemitic hatred. In these instances and so many others, Chaucer seems to go out of his way to foreground such ideological fissures – and then, as typical of his *modus operandi* of laconic profundity, leaves his own attitude toward those fissures more or less inscrutable. Consequently, while many critics have understood the Knight's Tale to voice a critique of patriarchy, just as many have seen the tale as a celebration of it. And for every reader who has interpreted the Prioress's Tale as an exposure of Christianity's capacity for antisemitism, another has taken the tale to be a horrifically unapologetic instance of it. As one scholar has remarked (in this instance, about Chaucer's *House of Fame*), "it is Chaucer who remains the slipperiest author of all" (Colley 2021, 74).

I don't want to underestimate the importance of holding authors ideologically accountable for their writings. Yet at least in Chaucer's case, the determination of his accountability tends to alternate between being too self-evident (in that he plainly holds some of the views of his time and place that most today would reject out of hand) and too uncertain (in the characteristic difficulty of pinning him down to a single position). Moreover, for the task of ascertaining what we today might get out Chaucer's writings, it's more helpful to focus on the ideologies we wish to judge Chaucer for than on the nature of the judgments themselves. As I've suggested, because those writings so often call attention to ideological fault lines, what we may obtain from them, regardless of Chaucer's own ideological positions, is greater appreciation of the nature, scope, interactions, and implications of the ideologies at play. The simultaneously complex and accessible manner in which Chaucer delves into these fault lines makes his writings a potential source of acute insights into the modern counterparts to those ideologies, which continue, for better or worse, to shape our lives. To be sure, as I've conceded above, Chaucer's writings are not unique in this respect. Yet to gauge whether he remains worth reading, alongside or instead of other authors who similarly dwell within ideological fault lines, we must follow where he leads. What I am proposing, therefore, is that the very complicities of Chaucer's writings, when they invoke ideological fissures that continue to matter us, quite often serve as the signposts toward why those writings may also continue to matter.

This book thus pursues a method of reading both *with* and *against* Chaucer. It reads Chaucer sympathetically in its attempts to do justice to the nuances and complexities of his craft, providing a sense of the literary and intellectual engagements involved in the passages that it considers, as well as of the subtleties of their literary expression. But it does not hesitate to cast a wary, critical eye at the ideological possibilities at play in those same passages, remaining on guard in no small part precisely because of their literary sophistication. If one of the outcomes of this procedure is that you'll have gained greater cognizance of both the ideologies that you wish to resist and those that you wish to embrace, then this book will have accomplished its basic aim of explaining why reading Chaucer remains worthwhile.

Notes

1 These assumptions rest in turn upon how we determine what counts as "literary," which, while self-evident in some respects, proves quite difficult to define. I've explored this topic some in Meyer-Lee 2023.
2 For a similar approach to Chaucer's writings, although one that draws on Gloria Anzaldúa's concept of borderlands, see Schirmer 2022.
3 I take up some of these issues in Meyer-Lee 2023.

1 The *Canterbury Tales*

Overview and General Prologue

This chapter has two functions. First, it introduces the *Canterbury Tales* as whole, serving in that way as a sort of preface for the next five chapters, which cover selected parts of that work. Second, it makes this book's initial text-focused foray into the question of why Chaucer continues to matter today, applying some of the ideas from the book's Introduction to a close reading of the famous first sentence of the *Tales*. In particular, with an eye toward the modern critical approaches of the new materialisms and gender and sexuality studies, this section of the chapter explores the ambiguously profound implications of the sentence's conjunction of the realms of nature and spirit. This conjunction matters today, the chapter will conclude, since in one way or another we necessarily continue to confront its implications in our own lives.

The idea of the *Canterbury Tales* and its affordances

In her 2015 book *Forms: Whole, Rhythm, Hierarchy, Network*, Caroline Levine influentially imported the term *affordance* from design theory into the literary critical lexicon. She recognizes that in the same way that the shape and materials of objects afford particular uses – so, for example, the shape and material of a fork "affords stabbing and scooping" – the shape and materials of literature, that is, specific literary forms, also have particular affordances. So, a "sonnet, brief and condensed, best affords a single idea or experience…while the triple-decker novel affords elaborate processes of character development in multiplot social contexts" (6). Some writers consciously choose the forms that they determine to be most suited to their particular creative impulses. Many others, I suspect, begin with a form that is simply comfortable or interesting to them, and that form then encourages their initially amorphous, semiconscious creative impulses to take some directions over others. As an analogy, at dinner, if on a whim you were to choose chopsticks rather than a fork, you would find your manner

DOI: 10.4324/9781003273318-2

of eating affected accordingly. Literary authorship frequently involves the same sort of whimsy. Sometimes, indeed, authors find the existing set of forms tiresome, and so for variety they innovate upon the inventory in some way. To extend the analogy, they decide to use both a fork and chopsticks. The result may be an awkward mess.

With the *Canterbury Tales* – Chaucer's final and incomplete literary tour de force – he innovated upon the inventory. As in the fork-and-chopsticks analogy, none of the individual elements of the work's overall form was entirely unprecedented. In fact, an Italian work with which he was almost certainly quite familiar, the *Decameron* completed by Giovanni Boccaccio some four decades before Chaucer began the *Tales*, brings together many of the same elements. Nevertheless, the particular array of elements that Chaucer assembles results in a set of affordances that, although sometimes indeed leading to awkward messes, on the whole possesses tremendous range and power. And this achievement is all the more remarkable given the rather simple basic idea of the overall form: a collection of stories, told by a group of pilgrims during their fifty-six-mile journey from London to the shrine of Saint Thomas à Becket in Canterbury Cathedral, as reported by one of those pilgrims, who also recounts some of the lively and often conflict-ridden interactions among the pilgrims between their turns at tale-telling.

This very simplicity, in fact, suggests that Chaucer may have happened upon the idea fortuitously before fully grasping its potential. There are clear indications that some of the items in the *Canterbury Tales* were compositions he had completed prior to his envisioning of this larger, later effort, and thus he may have been searching for some sort of framework just to collect those pieces together. Aspects of the text and some features of the surviving early manuscripts suggest that Chaucer's efforts at assembling the *Tales* were often opportunistic more than strategic and that his plans evolved in the process of writing. Indeed, while the *Tales* possesses a clear beginning and end, it's not, as I've mentioned, definitively finished. How many total tales Chaucer finally intended it to contain, and the precise order in which they were to appear, are just two of many uncertainties that scholars continue to debate. Their disagreements pivot on different assumptions about exactly how unfinished the work actually is. Some believe that Chaucer firmly decided that he was done with it as we have it, and so we can take it as complete in its incompleteness. Others contend that the scribes who copied the earliest manuscripts, working with the chaotic, chancy survival of materials found after Chaucer's death, had a heavy hand in organizing the work and were maybe even responsible for some of the dramatized interactions between pilgrims. And still others take a position somewhere between these views.[1] Whatever the truth of the matter, we can be sure that at some point Chaucer did become aware of the enormous potential of the overall form.

That potential, or the form's affordances, arises from the complexities and generative ambiguities that reside within the multifarious relations among the form's component parts. In particular:

- Each tale has its own distinctive formal and generic affiliations – there are romances in rhyming couplets, religious tales in seven-line stanzas, and serious moral or spiritual meditations in prose, among many other affiliations. And, in fact, *within* individual tales, there can be variation or hybridity in this respect.
- Each tale is given in the voice – and so, by implication, from the point of view – of a particular pilgrim, almost all of whom are given characterizing portraits in the work's General Prologue.
- Each tale occupies a specific place in the unfolding narrative of the pilgrimage, so that it often has a marked relation to the tales that come before and after, and to the exchanges among pilgrims between successive tale-tellings, as well as some relation to the overall idea of the journey to Canterbury.
- And finally, since Chaucer has set this fictional pilgrimage in the everyday world of his late-fourteenth-century present and places himself within the group as the reporter and, eventually, one of the tale-tellers, each tale emphasizes the possible distinction between its point of view and that of the work's author and his overall purposes, whatever those may be.

For some authors, such a framework might quickly become repetitious and predictable. The pilgrims would straightforwardly consist of goodies and baddies, with their tales in turn straightforwardly reflecting this preestablished moral judgment. Chaucer, however, was shrewd enough to realize (or, in reusing his already written works, discovered opportunistically) that the form's most potent affordances reside in the inconsistency, variety, and uncertainty of its component parts, both in themselves and in relation to each other. Sometimes the formal and generic affiliations of an individual tale have relatively definite significance, as with Chaucer-the-Pilgrim's Tale of Sir Thopas, which is a burlesque of then-popular romance/adventure stories. In other cases, the significance of the affiliations is more uncertain or may seem somewhat incidental, as with the moral fable told by the Manciple. The identity of the teller and that pilgrim's General Prologue portrait sometimes have enormous bearing on the tale they tell, as with the Wife of Bath and the Pardoner. Other times, the pilgrim/tale pairing may have less obvious or less far-reaching significance or may even be misleading, as with the Shipman. The General Prologue portraits of some pilgrims, such as the Friar, are self-evidently satiric depictions of corrupt hypocrites, and conversely, the portraits of others, such as the Parson, present them as embodiments of virtue. But many portraits – perhaps the majority – fall ambiguously somewhere between those moral poles. In some instances, the sequence of tales and the pilgrim interactions between them are obviously freighted with meaning, as we'll see in the next chapter with the work's initial sequence of Knight and Miller. But in other cases, the point of the sequence remains enigmatic despite centuries of readers' commentary, extending even to doubt over whether the responsibility for the sequence lies with Chaucer or the scribes who copied the first manuscripts. Finally, it's clear enough that the arc of the work's overall narrative traces a journey ostensibly undertaken, as I'll discuss below, for the cleansing of the pilgrims' souls and that in this respect the concluding 'tale' told by the Parson – a penitential treatise in prose – would appear to provide authoritative religious instruction for the reader as the textual double of that fictional journey's goal. Yet for many readers, all the inconsistency, variety, and uncertainty leading up to this finale leave plenty of room for doubting that the work's end provides any sort of definite closure.

In Chaucer's hands, therefore, the overall form of the *Canterbury Tales* affords a thematic scope of astounding capaciousness, flexibility, and depth, as each of its many component parts is evidently but in varying degrees ambiguously meaningful, and that ambiguity is then exponentially multiplied through those components' multifarious relations with one another. Admittedly, in trying to describe these affordances, I've perhaps made them sound overly complicated. So to reiterate what I earlier observed: in practice, the overall form's basic idea comes across to most readers as quite straightforward. Hence with this form, Chaucer has infused the work's very architecture with his laconic profundity – his technique, as I explained in the Introduction, of invoking weighty, complex matters in a deceptively simple and open-ended manner.

The next five chapters each consider specific tale-telling *performances*, which is a term I use throughout this book to denote the combination of a particular pilgrim identity, any chatter among pilgrims before or after that pilgrim's tale, and the tale itself. In these chapters, therefore, we will have ample opportunity to examine the kind and amount of literary hay that is made by the affordances that I've described. The remainder of this chapter focuses on a brief passage within the General Prologue that is, in contrast, relatively independent of these affordances yet nevertheless almost as famous.

The first sentence of the General Prologue

The fame of the first sentence of the *Canterbury Tales* likely derives in large part from the fact that generations of English majors have been required to memorize it as a kind of academic rite of passage. In our (that is, teachers') defense, we have imposed this assignment not for the sake of hazing but because there is so much going on in these initial lines. Here is the sentence in full:

> Whan that Aprill with his shoures soote
> The droghte of March hath perced to the roote,
> And bathed every veine in swich licour
> Of which vertu engendred is the flour;
> Whan Zephyrus eek with his sweete breeth
> Inspired hath in every holt and heeth
> The tendre croppes, and the yonge sonne
> Hath in the Ram his halve cours yronne,
> And smale foweles maken melodye
> That sleepen al the night with open eye –
> So priketh hem Nature in hir corages –
> Thanne longen folk to goon on pilgrimages,
> And palmeres for to seeken straunge strondes
> To ferne halwes, couthe in sondry londes;
> And specially from every shires ende
> Of Engelond to Caunterbury they wende,
> The holy blisful martyr for to seeke,
> That hem hath holpen whan that they were seke.
> (1.1–18)

I haven't supplied glosses along with this quotation, as I usually do elsewhere, since we will work through the language below. But if you don't yet have much experience with Chaucer, you may have wished for that assistance, as the passage's lexicon and syntax are more difficult than is generally characteristic of Chaucer's poetry. Chaucer here adopts a heightened style of expression, which elsewhere he uses rather sparingly and sometimes quite ironically. In Chaucer's day, this style was suited to introductions of events of epic proportions (and indeed one of Chaucer's possible models for the passage is a Latin account of Greek warships headed for Troy) or instances of intense religious adoration. It is a style whose very difficulty signals to readers that matters of great scope and deep import are at hand. Yet what this sentence actually introduces, as readers shortly discover, is a rather straightforward description of the mundane event of more-or-less ordinary English folks arriving at an inn on the outskirts of Chaucer's contemporary London. Such an apparently jarring discrepancy between style and content therefore seems to gesture toward the presence of some deeper meaning but without spelling that meaning out.

To launch the exploration of what Chaucer may be up to here, I, like many teachers, often ask students to paraphrase the first eleven lines in as few words as possible. Despite the passage's difficulty, they quickly arrive without too much trouble at something like "In springtime." The obvious follow-up question, then, is what the implications of all the excessive verbiage may be – in what directions does it develop the basic indication of seasonal setting? And again, students readily spot the emphasis on the renewal of life. Working next through some of the lines' details with the help of the glosses and footnotes in their editions of the text, they trace this renewal across a natural landscape. They register how its high stylistic features – such as the figuration of the west wind as the "sweete breeth" of "Zephyrus" and the description of the seasonal movement of the sun with the astrological periphrasis of "Hath in the Ram his halve cours yronne" – seem to raise the principle of renewal to cosmic proportions. One possible conclusion about the excessive verbiage of the first eleven lines, therefore, is that it evokes a happy vision of a universe of life-regenerating forces that work together harmoniously, cyclically, and endlessly.

The new materialisms

Such an affirmation of nature has resonance with a diverse collection of modern critical approaches and arguments that share enough basic positions to cohere under the label *the new materialisms*. This sort of work has emphasized the continuity between human corporeality and the material existence of everything else, rejecting such neatly categorical dualisms as those between subject (the human actor) and object (physical material acted upon), form and matter, culture and nature, soul or consciousness and body, and the distinctively human and the merely animal. The new materialisms inquire critically into the systemic conditions that give rise to such dualisms and into those dualisms' consequences (which include, for example, impending environmental catastrophe), and they seek to formulate possible alternatives. In a complicated way, the new materialisms are interested in the meaning of life, when that phrase is understood to denote, as I explain in this book's Introduction, the relations between our material, corporeal existence and those nonmaterial ideas, ideals, and values that shape our experience of that existence. The new materialisms, by situating life within the complex material systems from which it is inseparable, in effect ask, not what sort of meanings explain life but what sort of meanings life, in all its dimensions of embeddedness, has engendered – and may yet engender. (For a helpful introduction to the new materialisms, see Coole and Frost 2010, and, for their relevance to the Middle Ages, Robertson 2008 and Wright 2020.)

If we bring this lens to the first eleven lines of the *Canterbury Tales*, we notice that the passage puts emphasis on life precisely in its rich continuity with its material environment. We see, for example, that rain ("shoures"), flowers ("flour"), wind, woods ("holt"), heath ("heeth"), sun ("sonne"), and birds ("foweles") constitute a dynamic system of life-regenerating interdependencies that we might term *ecological*. To our initial happy conclusion, then, we may add that the particular way that the passage develops the principle of renewal dovetails with the new materialisms' conception of material existence as active, relational, and systemic – an existence that is ceaselessly "becoming" rather than statically "being." We may declare that the cyclic regeneration that the passage celebrates is *environmental*, in something like the way we use that term today.

Gender and sexuality studies

Less happy conclusions, however, may emerge if we draw upon the resources of the modern critical framework of gender and sexuality studies. Covering an array of approaches and arguments perhaps even broader than that of the new materialisms, the label identifies the common thread of emphasizing the embeddedness of gender and sexuality within political, social, economic, and cultural systems. As exemplified in the work of, for example, Judith Butler and Eve Kosofsky Sedgwick, this framework examines the ways in which norms of gender and sexuality are at once effects and perpetuators of the status quos of the social orders that contain them. Those norms are defined, disseminated, and enforced, sometimes quite consciously but often reflexively, by means of a vast collection of mechanisms and media, including, say, schooling, accepted styles of dress and speaking, beer advertisements, and canonical poetry by dead white men.

In comparison with the new materialisms, gender and sexuality studies may not appear especially applicable to the first eleven lines of the *Canterbury Tales*, since there are so far no human beings present. Even what might seem to be the masculine personification of "Aprill" is undone by the fact that in Chaucer's English the possessive determiner "his" was used for both the modern "his" and "its" (which might indeed be a topic for gender and sexuality studies, albeit not one specific to this passage). Closer scrutiny, however, brings into view the significance of a vein of imagery that runs through the lines – namely sexual and specifically heterosexual imagery of a masculinist character. The first four lines tell us that new life, the engendering of flowers ("engendred is the flour"), comes about through a process that involves penetration ("perced") and a potent liquid that washes through the passive vessels of plants (the "shoures" and the "licour" that possesses "vertu" or power that "bathed every veine"). In the following line, this imagery activates the masculinity latent in the otherwise conventional name for the west wind, "Zephyrus," whose "sweete breeth" similarly penetrates ("Inspired" or breathed into)

"The tendre croppes," with the adjective "tendre" possessing a range meanings that includes feminizing ones similar to today's *tender*. With the little birds making music ("smale foweles maken melodye"), then, we are given an almost literal explanation of the preceding imagery. The narrator tells us that Nature so penetrates the birds' hearts ("priketh… in hir corages") – that is to say, they are so physically stimulated – that they stay up all night ("sleepen al the night with open eye"), presumably making more than just "melodye." Norms of heterosexuality, masculinity, and femininity hence circulate through the passage, and, crucially, these norms cannot be disentangled from the passage's simultaneous development of an ecological principle of cosmic renewal. Indeed, as one scholar puts it, from our post-#MeToo perspective, the passage's "cosmic beauties and gorgeous pleasures" may be understood to naturalize patriarchal violence, so that the "consent, agency, and subjectivity of the [feminized] object have no place" (Solberg 2021, 138). What seemed an upbeat vision of cosmic environmental harmony may also serve to transmit ideologies of heteronormativity and male supremacy, precisely by representing those ideologies as necessary facts of nature.

Indeed, if the remainder of the sentence proceeded in the way that its first-time medieval readers (and perhaps still some of its modern ones) had reason to expect, those ideologies would likely be straightforwardly in play. In the conventions of late medieval narrative literature on which Chaucer here is riffing, such an introductory description of the physical renewal of springtime serves as a typical opening for a *romance*. This narrative genre, with its stereotypical plot of a brave knight rescuing a beautiful princess, characteristically involves hyper-masculine male protagonists in violent competition with one another (or some other entity), with the victor obtaining the sexual possession of a desired, idealized female object.[2] In such stories, the movement of the characters through the plot – culminating, say, with the heterosexual coupling of masculine hero and feminine desired object, after the former has overcome the "winter" of a series of violent trials – serves as an expansive insistence that what's natural in human life are the principles that supposedly govern nature as a whole. The knight and the princess are, at the end, the happy birds making "melodye." Accordingly, the reigning social order is understood as underwritten by those same universal principles of nature.

Penitence

Obviously, however, the sentence does not proceed in this direction. Instead, when Chaucer on the twelfth line finally supplies the sentence's long-delayed main subject and verb, he makes an abrupt U-turn in respect to conventional narrative, thematic, and ideological expectations. Instead of his telling us, say, "In springtime a doughty knight rides through a forest," we learn that this is the season when "folk" "longen" or desire "to goon [go] on pilgrimages." On the one hand, in respect to the initiation of an adventure in a faraway place and time that readers had reason to expect, this comes across as a sudden, rather deflating observation about ordinary life in Chaucer's England: in springtime, when the weather makes travel more feasible, English folk are able to go on pilgrimages. But on the other hand, this seemingly ordinary observation potentially cancels all that has led up to it, supplying a vision of the cosmos (an ideology) that may seem directly antithetical to the one painted by the preceding lines.

To appreciate the stakes of this U-turn, we'll need some additional historical background. Chaucer lived before the Reformation, the sixteenth-century fracturing of the centuries-long religious, cultural, and intellectual European hegemony of the Roman Catholic Church. He also lived before the Enlightenment, the seventeenth- and eighteenth-century transition in the West toward a deeper centering of human rationality, which manifested in many ways, as in the privileging of scientific knowledge, the revival of political alternatives to monarchy, and a general if uneven circumscription of the place of religion in human affairs (and, as well, in the acceleration of European imperialism, colonialism, and trade in enslaved African peoples). For Chaucer, therefore, religion, and specifically a late medieval English version of Roman Catholic religious practice and belief, comprehensively infused his experience of the world in a fashion that would be unfamiliar to many of us today. Nonetheless, in the modern world, there obviously remain many individuals, and some entire communities, who would find such deeply infused religiosity entirely relatable, once adjustments for religious differences are made. It is a mistake, therefore, to divide medieval and modern between the respective stereotypes of "Age of Faith" and "Age of Reason." Not only are both faith and reason crucial to both past and present, but also the Middle Ages did not and modernity does not possess anything close to the unified worldview that the "age of" locution implies. While religious belief and practice were in Chaucer's day more immediate to the everyday experiences of the people living on the island of Britain than they are to most of their counterparts living there today, there was no single, monolithic, untroubled medieval worldview that individuals in Chaucer's society simply and unquestioningly shared. Instead, then as now, there was an assembly of ideologies, always evolving, sometimes reinforcing one another and sometimes conflicting, and shared to different degrees in different ways from one person to another.

The significance of the activity of pilgrimage and of the implied contrast with the first eleven lines of the General Prologue therefore necessarily depends upon the particular ideological lenses through which that activity is perceived. One such predominant lens in late medieval England was a conception of the meaning of life that views corporeal existence as a kind of spiritual trial. In this view, which remains familiar to many today, corporeal existence most essentially comprises a series of tests, the outcome of which determines one's eternal spiritual destiny. And these tests involve most basically the challenges of corporeality itself, the temptation to value the bodily (or, more pejoratively, the carnal) over the spiritual – a temptation that ever since Adam and Eve's disobedience necessarily accompanies our existence as physical bodies in a physical world. The umbrella term for the various manifestations of this temptation was *concupiscence*. The common narrower meaning of this term today – strong sexual desire – derives from the regular positioning of sexuality as the preeminent human corporeal temptation, which eventually entailed, for example, the requirement of celibacy for priests, which, of course, remains the rule in today's Roman Catholic Church. The man who became Pope Innocent III expresses this view of corporeality succinctly in the opening of *De Miseria Condincionis Humane* (*On the Wretchedness of the Human Condition*), a widely disseminated Latin admonitory treatise he wrote in 1195: "Man is formed of dust, of clay, of ashes: what is more vile, from the filthiest sperm. He is conceived in the heat of desire, in the fervor of flesh, in the stench of lust: in the blemish of sin" (94). Because of the seemingly inescapably sinful condition of carnality, of "the fervor of flesh," that commences with our very conception, "the prison of the soul" as Innocent later quips, "is the body" (128).

Although the Church's official and de facto positions on these matters in the late Middle Ages were considerably more complex and far from a stable, unified set of doctrines, various versions of a view like Innocent's constituted one of the everyday understandings of the meaning of a life lived under the Church's authority. One of the principal engines behind this view's propagation, but also a kind pressure-release valve for it, was the *penitential system*, a set of beliefs and practices that the Church developed over the centuries as a mechanism for managing the accumulation of failed spiritual trials – of sins – that seemingly inevitably attends corporeal existence. For the typical individual in the late medieval Christian West, the penitential system offered understandings of self, society, and cosmos, an accompanying set of practices, and institutional locations for promulgating those beliefs and practices. In this way, it promised and no doubt often provided access to a life experience that would be meaningful and good. (Within today's most secularized communities, there is no exact equivalent to the penitential system, although where psychotherapy is ubiquitous, the mental health system may serve as a rough analogue.)

For present purposes, the key piece of information that all this background discussion leads toward is that pilgrimage in Chaucer's day was not just a journey to some holy site but also a penitential act, specifically the act termed *satisfaction*. This category of action comprised the most visible manifestation of a kind of economic/judicial understanding of sin, in which, following an official acknowledgment of guilt (by way of confession to a priest), sinners must still somehow make restitution, or repayment, to God in order to restore their broken relationship. Since the penalty for failing to complete one's payments for sins of the 'fatal' kind is damnation, the development of the doctrine of purgatory provided the comforting assurance that payments may continue to be made after death, so that one's salvation did not depend upon having the opportunity and ability to complete them during one's lifetime. Nonetheless, as the many vivid, widely circulating accounts of the torments of purgatory made plain, it was much better not to put the payments off. Pilgrimage, as one of many officially prescribed forms of satisfaction (others included the giving of alms and the recital of prayers), was thus a physical activity in the physical world that served as a means to reverse the spiritual consequences of human physical existence.

One possible interpretation of the U-turn in the twelfth line of the first sentence of the *Canterbury Tales*, then, is that in the first eleven lines Chaucer purposely leads the reader astray in order to provide a shock of spiritual correction. Those first eleven lines develop an ideology that seems to celebrate material regeneration and even especially sexual reproduction. Life, in the specific sense defined above, seems valuable for its own sake, although the consideration of these lines through the lens of gender and sexuality studies cautions us against understanding this embrace of life as a simple prioritization of the material over the nonmaterial. Rather, as an ideology, it defines specific relations between the material and nonmaterial, by, for example, construing the material as signifying the idea of heteronormativity, which is elevated to a cosmic principle. What the U-turn may reveal is thus that that very elevation functions as a sort of concupiscent temptation to readers, an ideology in which their carnality, rather than a source of sin, epitomizes cosmic renewal. The final seven lines abruptly overturn that ideology by means of a sudden reversal of values in which the spiritual – the nonmaterial *par excellence* – emerges triumphant over the now evidently degraded material. Corporeal existence now signifies its own abjection and the greater value of precisely what it is not. The very structure of the passage in this way performs a penitential act in miniature, supplying a thematic act of satisfaction in recompense for the thematic sin of the sentence's long opening adverbial clause.

Ideological fault lines

Such a pious interpretation of the first sentence receives some support by the fact that, as noted above, the concluding pilgrim performance in the

Canterbury Tales, the Parson's, is no tale at all but a long penitential treatise translated from two standard Latin works on the topic. From what Chaucer tells us in his *Legend of Good Women*, moreover, we know that he translated Innocent's *De Miseria* itself, and he makes clear use of that treatise in the prologue to the tale told by the Sergeant of Law. Nevertheless, one difficulty with this pious interpretation is that there are no explicit lexical or syntactic markers of contradiction or reversal in the sentence, nothing that assuredly signals any logical tension between the first eleven lines and remaining seven. Rather, the opening adverbial clause connects smoothly and elegantly with the rest of the sentence. Here, then, we are confronted again with Chaucer's laconic profundity: what are we to make of a passage that apparently presents binary opposing ideologies but in its linguistic structure appears wholly unified?

In fact, while the Parson's Tale and Chaucer's translation of *De Miseria* may seem to point toward the pious interpretation, neither actually supplies definitive evidence in this regard. The aforementioned affordances of the overall form of the *Canterbury Tales* instead render their exact bearing on these lines at best ambiguous. In the Sergeant of Law's Prologue, the material from *De Miseria* is voiced not by Chaucer but by the Sergeant, and as we will see in Chapter 3, the Sergeant deploys this material in a highly equivocal if not simply ironic fashion. With the Parson's Tale, we may observe that this pilgrim performance is exactly just that: the Parson's contribution to the storytelling contest. As an earnest exhortation to repent one's sins, this 'tale' wholly suits the character of its teller. Accordingly, it does not necessarily possess authorial imprimatur more categorically than any of the other tales, some of which would seem ideologically incompatible with the Parson's.

Furthermore, we don't need to look very far to find evidence of Chaucer's awareness of different understandings of human corporeality. Despite the tendency in such writings as *De Miseria* to depict soul and body – and, more generally, the domains of spirit and matter – in a simplistic good-versus-evil opposition, the Church was doctrinally definitive in its rejection of such dualism. The official view insisted instead that since God is the creator of everything, and God is wholly good, then everything – body as well as soul, matter as well as spirit – must also be good. To account then for sin and evil, Church thinkers, influenced by Platonism, developed various sophisticated understandings of the cosmos as consisting of gradations of goodness. Sin consists of the error of privileging a lower level of goodness over a higher one, as in the original sin of choosing one particular material creation of God, the fruit of the tree of knowledge, over God's disembodied commandment not to eat it.

In this regard, it's important to recognize that Chaucer's most ambitious translation was neither of those already mentioned but rather the

Consolation of Philosophy by sixth-century Roman philosopher Boethius, the most widely known (albeit not specifically Christian) articulation of this Platonizing or Neoplatonic view in the European Middle Ages. In addition, we know that Chaucer was aware of even more affirmative views concerning the interrelationships among body, soul, and the physical environment. These ultimately derive from Aristotle and the second-century medical writings of Galen, were supplemented and transmitted to Europe in Arabic texts, and were broadcast widely to late medieval Europeans through such authorities as thirteenth-century Italian theologian Thomas Aquinas. According to these views, the body is not the prison of the soul but rather its sustaining home. The nonmaterial soul is dependent on the substrate of the material body in something like the way that electricity circulates through copper wire. The soul's knowledge arrives through the mediating doorway of the body's senses, and the body and its four humors, in turn, are interpenetrated by the physical environment in which the body resides. Indeed, in several ways, these views anticipate the aforementioned new materialist arguments against the very sort of binaries between matter and spirit that writings such as the *De Miseria* seem to propagate. (Expert considerations of the diverse medieval understandings of these topics include Minnis 2016, Walter 2018, and Orlemanski 2019.)

Perhaps, then, the supposed U-turn in the first sentence of the *Canterbury Tales* is not a U-turn at all. Taking our cue from the sentence's smooth syntactic transition, we might interpret the first eleven lines as establishing an affirmative context for or even prefiguring the final seven, so that the happy regeneration of the material world – which necessarily includes human regeneration through procreation – reflects and stands as evidence for the even happier spiritual regeneration provided by God's grace and available to humans in such penitential activities as pilgrimage. Yet as appealingly unifying as this interpretation seems to be, it creates at least as many problems as it solves. In its very identification of a parallel, it simultaneously calls attention to key differences between the physical world's cyclical recovery from winter and the spiritual penitential recovery from sin. Instead of providing ideological closure, the ambiguous stylistic, syntactic, and thematic features of this first sentence more likely serve as prompts for some of the central, open-ended ideological questions – questions about the meaning of life – that the rest of the *Canterbury Tales* explores.

Further scrutiny of the first sentence helps to give these questions more specificity. In particular, my characterization of the transition between the two main components of the sentence as "smooth" was admittedly a bit overstated, as in fact immediately prior to the transition, following a rhythmically fluid series of five couplets, we bump into the somewhat disruptive parenthetical remark, "So priketh hem Nature in hir corages." When the passage is recited aloud, this digressive, retrospective comment urges a temporary modulation in tone and pace, which is to say, the line calls attention to itself. One might notice then that not only is the line syntactically intrusive but also, along with the twelfth line, it forms a couplet whose union of terminal rhyme words sits uncomfortably astride both the grammatical division of adverbial and main clauses and the thematic division of matter and spirit. Situated in this way, the couplet focuses questions of ideological significance on specific parallels between its two lines: between the apparently sexual desire that "Nature" "priketh" in the "corages" of the "smale foweles" and the next line's apparently spiritual desire, that of the "folk" who "longen" (the verb "to long" or desire) "to goon on pilgrimages." What are the continuities and discontinuities between these two desires, between "corages" (hearts) and "pilgrimages" and between "foweles" and "folk"? Do the continuities ideologically outweigh the discontinuities, so that, as one scholar suggests, "Nature acts on people in their hearts and in their groins, and then they long to go on pilgrimage" (Stanbury 2004, 11; see also Orlemanski 2019, 15–16)? Or is it vice versa, so that the categorical superiority of the spiritual winds up being reinforced precisely through its momentary juxtaposition with the carnal? And to these inquiries we may add the further complicating piece of information that here "Nature," as evident by its editorial capitalization, denotes not just what we mean by "the force of nature" but also the Christian Neoplatonic figuration of that force as the goddess Natura, the vicaress of God, the divine agency responsible for the harmonious unity of the physical world. (For this topic, see White 2000, and for its connection to the new materialisms, Robertson 2017.) With the introduction of this figure, the question of the distinction or lack thereof between sexual longing and spiritual longing takes on cosmic proportions.

The figure of Nature and ambiguities generated by this couplet, in turn, amplify and complicate the significance of what we noticed about the passage by way of gender and sexuality studies. We may now observe that in contrast with Zephyrus, the penetrating actor – the goddess Nature – is (tacitly) gendered feminine, and the penetrated bodies, the "foweles," are not specifically gendered; either they're conventionally male songbirds penetrated by a female force, or the plural signifies general sexual activity regardless of gender. For these reasons, although the idea of procreation plainly still predominates, the eleventh line may seem to move some steps away from the sexual norms that the preceding lines develop, despite, again, my earlier suggestion of continuity in this respect. And perhaps it strays far enough to say that it *queers* those norms. Such moves, as formulated by *queer theory* – an important conceptual resource in gender and sexuality studies – consist of insinuations or outright declarations of alternatives to heteronormativity in particular and identity norms more generally

(Pramaggiore 2013). Notably, "folk" is also plural and seemingly gender-inclusive, as is "palmeres" (pilgrims who have visited the holy land), and these two collective actors govern the rest of the sentence. We might therefore understand the couplet's incipient queering of norms to extend to the spiritual realm, thereby further blurring the matter/spirit distinction. Alternatively, we might see that distinction as reinforced, with the genderless "folk" and "palmeres" signaling a turn away from sexuality by way of their very juxtaposition with the genderless "foweles." As with the lens of the new materialisms, that of gender and sexuality studies does not predetermine a single interpretation but rather brings into view a set of competing ideologies and the fault lines within and between them.

If you were to attempt an interpretation that sees the passage as pursuing one ideological direction or another (say, for a short essay on the opening of the *Tales*), you might look up key words such as "corages" and "longen" in the *Middle English Dictionary* in order to assess the implications of their connotations. You might consider the way in which, even after the sentence's alleged U-turn, Chaucer continues the landscape description of the first part of the sentence, albeit with different emphasis. And you might think through how the final pair of rhyming words, "seeke" and "seke," raise in miniature the question of the relations of body and soul, the relations, that is, between the pilgrims' *seeking* of "The holy blisful martyr" (the tomb of Saint Thomas à Becket in Canterbury, the destination of the pilgrimage) and the *sickness* (of spirit? body? both?) for which they desire healing. Does this concluding rhyme of homophones (a device known as *rime riche*, much prized in Chaucer's day) signify a figuration of the spiritual by the bodily, a fusion of body and spirit, or the degradation of the spiritual into the carnal? Or some other relation?

Chaucer, of course, neither explicitly asks nor answers such questions. Yet, as this section has sought to trace, the opening sentence of the *Canterbury Tales*, despite its ambiguity, nonetheless urges readers toward some overall, foundational inquiries into the meaning of life. It may prompt readers to contemplate, for example, whether corporeal existence has any value beyond the spiritual trials that it provides. If the answer is affirmative (and maybe even if it isn't), it asks then whether, in particular, the pleasures that corporeal existence affords can be good. And if they can, it further queries how one is able to discern when those pleasures cross the line into bad. In the Neoplatonic scheme familiar to Chaucer, that last question wonders about the extent or kind of attachments to lower forms of good that cross the line into sin. Today, with the requisite substitution of concepts of good and evil, this sort of question, even in the most secular of contexts, remains profoundly urgent. It underlies, for example, such everyday decisions as the determination of how much money to spend on a good bottle of wine versus sending that much more to an activist organization that is performing what you believe to be crucial work. At what point does attention to our own pleasure cross the line into doing harm? Here and elsewhere, Chaucer's laconic profundity, if we follow its piper's song, leads us into a forest of ambiguity from which emerge questions that demand answers that the text itself does not supply.

Notes

1 For more on this general topic, see Meyer-Lee 2013.
2 In fact, notwithstanding this basic formula, many medieval romances are in practice considerably more complex and ideologically self-reflexive, as evident in those foundational ones by twelfth-century French poets Chrétien de Troyes and Marie de France.

2 The Knight's and Miller's Tales

Perhaps the least surprising moment in the *Canterbury Tales* occurs at the end of the General Prologue when the Knight, invited by the Host before the rest of the pilgrims to draw lots to determine the initial tale teller, winds up winning the putative game of chance. "Were it by aventure [chance], or sort [luck], or cas [destiny]" (1:844), the narrator tells us, the Knight draws the short straw. The very uncertainty of the narrator's remark encourages us to think of alternative explanations, most obviously the Host's manipulation of the game to ensure that the socially highest-ranking member of the group is given the place of honor. The rest of the pilgrims, far from resentful, seem relieved by the result, however it came about: "Of which ful blithe [very happy] and glad was every wight [person]" (1:846). Indeed, given the sheer importance and ubiquity of protocols of social hierarchy in Chaucer's England, what *was* unexpected was the General Prologue's establishment of an apparently socially egalitarian tale-telling group. In principle, a peasant such as the Plowman and a bourgeois woman such as the Wife of Bath were given equal footing in the competition with male aristocrats such as the Knight and his son the Squire. Here, then, as the lead-in to the Knight's Tale, we encounter one of those deceptively complicated ambiguities that in this book's Introduction I name laconic profundity. Why in the General Prologue does Chaucer seemingly go out of his way to deviate from expected social protocols (a deviation that he calls attention to by having his narrator apologize for it: "I praye you to foryive it me,/Al have I nat set folk in hir degree [their social rank]" [1:743–44]) only to reestablish them at the outset of the pilgrimage?

DOI: 10.4324/9781003273318-3

Literary and social order

One ready answer to this question arrives in the aftermath of the Knight's performance. The Host attempts to pass the tale-telling on to the Monk – who, as the highest-ranking churchman in the group, would be the most socially apt successor – but is boisterously foiled by a drunken Miller, who, despite what the General Prologue suggests about his prosperity, as a rural agricultural laborer ranks quite low in English society. Chaucer thus reestablishes social hierarchies at the outset of the pilgrimage precisely in order to set up their rather spectacular overturning. Yet this answer just prompts a sort of reiteration of the initial question, which now asks what Chaucer may be up to by making social hierarchies so unusually visible by alternatively fulfilling and defeating expectations regarding them. Social hierarchies, like all ideological social structures and practices, operate best when they are invisible, which is to say, when they are taken as simple facts rather than as mutable social constructs. A straightforward initiation of the contest beginning with the Knight and transitioning to the Monk would likely have seemed natural to Chaucer's fourteenth-century readers. In this way, it would have served not just as a literary reflection of that hierarchy but also as an instrument of the hierarchy's perpetuation. At the very least, therefore, Chaucer's departures from social expectations present social hierarchy as an object for the reader's contemplation – a topic for scrutiny rather than just a supposedly neutral description of the world.

Another way of putting this is that the dramatized interactions among pilgrims immediately prior to and following the Knight's Tale provoke questions about the social order itself. Such questions might include, for example, what justifies social hierarchy, what are the mechanisms with which that hierarchy is maintained, and how much and what sort of hierarchy is necessary. In the late 1380s when Chaucer likely began work on the *Canterbury Tales*, these sorts of questions were urgent, fraught, and edgy. Just a few years before, England experienced a violent collective uprising of many in the oppressed classes. This was the insurgency that scholars used to call the Peasant's Revolt but is now more commonly known by the less pejorative and more accurate descriptor (given that the participants were not restricted to peasants) of the Rising of 1381. The violence and antiestablishment social ideologies that accompanied the Rising were particularly marked in London, where Chaucer was living at the time. There, the insurgents forced a fourteen-year-old King Richard to flee into the Tower of London and, among other actions, executed Simon Sudbury, the Lord Chancellor and Archbishop of Canterbury, and burned down the London palace of John of Gaunt, the king's uncle and a patron of Chaucer's. The walls of medieval London proved ineffectual, as the insurgents streamed in unchecked through Aldgate (left open for still uncertain reasons), the very portal above which Chaucer then dwelled in an apartment granted to him by the royal government for his civil servant work as controller of the wool custom. The Rising proved short-lived, with King Richard retracting all the promises that he made to the insurgents not long after the killing of their leader, Wat Tyler. But it made plain the fragility of the reigning social order, and for acute social observers such as Chaucer, it appears to have prompted reflections on the foundations of social order per se.

Characteristic of Chaucer's slipperiness, these reflections do not take the form of direct commentary on the Rising but rather emerge by way of various more-or-less subtle literary displacements. In particular, as Chaucer scholars have noted (e.g., Patterson 1991 and Lavezzo 2017), with the Miller's unruly disruption of what could have been a smooth transition from Knight to Monk, Chaucer has projected into the opening structure of the *Canterbury Tales*, if less obviously into its content, the Rising's threatened overturning of the reigning social order. In this chapter, I'll point you toward the implications of this and related literary displacements in the Knight–Miller sequence. I'll suggest that with these displacements Chaucer meditates on the conditions and costs of social order. For Chaucer, as we will see, such meditations necessarily involve even more foundational considerations of the meaning of life, or, as I define that admittedly hackneyed phrase in this book's Introduction, of the relations between our basic material existence, our corporeal life as such, and those nonmaterial ideas, ideals, and values that shape our experience of that existence. Although social orders are all too often experienced as in some way oppressive, for Chaucer and indeed most of us today, some sort of order, as every bad post-apocalyptic movie readily dramatizes, is nonetheless an aspect of life that we would rather have than not. Simply put, social orders, in principle, ought to enable us to live our lives as we hope to live them. How we conceive of the meaning of life, in the sense given above, thus bears directly on how we evaluate what existing social orders do and do not accomplish.

The Knight's Tale meditates upon a social order that has at its apex a male sovereign who possesses something close to absolute power. In today's terminology, such a social order is *authoritarian* and *patriarchal*, and merely by recognizing the most obvious continuities of this order into the present – for example, the many male heads of state still wreaking havoc in the twenty-first century with their relatively unchecked power – we may expect that Chaucer's meditations will have contact points with our experiences. In particular, as this chapter explores after the following summary of the Knight's Tale, Chaucer exposes the relays between the political and the sexual in a way that resonates with feminist, gender, and queer theoretical frameworks. The Miller's subsequent riff on the tale of the Knight, we will then see, adds social class to the mix, extending Chaucer's scrutiny of the grounds of patriarchy even while replaying the collision of ideologies that the events of 1381 brought to the surface.

The Knight's Tale

Principal source and summary

First-time readers of the *Canterbury Tales* who have heard of Chaucer's reputation for raunchy humor may be taken aback by the Knight's Tale, a sprawling, philosophically ambitious blend of romance and epic set in ancient Athens. It's not just the first but also the longest of the pilgrim performances, except for the concluding Parson's Tale (a lengthy, sober, systematic penitential guidebook in prose, which, in contrast with the Knight's Tale, doesn't often appear on Chaucer course syllabi). As was usual and indeed expected for literary composition in Chaucer's day, the story did not spring directly from Chaucer's mind. It was prompted, rather, by *Il Teseida delle nozze d'Emelia* (*The Story of Theseus Concerning the Nuptials of Emily*), completed by Italian author Giovanni Boccaccio in the early 1340s. Boccaccio was a writer of great aspiration; in the *Teseida*, he sought to rewrite classical epic in what was for him a modern Italian idiom. Along with the work of Dante Alighieri, the more famous Italian author from the generation just before, Boccaccio's writings exemplified for Chaucer a literary grandiosity not usually attempted in the vernacular (that is, in any language other than Latin). Characteristically, Chaucer seems to have been both inspired and provoked by this grandiosity. He returns repeatedly to Boccaccio for his primary source texts – most significantly, for *Troilus and Criseyde* and perhaps even for the frame structure of the *Canterbury Tales*, which carries several resemblances to that of Boccaccio's *Decameron*. But in each instance, while some amount of the literary grandiosity remains, in Chaucer's hands it also turns in on itself, becoming a vehicle for inspecting the ideologies in which it participates. (For more on Boccaccio's complicated influence on Chaucer, see Schwebel 2024.) In the case of the Knight's Tale, one of those ideologies is patriarchy.

The Knight's Tale seems to have been one of the originally independent works that Chaucer later incorporated into the *Canterbury Tales* framework. In the *Legend of Good Women*, which he composed before conceiving that framework, he mentions that he had written about "al the love of Palamon and Arcite/of Thebes" (F 420–21), and this remark clearly identifies the center of the Knight's Tale's plot. How much he revised this earlier version, beyond making the changes required to integrate the story into the fiction of the pilgrimage to Canterbury, is impossible to ascertain with any certainty. Scholars have traced quite closely the ways in which Chaucer adapts the *Teseida*, identifying how he reshapes its story, where he incorporates material from other sources, and what portions are his own innovations. But because Chaucer's earlier version doesn't survive, we cannot with similar confidence trace the changes that he makes to his own work. Yet even if such changes were minimal, merely by way of the story's incorporation into the tale-telling framework and its assignment to the Knight, Chaucer leverages what I describe in the preceding chapter as the capacious affordances of the *Tales*' overall form. In this way alone, Chaucer connects the tale's meditation upon patriarchy in ancient Greece to his own present in a powerful manner.

That meditation upon patriarchy is lengthy, with a complicated but relatively easy-to-follow plot. Theseus, duke of Athens, is on his way back from conquering the Amazons ("the regne of Femenye" [1.866]), having taken the Amazonian queen Ipolyta as his bride, with Ipolyta's younger sister Emelye accompanying them. He encounters a group of widows from the city state of Thebes and, moved by their request, defers his return in order to wreak havoc upon Thebes (he "rente adoun bothe wall and sparre [beam] and rafter" [1.990)]) and kill its ruler Creon. In the pile of Theban corpses, "Two yonge knyghtes" (1.1011), Arcita and Palamon, are found still alive. They happen to be first cousins "of the blood royal/Of Thebes" (1.1018–19) and also, as we later learn, best friends as consecrated in the publicly recognized form of sworn brotherhood. Theseus imprisons them both in the same cell, apparently for the remaining duration of their lives.

Years later, Palamon spies Emelye walking in the garden below the prison window and, in stereotypical romance fashion, falls immediately and tortuously in love. When Arcite asks Palamon what's wrong and spots Emelye himself, he, too, is overcome in almost precisely the same fashion – greatly to Palamon's displeasure. Sworn brothers become, in an instant, sworn enemies, despite the fact that neither seemingly will ever have any sort of access to the object of their rivalry. Time passes. A close friend of both Theseus and Arcite visits Athens and persuades Theseus to free the Theban prince. Theseus does so on the condition that if Arcite is found "In any contree of this Theseus," that is, in any realm under Theseus's sovereignty, "with a swerd he sholde lese his heed," that is, be executed on the spot (1.1213–15). Arcite, now bereft of even the sight of Emelye, falls into erotic despair, the bodily impact of which eventually severely alters his physical appearance. Prompted by a message from the god Mercury, Arcite realizes that, so disfigured, he may return to Athens without being recognized. Thus he does so, becoming a servant in Emelye's home and, when his qualities become known, being later elevated to the position of Theseus's own trusted squire.

Meanwhile, Palamon manages to escape from prison and, on his way back to Thebes to raise an army against Theseus, conceals himself during the daytime in a nearby grove. Coincidentally, Arcite, out for a ride with his horse to enjoy the springtime weather, dismounts before that very grove to make a garland for himself. But his very attempt at such jollity reminds him of his inner turmoil. He laments aloud his plight: his unrequited love for Emelye and betrayal of Thebes in his service to Theseus, his "mortal enemy" (1.1558). Palamon, overhearing, is incensed and leaps out from his concealment to confront him. Since Palamon has no weapon or armor, they resolve to meet in the same place the next day to battle to the death in knightly fashion, with Arcite, despite his betrayal of Thebes, still honorable enough to bring the appropriate equipment for a fair fight. As appointed, they engage in brutal combat – "Up to the ancle foughte they in hir [their] blood" (1.1660). Before either is able to finish the other off, Theseus, out hunting with the full royal party, encounters them. When Palamon discloses to Theseus his and Arcite's identities, Theseus quickly determines to execute them on the spot for their several manifest crimes against his authority. At the plea of Ipolyta, Emelye, and "alle the ladies in the compaignye" (1.1750), however, he changes his mind. Instead, he decides that after fifty weeks each cousin is to return, accompanied by one hundred knights. He will host a lavish tournament between the two Theban princes and their respective military entourages, and he will reward the winning prince with Emelye.

Theseus orders the construction of a huge, elaborate, circular arena, with a temple to Venus above the east gate, a temple to Mars above the west, and a temple to Diana above the north. On the appointed day, the cousins return, each accompanied by one hundred of the most celebrated warriors of the day, including rulers of other realms. Two nights before the tournament, Palamon prays to Venus in her temple, requesting that he obtain Emelye, regardless of whether he wins or loses the battle. Arcite prays to Mars, requesting that he be the victor of the battle. Both gods appear to signal to their respective devotees that his request will be granted. Emelye goes to the temple of Diana and, in the only words she has in the 2,249 lines of the tale, requests that both Palamon's and Arcite's desire for her be extinguished, peace be restored, and she be allowed "to walken in the wodes wilde [i.e., to hunt as the Amazonians are wont to do]/And noght to been a wif and be with childe [i.e., become pregnant]" (2309–10). Diana says no.

The seemingly mutually exclusive promises of Venus and Mars lead to some divine squabbling. In response, the pre-Olympian god Saturn pledges to provide a resolution when the time arrives. The tournament begins. Eventually, Palamon is overcome and taken prisoner, and Theseus declares the tournament over with Arcite the winner. As Arcite rides up to greet Emelye, Saturn prompts the god Pluto to send "Out of the ground a furye infernal" (1.2684). This frightens Arcite's horse, throwing him to the ground and wounding him – fatally, as it turns out. At the culmination of a drawn-out (and ostentatiously medicalized) death scene, Arcite encourages Emelye to marry Palamon. An elaborate funeral follows. Some number of years later, Theseus, in response to a political exigency involving Thebes that apparently requires its total "obeisuance" (1.2974) or submission to Athenian overlordship, invites Palamon and Emelye – whose marriage clearly did not follow upon Arcite's death – to parliament. He gives a long speech invoking Neoplatonic metaphysics (which we'll examine below), at the end of which he declares that Emelye shall take Palamon "for housbonde and for lord" (1.3081). The tale ends with the Knight telling us that the couple lived happily ever after, although notably no direct speech from either is recorded: we hear only Theseus's pronouncement and the Knight's supposition of the outcome.

Homosociality and its discontents

As I hope the above summary suggests, the ideological stakes upon which Chaucer meditates in the Knight's Tale are considerable. To help illuminate these stakes, we may bring to our aid the influential formulations regarding homosociality developed by feminist, queer, and gender theorist Eve Kosofsky Sedgwick in her book *Between Men*. Sedgwick builds upon French theorist René Girard's idea of mimetic desire, which holds that our desires arise as an imitation of another's desires, so that we learn to want what another already wants. Examples of this phenomenon are pervasive. A ready instance is the playground swing that stands empty for hours before one child notices it, prompting immediate challenges from others. And many thousands of us experienced it in the first months of the 2020 COVID pandemic when we suddenly felt we needed ninety rolls of toilet paper.[1] Sedgwick is especially interested in the triangular relationships that mimetic desire often produces, in which two rivals desire the same object. In literary studies, this formation is instantly recognizable as the ubiquitous love triangle, but what Girard helps us to see is that, as Sedgwick summarizes, "the bond that links the two rivals is as intense and potent as the bond that links either of the rivals to the beloved." Or, indeed, the bond between rivals may be "even stronger, more heavily determinate of actions and choices, than anything in the bond between either of the lovers and the beloved" (21).

Sedgwick brilliantly extrapolates from this insight to identify the gender – and potentially queer – dynamics of the deep structure of patriarchal social orders. Observing that in both literature and actual social practice the triangular structure most often features two men in rivalry over a woman, she sees this rivalry as productive of the social bonds between men that constitute the fabric of patriarchal society. As Sedgwick writes, "large-scale social structures are congruent with the male-male-female erotic triangles described most forcefully by Girard," and in fact "in any male-dominated society, there is a special relationship between male homosocial (*including* homosexual) desire and the structures for maintaining and transmitting patriarchal power: a relationship founded on an inherent and potentially active structural congruence" (25, italics Sedgwick's).

Today, insofar as men worldwide still occupy the majority, and in many instances the vast majority, of positions of power within political, business, church, and many other hierarchies, we may conclude that relationships between men continue to comprise the infrastructure of most social orders. The butt-slapping that one often witnesses between two male professional sports opponents is thus, for example, not merely random rivalrous affection. It is, rather, a kind of distillation of the essence of patriarchy. In the context of a sometimes-brutal physical competition in which the financial stakes may be considerable, the slap on the butt – when delivered by, say, an NFL cornerback after he helps up a wide receiver following a vicious mid-air tackle – marks the recognition of the bond, in this case a physically affectionate and perhaps even sexually suggestive bond, that links otherwise bitter rivals. At the same time, it underscores how that bond constitutes the very fabric of this particular highly competitive social order, since there would be no game of football unless everyone involved (which is to say, the male players, coaches, owners, etc.) cooperates. From the football gridiron, we may extrapolate to boardrooms, halls of congress, church offices, etc. Though not always as starkly masculinist as football, these other arenas of competition depend upon relations between men – homosociality – for their very continuance.

The structural role of women in the example of football may not be immediately evident, but if we transpose this example to its medieval equivalent, the tournament between knights, that role comes more readily into view. As depicted in countless medieval romances, in such a tournament a woman – her 'favor' of some sort or even her hand in marriage (that is, the rights to her body) – serves as the immediate object of the competition. She is what the male combatants are trying to kill each other to obtain, whether that combat is literally to death or only figuratively so, as in football, with fatality an unusual but still possible outcome. At the same time, this manifestly heterosexual objective is only the most visibly immediate one. It more crucially functions as the hinge that holds together an ordered, hierarchical system of competition between men, which is to say, it holds together homosociality.

Insofar as the notion of 'trophy wives' is still current (and my students tell me that it is), we can be confident that this structural role of women, so obvious in the Middle Ages, not only persists into the present but does so in rather similar ways. Indeed, this modern-day version of that role – that of a woman (and, specifically, rights over her body) as the now-obtained 'trophy' – suggests her further function in maintaining homosociality. Once she has been decisively possessed as such a prize, the trophy wife's function has not ended. She still occupies one position of a triangular structure, but instead of serving as the actual object of competition between men, she now represents for her husband his *ownership* of that object – that is, his possession of the object of desire of other men. He *wants* those *other* men to want her, because inasmuch as they do, his status as the winner, as the superior in the competitive relations among men – which is to say, his top position in the hierarchy – is confirmed and hence perpetuated. So he shows her off, encouraging other men to feel desire for her, but at the same time communicating in some fashion that such desire, of course, may not be realized. He communicates, in effect, you must *want* my wife, but you cannot *have* my wife. If the other men play their roles, the bond between the alpha male and his entourage is strengthened, since in their shared, rivalrous desire for an object that is actually available to only one of them, they acknowledge the hierarchy in place and function cooperatively within their positions in that hierarchy.

The fragility of this triangular structure of relationships is evident. Since men's understandings of self and purpose are shaped from birth by a society that prioritizes male competition, there will always be at least some members of the entourage who have alpha-male aspirations. Those men, accordingly, have strong motivation to literalize what has become the merely symbolic structure of rivalry, which is to say, to act upon the desire that they're already compelled to feel for the trophy wife. With their erotic desire and sociopolitical ambitions inextricably entangled in the structure of rivalry, they bring down the alpha male and seize the trophy wife in the name of love. This is the plot, obviously, of countless novels, movies, television shows, operas, comics, etc. Folks in my generation might think of the 1983 film *Scarface* and the rivalry between Tony Montana and Frank Lopez over Lopez's wife Elvira, as memorably portrayed by Al Pacino, Robert Loggia, and Michelle Pfeiffer. But the archetype of this plot is quintessentially medieval, most famously and enduringly realized in the love triangle of King Arthur, Lancelot, and Guinevere. In Sir Thomas Malory's formative fifteenth-century version of this story, knights in service to a feudal lord were expected to display formalized expressions of adoration toward that lord's lady as part of their recognition of their loyalty to that lord, precisely as the logic of the trophy wife structure demands. When that adoration becomes something more than merely formal in the case of Lancelot and Guinevere, the consequences, as Malory records, are not just interpersonal conflict but bloody internecine strife that extends throughout the social order and eventuates its collapse.

At the heart of homosociality is hence a paradox, which is that its very mechanism of cohesion, rivalry between men, is also the means of its potential undoing. From Sedgwick's observation about "the slippery relation…between desire and identification" (24), we may see that the crucial pivot in the rivalry, which enables it to be constitutive rather than destructive of order, occurs when one of the rivals acknowledges the superiority of the other. He then determines that if he cannot be better than his rival, he will instead love that rival and fashion himself in the rival's image. He will transform his desire *for the same object as his rival* into a desire instead *for that rival*, a desire that takes the form of identifying with that rival, of trying to be *like* him, instead of trying to *outdo* him. As then a lesser version of his rival, he will have a lesser version of a trophy wife. In traditional patriarchal societies, this wife will be a woman somehow (perhaps just symbolically) granted to him by the alpha male. At this point, a triangular structure of rivalry has become one of allegiance. The structure of a conflict between men over a woman is replaced by a structure in which the superior man passes a woman, in some way under his authority, to one of his loyal subjects, thereby further strengthening the bond between men. This transformation, Sedgwick observes – drawing on the formulations of anthropologist Gayle Rubin – depends upon women functioning as *commodities* in relations between men. As Sedgwick writes, "patriarchal heterosexuality" rests upon "one or another form of the traffic in women: it is the use of women as exchangeable, perhaps symbolic, property for the primary purpose of cementing the bonds of men with men" (25–26).

In today's patriarchal societies, the continued function of this "traffic of women" is not hard to spot, even in those that seem most far removed the feudal ideals of the King Arthur story, even in societies in which marriage is understood to be the wholly consensual decision of two autonomous individuals. It's detectable at a symbolic level, for example, in the still-common practice of fathers "giving away" the bride in wedding ceremonies and in the perhaps less common but still-widespread practice of men asking their hoped-for bride's father for her "hand in marriage." In the homosocial ideal, a son-in-law and father-in-law form an alliance by way of the latter granting the former the hand of his daughter, and, as one generation yields to the next, that son-in-law himself ascends to the position of father-in-law, granting the hand of his own daughter to a young man who comes to ask for his permission. But underneath such a smooth reproduction of this social order lies the only temporarily dormant volcano of rivalrous energies, the energies that both keep that order in motion and threaten its annihilation.

Fractured homosociality in the Knight's Tale

The light that all this theorization casts upon the Knight's Tale is in some respects rather obvious. With the "strif" (1.1187) between Arcite and

Palamon over Emelye, we have almost a caricature, or something like a laboratory study, of Girard's mimetic rivalry. Locked up together in the same prison cell, when one of the two men (Palamon) expresses desire for a female object (Emelye) passing into their view, the other (Arcite) almost immediately claims stronger desire. They are, in a sense, inflated versions of those two children striving for the one empty swing on the playground. Their bond as cousins who had sworn an oath of brotherhood (see lines 1.1131–32) is instantly torn asunder. And this is despite the fact that since they are under perpetual sentence of imprisonment, neither seemingly will ever have access to Emelye (who at this point has no knowledge of them whatsoever), and so there is no foreseeable resolution to this rivalrous triangle. Instead, they face a lifetime of nothing but rivalrous enmity, competing for something neither can win, with their ever-deepening conflict totally consuming them.

In fact, that the two cousins fall so quickly into this conflict – which is clearly among the worst possible outcomes for the triangular dynamics of homosocial relations – points to one of the reasons they were in prison to begin with. The Theban ruler killed by Theseus, King Creon, had taken the throne following the decimating civil war between the twin sons of the prior king, who was none other than Oedipus, the notoriously uninformed killer of own his father, who was the king before him. (This back story is not in the Knight's Tale but is alluded to in its epigraph from the *Thebaid*, a Latin epic by Roman poet Statius, that accompanies some manuscript copies of the tale.) The conflict between Arcite and Palamon is thus the end product of generations of violent, internecine conflict – of rivalry undoing homosociality. The cousin's rivalry is a representative recapitulation of the larger, multigenerational story of Theban self-destruction.

To the medieval reader, Athens, in contrast, was the epitome of civilization, which is to say, of successful patriarchal social order, the ground of a historical sequence (termed *translatio imperii*) realized next in Rome and subsequently in the kingdoms of Western Europe, including Chaucer's England. Athens's ruler Theseus therefore epitomizes a form of patriarchal rule that seeks to draw upon the energies of violent masculine rivalry as a means of maintaining and extending social order, using, for example, the rivalries that tore Thebes apart to consolidate Athenian dominion. While the Knight's Tale doesn't tell us why Theseus decides to imprison Arcite and Palamon interminably, from later events we may surmise that it's part of this strategy, with them serving as possible future bargaining chips or just as Theseus's literal control over the Theban royal line. Whatever the reason, the effect is that the self-destructive mode of rivalry practiced by the cousins is contained, shut off from the functional homosocial society of Athens.

Thus, when Theseus discovers that the two cousins not only are no longer his prisoners but also have unleashed the self-destructive force of their rivalry within the very precincts of his dukedom, his first impulse is to eradicate that force by killing both on the spot. "Ye shul be deed," he pronounces, "by mighty Mars the rede" (1.1747). This provokes an outcry by Ipolyta, Emelye, "And alle the ladies in the compaignye," who once again are faced with witnessing deadly violence between men (1.1750). Anachronistically, we might imagine a lightbulb snapping on in Theseus's mind. Here is an opportunity to exhibit and secure, in the most grandiose fashion, the transformation of rivalry into social order. He will orchestrate a grand competition between two groups each of one hundred of the best knights of the world. All these competitors will fight under the strict dictates of his near absolute authority, and the outcome of their controlled and limited violence (again, think football) will be his awarding the body of the sister of his Amazonian bride to the winner. The result will be that one of his Theban political antagonists will become something like a son-in-law, no longer a threat but instead happily bringing Thebes (as well as Scythia) within his political sovereignty. This clever and even elegant plan, of course, fails.

Theseus's Neoplatonic stratagem

The significance of the specific way in which Chaucer represents the immediate cause of this plan's failure, with the unexpected death of the tournament's winner, is a topic we'll revisit later when considering the Miller's response to the Knight. Here, we'll move on to that event's aftermath and note, first, the irony of the exceptionally elaborate funeral that Theseus engineers for Arcite. This supposed fallen hero, after all, was an enemy solider whom Theseus had unceremoniously thrown into prison, who traitorously returned to Athens and insinuated himself into Theseus's household and, when Theseus learned of his identity, was about to be executed by the duke on the spot. Arcite's only actual achievement was to edge out his cousin, another enemy solider, in a rather splashy sort of football game. Plainly, then, the sheer ostentation of his funeral, rather than reflecting Arcite's supposed accomplishments, seeks to plug a hole in the barrel of Theseus's attempt to use male rivalry to extend his power. Theseus has failed to make violent masculine competition the avenue for an alliance between men, cemented by the transfer of a woman's body, with him in the superior position. So he now wants everyone to pretend that Arcite was a great hero who died performing some noble deed in service to Theseus's dukedom. With this stratagem, we witness how a cultural ritual becomes an ideological, even propagandistic stage trick of misdirection, one manipulated by an autocrat to shore up his power. (And, alas, one does not have to search long to find ready correspondences to such manipulative stage tricks in the public ceremonies overseen by today's autocratic patriarchs.)

Chaucer, in added material that has no parallel in Boccaccio's *Teseida*, goes on to provide another instance of Theseus's patent ideological manipulation in a way that greatly raises its stakes via its bearing on the meaning of life, as I defined that phrase above. In the final passages of the tale, he gives Theseus a long, philosophical speech in which the duke situates Arcite's death in an account of the cosmos as an ordered, stable, hierarchical organization of space, time, matter, and spirit. At the top of the hierarchy is the wholly spiritual "Firste Moevere," who "made the faire chaine of love" that is the cosmos; "thilke [this same] Moevere stable is and eterne," and "every [lesser] part deriveth from his hool [whole] … Descending so til it be corrumpable [not eternal or stable]":

And therfore for his wise purveyaunce* — foresight, planning
He hath so wel biset his ordinaunce* — rules
That speces of thinges and progressiouns
Shullen enduren by successiouns,
And noght eterne, withouten any lie.
(1.2987–3015)

According to Theseus's speech, that human life is material and finite reflects the place of the human in the cosmic "faire chaine of love" and in particular our relative distance from the perfect "Firste Moevere" who created everything. Happiness in life requires acceptance of one's place in this cosmic hierarchy: "And who so gruccheth oght [whoever at all complains about this condition], he dooth folye [folly],/And rebel is to him that al may gie [guide, rule]" (1.3045–46).

This philosophical position would've been familiar to Chaucer's contemporaries, at least the more learned ones. With what has come to be known as Neoplatonism, medieval philosophers (and poets) sought to reconcile the principles of Christianity with those of Plato's idealist metaphysics, in which ultimate reality consists of timeless, nonmaterial forms. Among the most influential medieval articulations of this position (if not the most specifically Christian) was the *Consolation of Philosophy* by sixth-century Roman philosopher Boethius, a work that Chaucer himself translated into English. Chaucer puts paraphrases of passages from this work into the mouths of several characters in the tale, with varying degrees of irony or distortion. Theseus's speech here is the most prominent instance of this Boethian borrowing, and in this case the ideas he expresses are, in themselves, wholly consistent with the *Consolation*'s views. In this way, Chaucer makes Theseus a mouthpiece for one of the reigning medieval explanations of the meaning of life, in which a wholly spiritual, wholly absolute, eternal Creator God – a "Firste Moevere" – creates a less perfect material universe that is hierarchically ordered according to a beneficent divine plan, the Creator God's "faire chaine of love."

Yet as obvious to medieval readers as this Neoplatonic vision of the cosmos would have been, also standing in plain sight is Theseus's baldly political deployment of it. Theseus, near the conclusion of his speech, asks his audience, "Why grucchen we, why have we hevinesse,/That good Arcite, of chivalrye flour [the flower of chivalry]/Departed is, with duetee [duty performed] and with honour,/Out of this foule prison of this lif?" (1.3058–61). The aim of his speech, he clearly emphasizes, is to urge Athenians to move beyond the paralysis of mourning by accepting the lowly position of humanity, corporeally entrapped in "this foule prison of this lif," within the cosmic scheme of a nonmaterial absolute Creator God. But, as Chaucer (or, rather, the Knight) is careful to tell us just before Theseus begins his speech, no one is in fact still mourning:

> By process* and by lengthe of certayn yeres, — the course of time
> Al stinted is the moorning* and the teres — ended is the mourning
> Of Greekes by oon general assent.
> Thanne semed me ther was a parlement
> At Atthenes, upon certayn points and cas;* — topics and concerns
> Among the whiche points yspoken was
> To have with certayn contrees alliaunce,
> And have fully of Thebans obeisaunce.* — submission
> (1.2967–74)

The occasion of Theseus's speech, we learn here, isn't some society-wide struggle to cope with the trauma of unexpected death. It's rather – some "certayn yeres" after that event, when all the "Greekes" have in fact moved on – a parliamentary meeting to consider political alliances with "certayn contrees" and in particular to secure total dominance over Thebes. Theseus is thus not really trying to convince the parliament to accept humanity's lot in the cosmos. Rather, after taking a moment before his speech to assume a solemn expression and beginning, performatively, with a sigh ("with a sad visage he siked stille" [1.2985]), he attempts to persuade them that the best way to secure Theban submission is by marrying Emelye to Palamon. He would thereby forge a homosocial alliance that places him in the alpha-male position and extends the dominion of his own political authority. His apparent success at this attempt quickly leads to the tale's happily-ever-after conclusion, although notably we hear no direct speech from anyone involved except for Theseus.

On the one hand, then, Theseus's "First Moevere" speech supplies a suspiciously convenient autocratic metaphysics for a ruler who is praised, at the tale's outset, as "swich [such] a conquerour,/That gretter was ther noon [none] under the sonne" (1.862–63). On the other hand, not only is that metaphysics one that we may be confident that Chaucer took quite seriously (although his ultimate attitude toward it, as toward most things, is much less certain), but also, in the context of the Knight's Tale, the social order underwritten by that metaphysics would seem to be the more desirable alternative to the bloody mess of Theban mimetic rivalry. Does Chaucer mean us then to embrace the autocratic political ramifications of Neoplatonic metaphysics, with its vision of the meaning of human life as subject to an absolute, nonmaterial God, as the most promising way to navigate the "thurghfare [thoroughfare] ful of wo" (1.2847) that, according to Theseus's father Egeus, constitutes the temporary space of our corporeal existence? Or is Chaucer here exposing this metaphysics as an ideological feint, deployed by an autocratic ruler with imperialist ambitions, in order to consolidate and extend his power?

In fact, much of the long history of scholarly disagreement about the Knight's Tale boils down to whether or how much one understands Chaucer to be with Theseus or against him. Because of the multiple levels of indirection afforded by the overall form of the *Canterbury Tales*, this question also necessarily involves the Knight, the teller of the tale who is himself a fictional character, whose performance is related to us by yet another fictional character, the pilgrim version of Chaucer who is along for the ride to Canterbury. To ask whether Chaucer's views align with Theseus's, then, we must ask the same question for each of these fictional narrators and then determine how each answer relates to the others. This structure seems perversely designed to occlude any easy identification of the author's attitude toward the views of his characters. Yet this has not prevented scholars from readily assuming either ideological harmony or hostility between Chaucer and Theseus and producing, accordingly, vastly different interpretations of the tale.

Without discounting the likelihood of either view, we might alternatively consider how the tale itself may be exploring the very question. With this tale, that is, Chaucer may be weighing the benefits and costs of the political/theological metaphysics that Theseus promotes. As I mentioned above, when Chaucer first wrote the story of the Knight's Tale, he had recently witnessed the insurgency of 1381. In the years that followed that event, Chaucer also witnessed (at first hand, in his role as a government official) the political "strif" provoked by the absolutist tendencies of an autocrat, in this case, King Richard II. Eventually, this strife resulted, in the year before Chaucer's death, in Richard's throne being seized by his own cousin Henry of Derby, shortly after which Richard was murdered in prison. Sometime in those months, after his decades of service to King Richard, Chaucer wrote what may have been his final literary composition: a short poem, known as "The Complaint of

Chaucer to His Purse," that requests payment of his annual salary from the newly ascended King Henry. This is all just to suggest that in his historical moment, Chaucer would have had good reason to wonder whether Theseus's absolutism was a satisfactory or even viable solution to Theban chaos.

Emelye and the plight of women

One of the costs of Theseus's version of social order that is unmistakably foregrounded by the tale takes us back to that order's gendered organization. As the Knight's Tale epitomizes, to produce social stability, the triangle of homosociality requires the total nonagency of the woman occupying the female position. Whether that woman is the token to be passed from the alpha male to his subordinate or the object of competition between rivals, if she refuses to play along, the triangle's sociopolitically consolidating circuits of desire fail. Not at all coincidentally, therefore, Chaucer reshapes the plot that he takes from Boccaccio to reduce its representation of female agency dramatically and starkly to call attention to that very reduction.

By indicating the Amazonian identity of Ipolyta and Emelye at the outset of the story, Chaucer ensures that all the subsequent events involving them happen in some relation to an idea of a female agency exercised wholly independently of patriarchal social orders. Yet Chaucer drastically abbreviates their introduction into the tale, merely mentioning, rather than describing (as Boccaccio does at length), Theseus's conquering of "the regne of Femenye" (1.866). Consequently, as the male-versus-male rivalrous plot unfolds, readers may well forget this important fact about the background of the female object over whom Palamon and Arcite are contending. When she finally gives her first and only direct speech, then, we are all the more stunned. Emelye, slated to serve as Theseus's prize to the winner of a violent and perhaps deadly combat between men, pleas to Diana, the virgin huntress goddess, for a way out. She asks, in effect, precisely for her former Amazonian female agency, independent of Theseus's patriarchal social order, that her very situation is denying her:

> Chaste goddesse, woostou* that I — *you know well*
> Desire to been a maiden al my lif,
> Ne never wol I be no love ne wif.
> I am, thou woost,* yet of thy compaignye, — *you know*
> A maide, and love hunting and venerye,* — *sport hunting*
> And for to walken in the wodes* wilde, — *woods*
> And noght to been a wif and be with childe* — *pregnant*
> Noght wol I knowe compaignye of man.
> (1.2304–11)

She requests, moreover, that the whole rivalrous structure of homosociality be overturned:

This grace I praye thee* withoute moore:	ask of you, Diana
As sende love and pees* bitwixe hem two,	peace
And fro me turn away hir hertes* so	their hearts
That al hir hote* love and hir desir,	hot, violently agitated
And al hir bisy* torment and hir fir,*	anxious; fire
Be queint* or turned in another place.	extinguished
(1.2316–21)	

In a striking remodulation of Boccaccio's corresponding passage, Emelye here movingly protests against the very role in which she has been cast, speaking thereby on behalf of everyone whom the triangular structure of patriarchal homosociality slots into that role.[2] She offers a vision of an alternative to what feminist theorist and poet Adrienne Rich diagnoses as the *compulsory heterosexuality* of patriarchal societies. She asks for a world in which women are encouraged to follow their own inclinations, "to walken in the wodes wilde," and not face the normative demand that they be "a wif and be with childe." For men, in place of violent rivalry, she imagines relations of "love and pees," with the fires of mimetic desire either wholly "queint" or redirected so as not to include women as the necessary third party.

Diana curtly and categorically denies her request, with very little explanation. Flatly reasserting the structure of homosociality, she declares, "Thou shalt be wedded unto oon of tho [the two]" (1.2351). Emelye expresses bewildered astonishment, and then her voice vanishes from the tale as quickly as it finally and belatedly emerged. The effect is haunting. This one glimpse of her perspective, in its sheer contrast with what comes before and after, ensures that her desperate plea hangs over the tale's ending sequence. Our knowledge of her desire makes it present in its absence, firmly establishing that desire's denial, or indeed its total lack of recognition, as one of the flesh-and-blood consequences of the absolutist metaphysics of Theseus's speech. According to that metaphysics, everything in the cosmos has its place. The silent refusal to recognize the female desire that Emelye so eloquently voices thus signifies that the place of women is to serve as the passive objects that enable rivalrous relations between men to stabilize into patriarchal, hierarchical social order, regardless of what women themselves may want.

The question of whether or how much Chaucer is with Theseus or against him, therefore, necessarily also raises the question of whether or how much Chaucer is rationalizing the subjection of women or critiquing it. Not surprisingly, this also has been a topic of great disagreement.

But regardless of which direction one takes, any informed answer must begin by acknowledging that, at the very least, Chaucer is not here disguising or covering up patriarchy's structural requirement of the subjection of women. He is rather calling attention to it, explicitly pointing to the denial of female agency and female suffering as necessary consequences of the ideology expressed and represented by Theseus. As much of this book attests, this sort of recognition of women's subjection, whatever it means, is in fact not at all unusual for Chaucer. It rather serves for him as a primary source of creative energy.

Saturn's speech, the Rising of 1381, and the Miller's intrusion

In light of Theseus's vision of the cosmos as a stable, eternal, hierarchical "faire chaine of love" descending from the absolute authority of a "Firste Moevere," we're now in better position to appreciate the stakes involved in the Miller's boisterous interruption of what would've been the socially appropriate transition from Knight to Monk. As I mentioned at the outset of this chapter, that interruption's overturning of social hierarchies possesses a suggestive parallel to the Rising of 1381, the so-called Peasant's Revolt in which, across the kingdom, groups of individuals from the lower strata of the social hierarchy demanded – by argument as well as acts and threats of violence – rights, privileges, and resources denied them. Against the backdrop of Theseus's speech, we have reason to suspect that this parallel extends from the sociopolitical to the metaphysical, presenting thereby a rather different understanding of the meaning of life in relation to questions of social order. And in a characteristic moment of laconic profundity, Chaucer plants a seed for this suspicion in the Knight's Tale itself.

Notably, although Chaucer rarely directly refers to the Rising of 1381, one place he does so is in the Knight's Tale. This occurs in the speech of the god/planet Saturn, a passage with no precedent in Chaucer's sources. When Venus and Mars squabble over their mutually exclusive respective promises to Palamon and Arcite (a conflict that itself undercuts the vision of stable order and balance of contending forces that Theseus's circular stadium is presumably meant to symbolize), Saturn intercedes. He pledges to manipulate the circumstances so that both promises will be kept, explaining to his grandchildren gods (as he names them), "Bitwixe you ther moot [must] be som time pees [peace]" (1.2474). But rather than disclosing his plan, he devotes most of his speech to describing his own nature, which seems to be one of violence and death, often of the random, uncontrolled, or malevolent sort. He hence represents a cosmic force that would seem to be the stark opposite of that of the "First Moevere" with his "faire chaine of love." Examples of Saturn's "power" are drowning, strangling, the collapse of towers upon carpenters, the plague, and, casually and ambiguously dropped among these, "The murmur and the cherles rebelling [the discontent and rebellion of the churls or lower classes]" (1.2455, 2459).

For Chaucer's fourteenth-century audience, this rather specific reference to a recent sociopolitical trauma likely raised eyebrows, as it was perhaps too uncomfortably close to home. What makes it profound rather than merely winkingly provocative is that it appears here not just as an instance of Saturnine chaos but also, paradoxically, as a manifestation of a force that seeks to resolve Palamon and Arcite's self-destructive rivalry. Significantly, it seeks to do so in a rather different fashion than planned by Theseus: namely by arranging events so that the rivals themselves acknowledge the pointlessness of their competition. Shortly following the misfortune, orchestrated by Saturn, of Arcite's being thrown from his horse, the internecine strife between the cousins abruptly ceases. With his dying words, Arcite wonders aloud about the meaning of a life that has precisely the same outcome for any man, regardless of his successes and failures – which is to lie "in his colde grave,/Allone withouten any compaignye" (1.2778–79). Acknowledging then the "strif and rancour" between himself and Palamon, he moves to resolve the homosocial triangle by gifting his claim on the female object to his rival, telling Emelye, "if that ever ye shal been a wif,/Foryet nat Palamon, the gentil man" (1.2796–97). That this resolution, this passing of Emelye to Palamon, does not actually occur until much later is, as we know, the result of Theseus reinserting himself and his political ideology into the homosocial triangle in the aftermath of the surprise failure of his original plan.

Chaucer therefore situates the Rising of 1381 within a quite different vision of the cosmos than the Neoplatonic one of Theseus's speech. That entire speech, as we considered above, may be understood as Theseus's attempt to reimpose his vision in the wake of the tale's Saturnine turn of events – "To maken vertu of necessitee" (1.3042), as Theseus himself puts it. The alternative, Saturnine vision, in so provoking Theseus, lays claim to a more basic, fundamental truth of human experience, the truth that Theseus seeks to paint over. Insofar as the Knight may be aligned with Theseus, then, the Miller's intrusion into the orderly sequencing of the *Tales* may be aligned with Saturn. That intrusion, as precisely the action of a rebellious churl like those whom Saturn mentions, serves as a parallel in the work's frame narrative to the "furye infernal [hellish fury]" (1.2684) whose sudden appearance, causing Arcite's horse to throw him from the saddle, foils Theseus's orderly plan. In this way, the intrusion cues us to understand the Miller's ensuing performance as Chaucer's further articulation – and also, as we will see, evaluation – of a Saturnine/churlish understanding of the meaning of life as a potential alternative to that of the Knight's/Theseus's. And lest we miss this cue, Chaucer makes sure early on to signal the general rivalrous nature of the relation between the two tales by importing verbatim Arcite's moving deathbed remark about being eternally "Allone withouten any compaignye" into a vastly different literary context.

The Miller's Tale

Genre and summary

That vastly different context is supplied by the literary genre known as the fabliau. Short narratives possessing a comic element of some sort, fabliaux would've been known by Chaucer primarily as compositions in French, mostly from the century that preceded his own. Notably, among the very first English instances of the genre are several of the tales told by Canterbury pilgrims, including the Miller's and the immediately following Reeve's. This suggests that Chaucer's choice of this genre for the Miller was far from preordained but rather represents a calculated literary innovation on his part. We may therefore consider the relation between the Knight's and the Miller's performances by first contemplating what it was that prompted Chaucer to try his hand specifically at a fabliau for the purpose of representing the Miller's attempt, as that character puts it, "Somewhat to quite with [repay, pay back, or get back at] the Knightes tale" (1.3119).

What distinguishes fabliaux as a genre are not so much any particular formal features but rather a readily apparent overall attitude toward human life. As scholar Derek Pearsall (1985) describes, with a fabliau, "the common understanding of author and reader is that there are no values, secular or religious, more important than survival and the satisfaction of appetite" (167). To read or write a fabliau according to how the genre prompts is to adopt a set of values that give priority to the material, corporeal aspects of human experience and conversely to deprioritize, if not wholly put aside, values of other sorts, especially those "secular or religious" values whose sources are ultimately nonmaterial. Built into the genre itself is thus a competition between contrasting understandings of the meaning of life, and indeed very often this competition is staged directly in the narrative, with, say, the winners duping the losers by means of the latter's deluded embrace of nonmaterial values.

In the Miller's Tale, a university student named Nicholas dupes his landlord, a carpenter named John, by manipulating John's earnest if rather unsophisticated piety. But more than spiritual values, sighted in the crosshairs of this tale are the values promoted by medieval romance: the elevation of love, and especially the pursuit of love, into an all-encompassing principle of being. Of course, this pursuit of love usually has a straightforward erotic component, and thus it would seem already more corporeal than not. Nonetheless, what fabliaux such as the Miller's Tale target in the medieval romance is precisely its error (according to fabliaux) of believing love to be something *more* than a matter of sexual appetite or physical domination. In this view, Arcite and Palamon were right to pursue the sexual possession/domination of Emelye and thereby gain an alpha-male edge on the other. Their mistake was to believe that this pursuit held any larger meaning than that, whether of a personal, social, or cosmic nature. What these fabliaux expose and mock, that is, is the *idealization* of love, or, literally, the turning of the physicality of love into an idea which, like the idea of God, can be worshiped and centered as the ultimately nonmaterial value around which one organizes one's life.[3]

The Miller's Tale unmistakably signals this target just a few lines in, when in his introduction of the main characters the Miller remarks, "This clerk [university student] was cleped [called] hende Nicholas./Of derne love he coude [knew], and of solas [pleasure]" (1.3219–20). The now obscure terms "hende" and "derne love" are the giveaways here. By Chaucer's day, "hende" had long served as the English adjective for encompassing a range of positive and usually (though not always) masculine romance hero traits. The *Middle English Dictionary* defines the word as "Having the approved courtly or knightly qualities, noble, courtly, well-bred, refined, sportsmanlike." The phrase "derne love" held something like the meaning of "courtly love," a phrase not used in the Middle Ages but invented by nineteenth-century scholars as an umbrella term for the many manifestations of the idealization of love that they found in medieval romances. "Derne" had a primary meaning of "secret," and so the phrase "derne love" emphasized the private, intimate, hidden, and perhaps adulterous elements of courtly love (as in the famous example of Guinevere and Lancelot) but also its mysterious power. With these two lines, then, the Miller's Tale in one stroke decimates romance idealism through a gross misapplication of the terms to Nicholas. The events of the tale make plain that Nicholas's only "approved courtly or knightly qualities" are ones that he farcically assumes either to delude others or simply out of mockery. Likewise, the secrecy of his "derne love" consists of his deceiving the gullible John.

All the components of the tale's plot Chaucer could've found in existing stories, and a Dutch tale of uncertain date puts most of those pieces together. But the sheer elaboration of the tale's parodic and ironic detail is entirely Chaucer's. For example, unusually for a fabliau, Chaucer devotes a significant portion of the story to descriptions of his four main characters, some 111 lines of the total 668. The beginning of the tale tells us about the old, "sely" carpenter John, with "sely" (our modern "silly") having an ambiguously expansive meaning encompassing "gullible" but also "innocent." We learn of the Oxford university student Nicholas, who rents a room in John's house, where he dwells (as the Miller sardonically adds) "Allone, withouten any compaignye" (1.3204). And then we hear about John's young wife Alisoun, for whom the Miller provides a notoriously leering *effictio* (the rhetorical term for a head-to-toe description). Later he tells us about "joly" Absolon, a parish clerk (a low-level assistant to the parish priest), with "joly" (our modern "jolly") also an expansive adjective, here encompassing a self-presentation that we might now call dandyish, with an unintentional foppish result.

Chaucer weaves together two basic plot lines: the machinations of Nicholas and Alisoun to secure an entire nighttime of sex, and the rivalry between Nicholas and Absolon over Alisoun's 'love.' Nicholas devises a ruse so overly elaborate for the former purpose that we quickly understand that its point, much beyond its immediate appetitive end, is to serve as an ostentatious display of Nicholas's conniving masculine superiority and to mock the naïve piety that is its instrument of deception. He convinces John that he alone has learned, through his "astrologye" (1.3514), about God's decision to cause a second world-destroying flood. He offers to include John and Alisoun in his plan to survive. John is to secure three large tubs, load them with "breed and cheese and good ale" (1.3628), and hang them from the rafters. They will sleep each in their own tub until the flood arrives, then cut the cords and float safely until the waters recede. Meanwhile, Absolon repeatedly attempts to woo Alisoun. One night, he serenades her in courtly style outside her bedroom window but succeeds only in waking John, who was of course lying next to her. On the day whose night would supposedly see the earth flooded, Absolon, hearing that no one has seen John and so believing him to be away, determines to attempt another nighttime wooing of Alisoun outside her window. But readers know that no one has seen John because he has been carrying out Nicholas's plan, and, by evening, John, Alisoun, and Nicholas have climbed into their respective tubs. When they hear John snoring, Alisoun and Nicholas climb out of their tubs and "Withouten words mo [more] they goon [go] to bedde/Theras [where] the carpenter is wont to lie" (1.3650–51).

The two plot lines spectacularly collide in the tale's conclusion. Once more, Absolon in courtly style serenades Alisoun outside her window, and once again he does so while another man – albeit a different one – lies in bed next to her. In response to his entreaty, which begins, "What do ye, hony-comb, sweete Alisoun,/My faire brid [bird], my sweete cinamome," he receives from Alisoun the curt, unequivocal rebuff, "Go fro the windowe, Jakke fool" (1.3698–99, 3708). According to the masculinist tradition of courtly wooing, Absolon interprets this rejection as an invitation to keep trying, and so he promises to leave if Alisoun grants him a kiss. She agrees,

> And at the windowe out she putte hir hole
> And Absolon, him fil no bet ne wers* — *it befell him no better or worse*
> But with his mouth he kiste hir naked ers* — *ass*
> Full savourly, er he was war* of this. — *before he was aware*
> (1.3732–35)

Enraged at being so tricked, Absolon walks away vowing revenge. He happens upon a blacksmith and borrows from him a "hote cultour" – the part of a plow that cuts the earth, still hot from the forge. Returning to Alisoun's window, he asks for another kiss. But this time Nicholas, having "risen for to pisse" and deciding that he will outdo Alisoun's "jape," opens the window and puts "out his ers [ass] ... Over the buttok to the haunche-bon [sacrum]" (1.3798–3803). Absolon entreats Alisoun to speak, and in response Nicholas "leet fle [let fly] a fart/As greet as it hadde been a thonder-dent [thunderclap]" (1.3805–6). Although "almost yblent [blinded]" by the fart, Absolon "was redy with his iren hoot,/And Nicholas amide the ers [ass] he smoot [struck]" (1.3808–10). In literally searing pain, Nicholas cries out for water. John, awakened by the cry and believing it to announce the flood's arrival, cuts the rope to his tub and crashes to the floor, breaking his arm. The townspeople gather and proceed to have a good laugh at John's plight, turning "al his harm unto a jape [into a joke]" (1.3842). Upon hearing his explanation, they assume that he has lost his mind: "he was holden wood [insane] in al the toun" (1.3846).

The Miller's complementary counter-ideology

Cued by the Miller to anticipate parallels between his tale and the Knight's, we can easily spot them. We notice the same basic set of main characters and plot structure: both tales feature three men and a woman, with the two younger men positioned as rivals for the woman, who is in some sense in the possession of the third, older man, who is in some way the 'ruler of the realm' (with duke = landlord). The plot's climax in each case involves the older man's using the resources under his control to build a structure designed to organize future events in his favor (with Theseus's stadium's three temples = John's three tubs), and in both cases the structure fails to achieve its purpose. These parallels, of course, serve to highlight the sheer contrasts evident at each point of comparison, which then carry the critical force of a mocking imitation. As a result, every ideological position, every espoused value of the Knight's Tale is potentially exposed as either a delusion or a means to delude others. If we join in the laughter that the Miller's Tale invites from its readers, we're also therefore laughing at the Knight's Tale's vision of the world. But what sort of counter-vision does the Miller offer in its place?

As I earlier mentioned, fabliaux in general emphasize the corporeal level of human experience. They understand human beings as motivated primarily by physical appetite and the desire to dominate. When the Miller supplies this perspective on human life as part of his ironic mimicry of the preceding tale, it thereby serves, in one sense, as an alternative to that tale's spiritualized Neoplatonic perspective, as voiced by Theseus. Yet in another sense, given the Saturnine undercurrent to the Knight's Tale that becomes explicit with the god's speech, the fabliaux perspective is not as much an alternative as a further development of what the Knight's Tale itself at some level recognizes but then seeks to gloss over. In this respect, Theseus may be understood as accepting that human life is in fact a matter of appetite and domination and thus, precisely as *a means of domination*, shrewdly promulgating the ideology that instead sets human experience in relation to the ultimate spiritual value of the "Firste Moevere." Arcite and Palamon might be understood as making the mistake of believing that their total surrender to appetite and the desire to dominate represents a noble commitment to an ideal of love, thereby ensuring that the self-destructive force of those motivations has full scope.

In this view, the lesson that the Miller's Tale seems to take from the Knight's Tale is that in this life you ought to grab what's in reach by whatever means are at your disposal and not be duped by the belief that there is anything more to your or anyone else's motivations. If you attempt to grab what's out of reach – as Nicholas does in wanting to outdo Alisoun's trick and, perhaps as Chaucer thought, the 1381 insurgents did in the full extent of their demands – you will suffer the violent reprisal of those who catch your hand in the cookie jar. The bigger losers, however, are the earnest believers, as John with his piety and, again perhaps as Chaucer thought, Richard II with his sense of divinely ordained kingship.

Theseus oddly turns out to be a fabliaux winner in this understanding of the Knight–Miller sequence, as he neither overreaches nor, it would seem, is fooled by the metaphysics that he himself voices. Accordingly, the Miller's Tale's ideology, rather than overturning that of the Knight's Tale and the absolutist, patriarchal social order that it reinforces, would seem to complement it by endorsing a qualified version of it. The Miller's Tale would seem to tell us: accept that social order and the limits that it places on you as one viable response to the underlying, tumultuous reality of rivalrous individual desires, but don't believe that order's self-justifying ideology – don't be gulled into working against your own self-interest. The Miller's disruption of the social hierarchy in his refusal to allow the tale-telling to pass to the Monk would not then signal revolution as much as just *demystification*. It exposes the reigning social protocols as smoke and mirrors concealing the reality of domination and desire, but it offers no actual alternative to the social order that those protocols reflect and sustain.

In yet another sense, however, such a grim, bad-faith, Hobbesian "life is nasty, brutish, and short" attitude toward human life is rather strikingly at odds with what many readers find to be the overall festive spirit of the Miller's Tale, despite its rather sordid series of events. The Miller conveys the perspective that underlies this festive spirit in his prologue, especially in his response to the Reeve's irate accusation that he intends his tale to depict the Reeve as a cuckold. The Miller observes,

I have a wif, pardee,* as wel as thou,	by god
Yet nolde I,* for the oxen in my plough,	I would not
Take upon me more than ynough	
As deemen of myself that I were oon:*	i.e., a cuckhold
I wol bileve that I am noon.*	not one
An housbonde shal noght been inquisitive	
Of Goddes privetee,* nor of his wif.	secrets
So he may finde Goddes foison* there,	plenty
Of the remenant needeth noght enquere.	
(1.3158–65)	

The Miller suggests that desire (specifically here sexual appetite) may be satisfied and that if one does manage to get what one wants ("finde Goddes foison there"), then one need not begrudge others getting what they want (specifically here his wife potentially having sex with other men). He imagines, in other words, a *non*-rivalrous structure of social relations, a live-and-let-live ethos that by embracing ignorance ("I wol bilevel that I am noon") may produce stable contentment and hence peaceful interaction and even a measure of joviality. The Miller's equation here of the mysteries of God ("Goddes privetee") with those of his wife's fidelity levels the difference between the spiritual and the corporeal, as the fabliau attitude encourages. It thereby extends this principle of contentment across the full breadth of desire, from the physical to the metaphysical.[4] Whether or how this principle might be represented in the Miller's Tale itself, however, and hence what sort of alternative ideology the Miller's performance as a whole may represent, depends to a large degree on how we interpret Alisoun's character and role.

Alisoun and the question of female desire

Just as with the Knight's Tale, the energy and ambiguity of Chaucer's exploration of these themes in the Miller's Tale ultimately gravitate to the structural position of women within a patriarchal social order. To begin with the tale's resolution, the prologue's principle of contentment, at first glance, may not seem much in evidence. As the Miller sums up in the concluding lines, following his observation that all the townspeople considered John mentally broken ("They saide, 'The man was wood, my leve brother'"),

> Thus swived* was the carpenteres wif — screwed
> For al his keeping* and his jalousye, — despite John's surveillance
> And Absolon hath kist her nether eye* — i.e., one of her lower orifices
> And Nicholas is scalded in the toute.* — on his ass
> (1.3847–53)

John, Absolon, and Nicholas appear to suffer the fate of those who attempt to grab what's out of reach, and John and to some extent Absolon are further punished for believing in values beyond the merely appetitive. But what about Alisoun? We are told that she has been "swived," that is, that she has been the object of Nicholas's sexual penetration. But at the moment when it occurs, that sexual activity is described as follows:

> Ther* was the revel and the melodye, — i.e., in John's bed
> And thus lith* Alison and Nicholas — lie
> In bisinesse of mirthe and of solas.
> (1.3652–54)

With the caveat that this description was written by a male author for a fictional male narrator (and so any real or fictional female point of view is wholly absent), we may cautiously note the apparent contrast between its sensibility and that of "swived was the carpenteres wif." The nouns "revel" and "mirthe" emphasize the joyousness of the activity along with its "solas" or pleasure, and "melodye" – which has much the same range of meaning as our modern "melody" – potentially connotes the collaboration of the partners in that "solas."

In its most reduced and bluntest form, then, the question of whether the Miller's Tale has anything to offer other than a deconstruction-without-replacement of the ideology of the Knight's Tale rests upon the question of whether Alisoun actually wants to have sex with Nicholas. If she does, then she may represent the successful achievement of satisfied, even joyful contentment in a tumultuous world of material competition – a life that might be led in peaceful coexistence with others, as long as John follows the Miller's principle of not being "inquisitive" about his wife's sex life and Nicholas knows not to want too much. Crucially, the homosocial triangle involving those three characters has a rather different dynamic than that which is operative in the Knight's. As we saw, for the latter tale's triangles, social order depends on women's abject passivity, in respect to which female desire of any sort is either a hostile force to be vanquished or, at best, irrelevant. In the Miller's Tale, not only might the Alisoun-Nicholas-John triangle make space for female desire, but its potential to draw on the energies of the structure of male rivalry without their consequences would seem to depend on Alisoun's sexual agency. In privately agreeing to have sex with Nicholas, on the condition that John never find out, both men may be satisfied even while they remain positionally rivals. Hence when Alisoun, at very moment she verbally agrees, insists to Nicholas, "Ye moste been ful derne as in this cas" (1.3297), she does not only explode in one stroke the whole ideology of noble, courtly "derne love." She also coaches Nicholas about how to make the homosocial triangle work in a way that the sort of courtly love represented by Arcite and Palamon would scarcely recognize.

In the aftermath of #MeToo, however, we now know – if we did not already – that within a resolutely patriarchal social order what might appear to be female consent is often far from it.[5] In this case, the Miller tells us that following Nicholas's initial sexual entreaty,

> ...she hir love him graunted atte laste
> And swoor hir ooth by Saint Thomas of Kent[6]
> That she wolde been at his commandement,
> Whan that she may hir leiser wel espye.* — determine an opportune time
>
> (1.3290–93)

However unequivocal and even active these narratorially reported words may seem, their status as verbal consent is greatly vexed if not simply negated by the events immediately leading up to them. Nicholas first makes a demand for sex after he has, without invitation, grabbed Alisoun's groin (the text is notoriously courser: "And prively he caughte hire by the queinte" [1.3276]). He continues his entreaty, declaring (as courtly lovers are wont to do) that he will die without her love ("For derne love of thee, lemman [beloved one], I spille [die]") while holding her "harde by the haunchebones [hips]" (1.3278–79). The uncanny echo of this moment voiced by Donald Trump in the infamous *Access Hollywood* tape ("And when you're a star, they let you do it. You can do anything. Grab them by the pussy. You can do anything") ensures that readers today place it in the context of a social order in which toxic masculinity is a homosocial norm – what scholar Carissa Harris (2018) has perspicaciously termed "felawe masculinity."

For her part, Alisoun, in response to what must be characterized as assault – no matter how much the two before were engaged in "rage and play [flirtation]" (1.3273) – makes her refusal crystal clear:

> And she sprong as a colt doth in the trave,* — an enclosure for restraining horses
> And with hir heed* she wried* faste away; — head; twisted

> She saide, "I wol nat kisse thee, by my fay.* faith
> Why, lat be," quod she, "lat be, Nicholas!
> Or I wol crye 'Out, harrow,* and allas!' help
> Do way youre hands, for your curteisye!"
> (1.3282–87)

Here, in a pun that Chaucer surely intended, "hende Nicholas" turns out to be "handy" in a gross physical sense, and the supposed "courtly or knightly qualities" of the "hende" lover are, in the equivalence made here with physical assault, exposed as weapons of male sexual aggression. What is considerably less clear, then, is the nature of Alisoun's ensuing verbal consent. One might imagine a wide range of possible scenarios, from her arriving at an authentic expression of choice and sexual desire to her being wholly coerced into verbal surrender in response to a physical assault that might well have eventuated in rape. Before #MeToo, many readers assumed the former scenario, while today the latter has gained broader currency. Whichever one chooses (and there are, of course, many possibilities in between the two), one nonetheless has to acknowledge that they are indeed *imagined* scenarios – that is, scenarios that we're adding to the text – since between Alisoun's refusal and her agreement Chaucer gives us only two very terse and highly indeterminate lines.

For help, we might set this moment against the later one in which Absolon returns to Alisoun's window when she's lying in bed with Nicholas. Once again, Alisoun faces unwanted sexual entreaties, this time from Absolon. In this case, the homosocial triangle involves Nicholas and Absolon in the positions of male rivals. But the scene does not depict a direct competition between them for possession of a passive female object. Instead, Alisoun – having already chosen or been coerced into sex with Nicholas – chooses to provide (or is pushed into providing) Absolon a substitute act of physical intimacy, one that marks his failure to possess her in its very proximity to what would stand as success. As with the earlier moment of verbal consent to Nicholas, how much female agency is in evidence here is not a simple question and likely to elicit a range of competing answers. Yet even if there is little or no agency in this later instance, there does seem to be female *creativity*. Sticking her rear end out the window appears to be entirely Alisoun's own innovative response to Absolon's unwanted sexual advances. If she was coerced into some sort of response, the form of the response seems to be her own, one calculated to provide her and Nicholas amusement at Absolon's expense: "Now hust [hush]," she says to Nicholas, "and thou shalt laughen al thy fille" (1.3722). Perhaps, then, the possibility for an affirmative vision of human life in the Miller's Tale resides in this sort of creative response to the conditions into which human beings have been thrown – and in the momentary joy that such a response may elicit, as evident in Alisoun's laughter at her own success: "'Teehee,' quod she, and clapte the windowe to [shut]" (1.3740).

This joy is indeed only momentary, of course. While we don't know what happens to Alisoun following John's plunge to the floor, it's hard to imagine a happy ending. And we can't forget that as punishment for Alisoun's creative reworking of the homosocial triangle, Absolon's hot iron was meant for her. From Absolon's perspective, the fabliau world of desire, deceit, and domination yields the lesson that if you can't get what you want, then get revenge. And it is this lesson, rather than anything about creativity and satisfaction, that subsequently emerges into the dramatic frame of the *Canterbury Tales* when the Reeve, with his tale, determines to get back at the Miller for the latter's perceived insult. Whatever potential the fabliau held for Chaucer in its initial rollout, its devolution with the mean-spirited Reeve's Tale (which features rape as a form of revenge) and the following Cook's Tale soon becomes a dead end. Notably, and alas not surprisingly, the roles of women in these tales become even more abject than in the Knight's Tale. With the mysteriously abrupt termination of the Cook's Tale, Chaucer leaves this particular downward trajectory behind and, with the Man of Law's Tale, provides us with something of a new start, as the next chapter will explore.

Notes

1 I owe this example to a student at the time.
2 Boccaccio's Emilia does not specifically request a restoration of her Amazonian agency but just generally for a happy outcome for the next day's contest between Theban rivals.
3 Indeed, much medieval romance idealizes love in this fashion by drawing on explicitly religious language (and, reciprocally, some medieval religious writings draw on the language of romance). The most sophisticated medieval romances, such as Chaucer's *Troilus and Criseyde*, are quite aware of the tensions within the overlaps between these otherwise quite different sorts of compositions.
4 Indeed, that "privetee" in Chaucer's day could also mean "genitalia" (as in our modern "private parts") perhaps subsumes the spiritual entirely into the corporeal.
5 For much more on this topic, see Chapter 8 on *Troilus and Criseyde*.
6 That is, she swore an oath by Saint Thomas à Becket of Canterbury, the very saint to whose shrine the Canterbury pilgrims are journeying.

3 The Man of Law's Tale

Since the Cook's Tale seemingly breaks off abruptly without any dramatized transition to the Man of Law, we can't be absolutely sure that Chaucer was responsible for this sequence, given that the earliest manuscripts of the *Tales* all likely postdate Chaucer's death. It remains uncertain (and a matter of some debate) how much the scribes who assembled those manuscripts knew about Chaucer's plans for tale order or even how firm Chaucer himself had been about those plans when he stopped working on his final, unfinished literary project. Nearly all the manuscripts place the Man of Law's tale in this position, however, and the likeliest interpretation of the few that do not is that they have misplaced the tale (Meyer-Lee 2013, 66–67). The very absence of an explicit segue thus suggests that the placement does in fact go back to Chaucer, since without any internal cues about where the tale belongs, its consistent position among the manuscripts implies that the earliest scribes just left it where they found it.[1]

It seems likely, therefore, that – as mentioned at the end of the preceding chapter – Chaucer intends the Man of Law's Tale to represent something of a reboot of the unfolding literary experiment that is the *Canterbury Tales*, following upon the devolution of the tale-telling contest into mean-spirited efforts of one pilgrim to get back at another. The Host's elaborate opening calculation of day and time (occupying some fourteen lines) appears pointedly to echo the General Prologue's initiating astrological periphrasis. His following concern with the pilgrims' wasting of time ("Now for the love God and of Saint John,/Leseth [waste] no time as ferforth as [as far as] ye may" [2.18–19]) seems then to suggest that the pilgrims have done just that with the preceding fabliaux and that the tale-telling contest needs rejuvenation with something of the high seriousness, dignity, and thematic heft of the Knight's Tale.

The Host's choice of the Man of Law for this purpose possesses sound social logic. We know from the General Prologue that this pilgrim is not just any lawyer but holds the status of Sergeant of Law. As such, he belongs to what was in a Chaucer's day a very small, elite group of highly educated,

DOI: 10.4324/9781003273318-4

powerful, and wealthy attorneys with special privileges in the English legal system. Although in strict social-status terms the Man of Law is a commoner, in that he holds no aristocratic title, as a sergeant he in practice possesses a stature in some ways equivalent to that of the Knight and perhaps even a notch up the scale. Thus holding tale-telling promise at least socially, the Man of Law in many respects does not disappoint. The tale that he tells, with its sprawling narrative and far-reaching ideological scope, approaches the Knight's in its ambition. Like that tale, it is centrally concerned with the political requirements of a hierarchical, autocratic, patriarchal social order, which it similarly situates within a vision of the cosmos that serves as that order's justification. These rather plainly marked parallels, however, also cast into relief important differences, which point to several of the specific issues at stake in this *Canterbury Tales* reboot.

The Man of Law's Tale versus the Knight's: setting, narrator, protagonist, genre

For Chaucer's contemporary audience, the geopolitical setting of the Man of Law's Tale would've felt considerably more proximate to their world. The setting of the Knight's Tale in ancient, pre-Christian Athens and Thebes would've held a "once upon a time" quality for those readers, one that includes – with its depiction of Greek gods – a fantasy element. The correspondences that Chaucer's readers would find with their own historical moment would be similar to those that we might find with, say, the Star Wars saga. In contrast, although the Man of Law's Tale is set during the period of the Roman Empire, many centuries before Chaucer's time, its depiction of a Christian empire in conflict with Islamic peoples would've been understood as having direct bearing on the late fourteenth-century present. In Chaucer's day, the Pope had been crowning a succession of European monarchs as Holy Roman Emperor for centuries; Byzantium, or what was left of the Empire's eastern territories, still had a foothold around Constantinople (reclaimed in the preceding century not from Muslims but from Western Crusaders); and the Crusading dream of a Western conquest of the East persisted, despite the practical termination of that dream in 1291 with the loss of the sole remaining Crusader state of Acre.

The setting of the Man of Law's Tale, extending from northern England on one end to Syria on the other, is thus the stage for global geopolitical conflict, in which religion and the desire for political domination combine in ways that would have been acutely familiar to Chaucer's readers and remain, alas, all too familiar to us. More so than any other of Chaucer's writings, the Man of Law's Tale places the idea of a global Western empire at its center, an idea – and an actual Western ambition – with a continuous history from well before Chaucer's day on up to our own troubled present.

On the surface, the tale appears to endorse and indeed promulgate this idea. But even the most cursory of second looks suggests that like the Knight's tale-telling performance, the Man of Law's is staged in a way to inspect the very ideology that it seems to promote, in this case the ideology of empire. For this reason, considerations of the Man of Law's performance lend themselves powerfully to analysis through a postcolonial theoretical lens (see, for example, Schibanoff 1996 and Heng 2003). Strictly speaking, postcolonial theory, as its name indicates, pertains to the historical epoch following that of the European global colonization that began in earnest more than a century after Chaucer's death and extended through the Second World War. Nonetheless, the application of that theory to analogous imperial aspirations of earlier periods has proven generative of insights about those periods and about important continuities between imperial desires past and present.

The anti-Muslim bigotry voiced by the Christian Man of Law is, as we will see, one of those continuities. As I describe in Chapter 1, the form of the *Canterbury Tales* – and specifically the dramatization of tale-telling performances by distinctively characterized narrators – makes the attitudes and judgments of each tale teller potentially (though not necessarily) part of what Chaucer the author wants his readers to reflect upon. In this respect, another important difference between the Man of Law's performance and the Knight's is that the Man of Law's distinctive voice is considerably more prominent in his narration. The Man of Law is highly intrusive, quite frequently supplying his own opinions on the events and characters of his tale and doing so in a rhetorically excessive manner. Beyond the basic formal distinction between whatever might be the views of Chaucer the author and those of the Man of Law as fictional narrator, then, this intrusiveness gives us further encouragement to ponder the narrator's motives and to query his opinions. As we'll consider below, this encouragement is in fact rather baldly signaled right off the bat by the odd nature of the Man of Law's introductory comments.

Another crucial difference highlighted by the parallels between the Knight's and the Man of Law's Tales is where the focus falls in the tales' respective inspections of the patriarchal structure of male rivalry. As we saw in the preceding chapter, in the Knight's Tale the narrative camera almost exclusively tracks the principal male rivals, Arcite and Palamon, or the alpha male Theseus. The one moment in which the female object of rivalry, Emelye, is spotlighted is all the more jarring for its singularity. In contrast, while male desire in the Man of Law's Tale similarly propels the plot, the narrative camera is predominantly focused on the tale's female protagonist, Custaunce. Consequently, although most of what we hear about Custaunce is filtered through the opinionated and not especially trustworthy voice of the Man of Law, she is given more opportunity to speak directly than is Emelye. Those moments are striking, we will see, in a fashion similar to Emelye's single speech but recalibrated for the Man of Law's different vision of the cosmos.

That different vision points to one further contrast-within-similarity between the two tales. The twists and turns of the plots of both tales include the sort of adventure, conflict, and erotic interest that characterize the genre of medieval romance, whose modern-day equivalent is, again, more like Star Wars than drugstore romance novels. Both tales weave into this genre elements that widen its scope narratively and thematically. Those elements in the Knight's Tale include military engagements of epic scale and, as discussed in the preceding chapter, a somewhat secularized version of Neoplatonic philosophy. In contrast, the Man of Law's Tale's central focus on the trials of a Christian holy woman lends this romance the flavor of a hagiography, a term denoting the biography of a saint. In the Middle Ages, such biographies were ubiquitous and ranged from Church-authorized Latin narratives to popular vernacular renditions of greater and lesser literary ambition. They typically recount the purity, spiritual agency, suffering, and martyrdom of one of those select human beings whom the Church (today's Roman Catholic Church) has elevated to sainthood. Custaunce is not in that select group, and so, strictly speaking, the Man of Law's tale is not a hagiography. But inasmuch as the tale foregrounds her purity, spiritual agency, and suffering (and near martyrdom), it evokes a hagiographical view of the cosmos, which the intrusive narrator frequently makes explicit.

In this view, an all-powerful, all-knowing Father God, to help humanity recognize and embrace his absolute cosmic sovereignty, elects select individuals to perform superhuman deeds (the ones we call miracles) but also to undergo severe physical tribulation and, typically, a spectacularly brutal death. A hagiographical romance such as the Man of Law's Tale therefore necessarily stages an internal argument about the meaning of life, by which phrase I mean, as I discuss in this book's Introduction, an understanding of the relations between our basic corporeal existence and those nonmaterial ideas, ideals, and values that shape our experience of that existence. The genre of romance to some degree elevates sexual desire into an abstract principle that is worth killing and dying for, as Arcite and Palamon in the Knight's Tale illustrate. For romance, then, no matter how much that desire is idealized in transcendental language, the meaning of human life remains in a basic way rooted in the physical body. As we saw in the preceding chapter, at the end of the Knight's Tale, Theseus's Neoplatonic metaphysics, with its stark demotion of the physical, emerges as a politically autocratic answer to the failure of the romance ethos to produce social order. In contrast, in a hagiographical romance, the aim from the start is to situate human corporeality in the context of a greater, wholly spiritual value system. This sort of romance seeks to explain how suffering, death, and – especially when the protagonist is female – sexuality take on meaning in respect to an eternal Father God, one understood to be the creator and ultimately also the destroyer of the material universe. In the Man of Law's Tale, as in Theseus's metaphysics in the Knight's Tale, this vision of the cosmos – and the patriarchal social order that it legitimizes – demands the subjection of women. Hence, how we understand the nature of Chaucer's inspection of this ideology will once again rest upon how we understand the implications of his representation of that subjection.

Sources and summary

Many stories resembling the Man of Law's Tale circulated in the Middle Ages, suggesting an ultimately folktale origin. Chaucer's specific template was the account of Constance that early fourteenth-century Oxford friar Nicholas Trevet included in *Les Cronicles*, a history, written in French, from the creation of the world up to Trevet's present. Chaucer's friend and literary competitor John Gower also adapted Trevet's version of the story for his own compilation of short narratives in English verse, the *Confessio Amantis* (*Lover's Confession*), and the Man of Law's Tale shares some features with Gower's rendition. While Gower's work on the *Confessio* coincided with Chaucer's on the *Canterbury Tales*, most scholars believe that Chaucer consulted Gower's version rather than vice versa. It may indeed have been Gower's version that inspired Chaucer to include the story in the *Tales* and that served as his model for refashioning Trevet's account. Notice of the additions, deletions, and alterations that Chaucer makes to Trevet and Gower thus provides unusual access to his creative process.

One of those additions is, naturally, the Host's reinitiation of the tale-telling performance on the road to Canterbury. Following the aforementioned calculation of day and time, he asks the Man of Law, using tongue-in-cheek legalese, to "Telle us a tale anon [immediately] as forward [agreement] is" (2.34). The Man of Law, also spouting legalese, agrees. But then – suddenly and jarringly incorporating the reality of Chaucer's authorship into the fiction of the pilgrimage – he digresses to complain that though Chaucer's ability at writing verse is crude at best ("he can but lewedly/On metres and on riming craftily" [2.47–48]), he has already told all the good stories. The Man of Law goes on to provide a long list of those stories. Each features a female protagonist who suffers in some way, most often deadly, and in most instances is in some fashion the victim of men. Several of these stories are in fact included in Chaucer's *Legend of Good Women*, which is a framed collection of verse narratives that Chaucer seems to have abandoned in favor of the *Canterbury Tales* and which the

Man of Law names here as "the Saintes Legende of Cupide" (2.61). In an apparent non sequitur, he then observes that though Chaucer has told so many stories, he hasn't incurred the offense of repeating ones that involve incest, examples of which the Man of Law names. Chaucer's most immediate circle of original readers, which almost certainly included Gower, would likely have recognized those examples as stories that appear in the *Confessio Amantis*. On one hand, therefore, we are left to imagine how Chaucer in his fictional pilgrim persona would've reacted to these remarks by a fellow pilgrim. On the other hand, we might ponder how the real John Gower took this indirect jab at the *Confessio*, a jab that Chaucer has appended to the front of his remaking of a story that Gower had already included in that work.

Remarkably, the Man of Law has not yet finished with his introductory digressions. In another apparent non sequitur, just when he seems ready to begin his tale, he instead supplies a rhetorically ornate lament over the tribulations of poverty that concludes with a contrasting celebration of "riche marchants" (2.122). Only at the end of five stanzas do we understand that the point of all this is simply to acknowledge the merchant from whom the Man of Law supposedly learned the tale. That in turn finally provides a transition to the tale proper, which begins with a group of rich Syrian merchants visiting Rome, where they happen to hear about, and later witness, the wondrous virtues and beauty "Of th'Emperoures doghter, dame Custaunce" (2.151). When they return home and tell their Sultan about Custaunce, he declares himself in love with her. After some consultation, he determines that he, along with all his subjects, will convert from Islam to Christianity as a bid for her hand in marriage. Negotiations with the Pope and presumably the Emperor prove successful. Custaunce accordingly departs for Syria but not before she is allowed two stanzas of direct speech, unique to Chaucer's version, in which she makes quite clear that she's none too happy about her plight.

Meanwhile in Syria, the Sultan's mother is also none too happy, in this case about her son's decision to betray their faith and, presumably, to recognize Rome as their imperial overlords. She and her council hatch a plan to pretend to convert, invite the couple and all the newly Christianized Syrians to a feast, slaughter them, and take over leadership of the country. This they accomplish, although rather than killing Custaunce they put her out to sea in a rudderless boat "and bidde hire learne saile [tell her to learn to sail]/Out of Surrye againward to Ytaile [from Syria back to Italy]" (2.440–41). Custaunce does not succeed in that journey but rather floats around the Mediterranean for "Yeres and dayes" (1.463). To answer the question of why the Sultaness doesn't have her executed and how she survives so long at sea, the Man of Law in five rhetorically elaborate stanzas declares that it was God's will (e.g., "God liste [wishes] to shewe his wonderful miracle/In hire, for we sholde seen his mighty werkes" [2.477–78]).

Eventually, Custaunce's boat drifts through the Strait of Gibraltar and up the western European coast until finally reaching the early medieval English kingdom of Northumberland. As the Man of Law reminds his listeners, in this period the English of this region are "payens" or pagans. They follow the non-Christian religion of their Germanic ancestors, who invaded and colonized this portion of island, pushing the original Christian British population "To Wales" (2.544), except for a few who remain and practice Christianity in secret. Custaunce thus finds herself once more among a people whom the Romans would consider barbarians, presumably with an even starker appreciation for her vulnerability. When the constable of a nearby castle approaches her, her first request – uniquely in Chaucer's version – is that, out of mercy, he kill her. Notably, she conceals her identity as the Roman Emperor's daughter.

The constable doesn't kill her. Instead, as in Syria, these non-Christians convert, although this time more gradually, more by Custaunce's agency, and, the Man of Law implies, more authentically. The constable's wife Hermengild, powerfully attracted to Custaunce, converts first, followed by the constable. The Man of Law suggests that this irritates Satan, who inflames a local "yong knight" (2.585) with sexual desire for Custaunce. When she refuses him, the knight seeks revenge by (oddly) framing her for murder. He slits Hermengild's throat while she's sleeping next to Custaunce and stows the "bloody knif by dame Custaunce" (2.601). The King of Northumberland, Alla,[2] comes to judge the case, falling in love with Custaunce while hearing testimony. When the actual murderer swears upon a book (containing, for some reason in this pagan country, the Christian gospels) that Custaunce killed Hermengild, a disembodied hand appears that "him smoot [smote him] upon the nekke boon [bone]/[so] That doun he fel at ones [once] as a stoon,/And bothe his eyen broste out of his face" (2.670–3). A disembodied voice declares the man to be a liar. "And for this miracle," the Man of Law informs us, "And by Custaunce's mediacioun,/ The King and many another in that place/Converted was" (2.683–86). Alla and Custaunce then marry. Before long, she's pregnant with the heir to the kingdom, with the Man of Law spending a stanza worrying over what he characterizes as Custaunce's necessary sexual sullying.

Meanwhile, mirroring the earlier situation in Syria, King Alla's mother Donegild is none too happy at this turn of events. When the constable sends a messenger to Alla to bring him news about the birth of his son Maurice (Alla is away fighting the Scots), Donegild seizes the opportunity to intervene. The messenger stops first at Donegild's place, where she plies him with "ale and win [wine]" (2.743). While he sleeps off his stupor, she swaps out the letter that he's carrying with one that declares that Custaunce gave birth to a "horrible" "feendlich [fiendish] creature" and that Custaunce herself is not human but rather "an elf" (2.751–54). Alla, however, proves hardier in his faith than his mother supposed, and, although he secretly weeps, he sends back a letter stating that he must accept God's will. Fortunately for Donegild, the messenger, who obviously enjoyed her earlier hospitality, decides to stop again at her place. Once more, while "He sleepeth and he fnorteth in his gies [snores in his fashion]" (2.79), she performs a letter swap, changing her son's acceptance into a command to put Custaunce and her baby back out to sea in the same rudderless boat in which she arrived. The constable, agonized by Alla's apparent cruelty, nonetheless carries out his order. Custaunce submits once again to her fate, albeit after a rather eloquent lament of over four stanzas of direct speech.

When Alla returns and learns about what has happened, he tortures the messenger, who tells him all he knows. After quickly then determining the truth, Alla kills his mother. Meanwhile, Custaunce's boat reaches a shore somewhere outside Christendom. A steward of a nearby "hethen [heathen] castle" (2.904) comes down to the boat and attempts to rape her. Custaunce cries for help to the Virgin Mary and struggles with the man, who suddenly falls overboard and drowns.

The story then enters its concluding sequence. The Man of Law tells us that back in Rome, the Emperor has learned of the slaughter of the Syrian converts. In response, he launches a full-scale military assault, during which Romans "brennen, slayn, and bring hem to meschaunce/Ful many a day" (2.964); that is, they wreck utter destruction on the Syrians across a long period of time. The senator who leads the assault, when sailing back to Rome, encounters Custaunce and Maurice, who are then welcomed into the senator's household. Despite finally being back among her own people – and indeed, her own family, as we shortly learn that this senator is married to Custaunce's aunt – Custaunce again does not reveal her identity (and somehow neither senator nor aunt recognizes her, despite her earlier fame). Sometime after this, Alla journeys to Rome to seek the Pope's forgiveness for the sin of matricide. The official greeting party for such a distinguished guest is led by the senator and includes Maurice. Alla is struck by Maurice's resemblance to Custaunce and is even more intrigued once the senator tells him how he and his mother were found. Alla accompanies the senator back to his home, and the couple is reunited and eventually reconcile, with much weeping, fainting, and, for Alla, desperate explaining.

Custaunce stages one final event to join the ends of the circular plot. She has Alla and the senator invite her father to dinner, without revealing to him her presence. When they go to meet the Emperor, Custaunce kneels, declares her identity, and requests, in her final direct speech in the tale, "Now goode fader, mercy I you crye:/Sende me namore [no more] unto noon [no] hethenesse" (1.1111–12). Following this joyful reunion,

Custaunce and Alla return to England, although Alla dies just a year later, at which point Custaunce returns to Rome to live with her father. At the end, we are back where the story began, except (a) Rome has vanquished Syria, (b) Rome has converted Northumberland and brought that kingdom within its domain, and (c) the Emperor has an heir to his throne: Maurice, who, the Man of Law tells us, "was sithen [afterward] emperour/Maad by the People, and lived Cristenly" (1.1121–22).

The voice of the narrator

In the preceding summary, I've noted some examples of the Man of Law's intrusive narrational style. Ubiquitously, the Man of Law turns to his audience to offer moralizing, opinionated commentary on the tale's events and characters, and he does so ostentatiously, with ornately embellished lines filled with rhetorical questions, catalogues of learned examples, and the vocative "O." We may fairly suspect, from comparison with Chaucer's more restrained narrational style elsewhere, that he's up to something in giving the Man of Law such an overbearing voice, although precisely what that something may be is, not surprisingly, harder to discern. A likely place to start the inquiry, however, is with the odd non sequiturs of the Man of Law's introductory remarks. In having the Man of Law mention Chaucer and his *Legend of Good Women* by name, Chaucer places the entire performance into a self-reflexive, or metafictional, frame. Whatever meanings Chaucer's version of the Custaunce story may possess by itself, we are also to understand that it stages Chaucer's contemplation of his own storytelling.

As we will see in Chapter 7, the *Legend of Good Women* is already itself a very metafictional, writerly self-conscious work, one in which the purpose of literary creation, the motives and responsibilities of the writer, and the hazards of the unpredictable responses of readers are very much at issue. In the *Legend*'s prologue, the God of Love and his queen Alceste sentence Chaucer to spend the rest of his life writing stories about good women and the bad men who abuse them as punishment for his crime of disparaging love in general and women in particular in his *Troilus and Criseyde* and his translation of the *Romance of the Rose*. Each of the stories that Chaucer subsequently includes in the compilation, before apparently abandoning the project, has at its center a sexualized, suffering woman, who in the majority of cases is somehow betrayed, abandoned, or assaulted by a man. The challenge of what to make of all this – assuming that Chaucer did not actually believe that he deserved this particular punishment for writing *Troilus and Criseyde*, and so some sort of irony is at play – is one we'll confront in Chapter 7. Here, we need only notice that Chaucer has the overbearing Man of Law reference the *Legend* within the very project that Chaucer took up after abandoning it, and that that reference occurs in the introduction to a story, like those in *Legend*, about a woman who suffers at the hands of men. By framing the Man of Law's tale in this specific metafictional manner, Chaucer opens up for inspection the ethics and ideology of tales told by men about suffering women. The tale does not just repeat the story of Custaunce's suffering from Trevet and Gower: within its *Canterbury Tales* framing, it scrutinizes the values and ideological implications of male authors' compulsion to repeat such stories.

What happens next in the Man of Law's Introduction discloses something rather specifically damning about the ethics of this particular tale teller. When unpredictably and ostentatiously the Man of Law suddenly begins to pontificate about the evils of poverty – "O hateful harm, condicion of poverte,/With thirst, with cold, with hunger so confounded" (2.99–100) – that same inner circle of knowing contemporary readers who would've spotted the just-preceding allusion to Gower's *Confessio* would've recognized that Chaucer here is translating, relatively closely, from *De Miseria Condincionis Humane* (*On the Wretchedness of the Human Condition*), or perhaps quoting his own translation, which he mentions in the *Legend of Good Women*. The *De Miseria* was a widely known Latin treatise written by Pope Innocent III in 1195. It urges its readers to recognize the evils and resist the temptations of the physical world. Innocent's point, at the juncture in the treatise quoted by the Man of Law, is to emphasize not only that life in the physical world is terrible for the poor, as the Man of Law relays, but also that it entices the rich into sin. As he writes, "The rich man, however, is untied by superfluity and unbridled by boasting, he flies away to his pleasure and falls into unlawfulness, and they become the instruments of his punishments that had been the pleasures of his sins" (116). The Man of Law, of course, makes precisely the opposite claim about the rich, casting Innocent's treatise aside and instead moving seamlessly to his own celebration of "riche marchants" (2.21). For those readers who would've recognized the source of the Man of Law's comments about the poor – which now include you – the effect is instantly to undermine any certain trust in the narrator's pompous pontifications. This man, we now know, is happy to distort an authoritative text, twisting it for his own purposes 180 degrees from its intended meaning, no matter how inscrutable (or, in this case, apparently trivial) those purposes may be.

We are right to be wary, therefore, of every instance of the narrator's subsequent commentary. Nevertheless, it is far from clear exactly which instances are distortions and which are not – that is to say, which ones may align with Chaucer's own views and which ones may not. In effect, Chaucer has footnoted each instance of the Man of Law's commentary with a caveat like the one that newspapers attach to their opinion sections: "These views do not necessarily reflect those of the author." Indeterminate and evasive as it is, the caveat encourages readers to evaluate, rather than merely absorb, the voice of this narrator. We will follow Chaucer's prompt in this regard in considering the imperialist, religiously bigoted, and misogynist elements of the tale.

Empire, patriarchy, and women

Strikingly, for a tale written by a medieval Christian, its *initial* depiction of the relation between the Islamicate and Christian worlds is not particularly conflictual. The Syrian merchants who visit Rome – who appear directly in the wake of the Man of Law's celebration of merchants generally – are described in wholly positive terms. Their decision to travel to the capitol of the Christian empire, "Were it for chapmanhode or for disport [business or pleasure]" (2.143), does not seem unusual for either them or the Romans, and they seem welcome enough. In this context, Custaunce is introduced as an object of cross-creedal male mimetic desire. As discussed in the preceding chapter, *mimetic desire* denotes the idea, developed by twentieth-century philosopher and anthropologist René Girard, that our desires arise as an imitation of another's, so that we learn to want what another already wants. In this case, all men who hear about Custaunce, regardless of creed, desire her because it seems as though every other man already desires her. In medieval romance generally, the promptings of mimetic desire are typically represented, as here and in the Knight's Tale, as instantaneous, intense, and irresistible. When the Sultan learns from the merchants what he is supposed to desire, he must have it at any cost.

Because of the Sultan's position as leader of a Muslim patriarchal social order, his desire for the daughter of a leader of a Christian patriarchal social order carries tremendous implications. What seemed initially non-conflictual relations between Syrians and Romans gives way to an underlying geopolitical and religious competition, one which has often taken the form of military conflict. Feminist, queer, and gender theorist Eve Kosofsky Sedgwick, drawing on Girard, has taught us to recognize the structural position that women play in such rivalries between patriarchal social orders. While a woman may be the pretext for a rivalry – the object of contention – she may also be the means of its resolution. This present instance with Custaunce, the Emperor, and the Sultan begins as the latter, specifically the type of resolution in which one rival becomes father-in-law to the other. The son-in-law receives the woman at the cost of recognizing the greater authority of the father-in-law. That recognition, at least in theory, leads to peaceful relations in the form of an expansion of the father-in-law's domain of control, which now incorporates the domain of his son-in-law. In the Man of Law's Tale, the father-in-law's domain is the Christian Roman Empire, which, by way of Custaunce's marriage to the

Sultan, would regain some of what was lost in the initial spread of Islam. For Chaucer's fourteenth-century readers, that historical fantasy would in turn evoke the prospect of regaining eastern territories formerly secured by Crusaders but since, for about century, entirely lost.

The bartering of Custaunce's body to secure imperial expansion is narrated quite matter-of-factly. The Sultan's advisors straightforwardly recognize the problem of religious difference, observing that "no Cristen prince wolde fain [willingly]/Wedden his child under oure lawe sweete/That us was taught by Mahoun [Mohammad] oure prophete" (2.222–24). The Syrians' conversion to Christianity would acknowledge the superiority of Rome's religion, culture, and political dominion, and this the Sultan is willing to do to obtain what he wants. On the other side, all the male leaders of Christendom readily agree to seize this opportunity:

...by trestis and embassadyre*	treaty and diplomacy
And by the Popes mediacioun,	
And all the Chirche, and all the Chivalrye,	
That in destruccioun of Maumetrye,*	Islam
And in encrees of Cristes lawe deere,	
They been accorded so as ye shal heere:	
How that the Soudan* and his baronage	Sultan
And all his liges* sholde ycristened* be;	subjects; baptized
And he shal han Custaunce in marriage,	
And certayn gold—I noot* what qauntitee.	don't know
(2.233–42)	

The Pope, all the other leaders of "the Chirche" (all men, of course), and "all the Chivalrye" or secular political leaders (men again, including presumably the Emperor, Custaunce's father) are happy to trade Custaunce (or, more exactly, her sexualized body) for a chance to further the destruction of Islam, which is to say to expand the cultural and territorial dominance of the Christian empire. Bluntly underscoring Custaunce's function here as a material token of exchange between two patriarchal social orders, Chaucer adds the detail of the "certayn gold" that is part of the package, and the Man of Law's expression of uncertainty as to how much gold serves to call attention to this very detail.

For this resolution of patriarchal rivalry to work, the female token of exchange must be wholly passive. Female agency and desire have no place in the bartering and are in fact profoundly threatening to the androcentric political and social structures the two societies share. In this instance, Custaunce passively obliges but does so in a peculiar way that we'll consider below. At this juncture, we'll consider the actions of a different woman, Custaunce's intended mother-in-law. What goes horribly awry in the deal between Romans and Syrians is, according to the Man of Law, inseparable from the fact that this woman – the Sultaness – improperly exercises political agency. After relaying her views on the deal and plan for undoing it, the Man of Law, in one of his trademark intrusive and rhetorically overwrought editorial comments (which appears neither in Trevet nor Gower), hurls two stanzas of condemnation not just at her but at the female sex as a category:

O Soudanesse,* roote of iniquitee,	Sultaness
Virago, thou Semirame the secounde,	
O serpent under femininitee,	
Lik to the serpent deepe in helle ybounde!	
O feined* womman, al that may confounde*	falsely appearing; destroy
Vertu and innocence thurgh thy malice	
Is bred in thee as nest of every vice!	
O Satan, envious sin thilke* day	since the very
That thou were chaced from oure heritage*	i.e., expelled from heaven,
Wel knowestou to wommen th'olde way:	
Thou madest Eva bringe us in servage;*	bondage;
Thou wolt fordoon* this Cristen mariage.	destroy
Thyn instrument, so wailaway the while,	
Makestou of wommen whan thou wolt bigile. (2.358–71)	

The problem with the Sultaness, the Man of Law declares, is not just that she's the source of all wickedness ("roote of iniquitee") but that she is so specifically because she's a woman acting like a man. The epithet "Virago" names "a woman usurping a man's office" (*Riverside Chaucer* gloss), and "Semirame" is an allusion to the ancient Assyrian queen Semiramis, who in Chaucer's day was an archetype of an evil woman usurping power from a man. In this respect, the phrases "serpent under femininitee" and "feined womman" serve a pivotal (and logically nonsensical) function. They emphasize the disconnect between the sex of the Sultaness's physical body and what ought to be her nature as a woman. At the same time, they also enable sudden slippage from the evil wrought by this particular mother acting like a man to the evil wrought by the mother of us all, Eve, depicted here as both weak and vulnerable (to Satan) but also the active agent of the fallen condition of all humanity: "Thou [Satan] madest Eva *bringe* us in servage." In this way, the Man of Law elevates a specific political, ideological, and religious conflict to the level of the cosmic conditions of good and evil, thereby justifying patriarchy as the God-ordained order of the universe.

It takes only a moment's reflection to recognize that none of this is particularly relevant. Presumably, if, say, the Sultan's father came up with the same plan, the Man of Law would be just as disapproving. Recalling, then, that Chaucer has already given us reason to be suspicious of this narrator's editorial excursions, we may take a closer look at the Sultaness's actions and speech. Having gained knowledge of her son's plans, she calls her council together and states the following (the details of which Chaucer expands greatly from Trevet):

"Lordes," quod she, "ye knowen everichon*	each one of you
How that my sone in point is for to lete*	i.e., plans to abandon
The holy lawes of oure Alkaron*	Qur'an
Yiven by Goddes message Makomete.*	messenger Mohammad
But oon* avow to grete god I hete:*	one; promise
The lif shal rather out of my body sterte	
Than Makometes lawe out of myn herte.	
What sholde us tiden of* this newe lawe	come to us from
But thraldom* to oure bodies and penaunce,*	enslavement; suffering;
And afterward in helle to be drawe*	taken
For we renayed Mahoun oure creaunce?*"	i.e., renounced our religion
(2.330–41)	

If we keep to one side the Man of Law's insistence that the speaker here is the "welle of vices" (2.323), then we notice that the Sultaness's assessment of the situation is not wrong. The Sultan *is* about to betray their religion and country. The result *is* likely to be subjection to the Romans and, from the perspective of a faithful Muslim, eternal damnation. In fact, if we simply flip-flop the scenario, so that a Christian prince and his subjects plan to convert to Islam so that he can marry a Muslim princess whom he's never even met (substituting in the passage Christ for Mohammad and the bible for the Qur'an), we may readily imagine the Man of Law himself as unhesitatingly and passionately holding exactly the same sentiment as the Sultaness. (And in retrospect, we might notice the close verbal echo between the Sultan's counselors' mention of "oure lawe sweete" [2.223] and, just a few lines later, the Man of Law's mention of "Cristes lawe deere" [2.237].) While the Sultaness's response – the brutal, mass slaughter of all the converts, including her own son – is obviously rather extreme (to say the least), we are again left to wonder whether, if the tables were turned, the Man of Law would not make a similar recommendation. Christians, of course, have historically not been averse to committing great acts of violence when they believed their faith or salvation required it, as evident in, say, the mass slaughter of Muslims and Jews during and following the capture of Jerusalem in the First Crusade. For the Man of Law, the difference seems to be a matter not of actions but of the identity of the actors.

Empire and race

Postcolonial theory, and in particular Homi K. Bhabha's notion of colonial mimicry, will help to unearth the significance of this striking moment of likeness in difference. As Bhabha writes, "colonial mimicry is the desire for a reformed, recognizable Other, as a *subject of difference that is almost the same, but not quite*" (86, emphasis Bhabha's). This formulation succinctly expresses how the typical justification for colonization – bringing the so-called light of civilization to so-called savages – entails the project of reforming the colonized so that they are recognizable as *like* the colonizer. Not coincidentally, this project is also a very effective means of domination, since if the people you're trying to control want to become just like you, they're less likely to foment a rebellion. The colonizer's aim thus encompasses such minutiae as regimens of bodily hygiene up through large-scale institutions such as public education and key ideologies such as political and religious beliefs. All this seeks to realize the objective of making *them* more like *us*.

Yet if this objective were to be wholly realized, then the very distinction between *us* and *them* would vanish and along with it any justification for the rule of the colonizer. Hence colonial mimicry's hedges of "almost" and "not quite": the reform of the Other must go only so far; in other words, it must not really be *reform* at all. Any recognition of similarity must always be doubled by an insistence upon ineradicable, inherent difference – a difference that is always necessarily a bad one for the colonized and, moreover, almost always racialized (so that Bhabha varies his formula as "almost the same but not *white*" [89]). Colonial mimicry, beset with inner contradiction, says to the colonized: "you must be like us, but you can't possibly be like us; you must become enlightened, but, because of your inherent inferiority, you can't possibly become enlightened." In this way, it is profoundly ambivalent and self-conflicted, speaking, as Bhabha quips, with a forked tongue (85). In particular, it requires some sort of articulation of the dehumanizing bigotry that the stated aim of colonialism – to bring reform – would seem to deny but which its actual aim – to dominate – requires.

What we might expect in the Man of Law's Tale, then, is that the very attempt to Christianize the Syrians, and its subsequent failure, would be accompanied by a narratorial expression of explicit anti-Muslim bigotry. We might expect that in his characteristically inflated rhetorical manner, the Man of Law would insist upon the Syrians' inherent, racialized degradation. Certainly, this discourse of bigotry was available. As several scholars have pointed out, in the Middle Ages the difference between Christian and Muslim (as well as Christian and Jew) was very often conceived as racial as well as religious, that is, as somehow ineradicably corporeal.[3] There was thus a ready racist discourse at hand to ensure that the *them* in this instance, however much reformed, remains firmly not the same as the *us*. If the Man of Law were to racialize the Syrians at this point, however, he would necessarily imply that the Pope, the Emperor, and all the rest of the Roman political and religious leaders, in packaging Custaunce off with some gold to Syria, would be unhesitatingly, even enthusiastically enabling miscegenation. In effect, the plot of the tale has been cornered by the contradictions within its own ideology. For the "destruccioun of Maumetrye" to succeed, the bartering of the woman's body that aims to secure that destruction necessitates a racial mixing abhorred by the anti-Muslim bigotry that justifies that destruction in the first place.

It's in respect to this narrative dilemma that we may understand the logic of the Man of Law's hyperbolic condemnation of the Sultaness, as illogical as it in fact is. With race mostly off the table as an explicit rationale, the Man of Law needs some other ineradicable binary identity difference to separate categorically *us* from *them*. He turns therefore to a binary that is always readily available within a patriarchy, that of sex. From his viewpoint, women's inherent inferiority to men, while it does not necessarily make women evil, becomes the ready entry point for evil (here that of Satan, the ultimate spiritual evil for both Christianity and Islam) inasmuch as *they* (women) try to be like *us* (men). The Sultaness's status as "Virago" and "Semirame the secounde" – her violation of the male/female boundary – therefore stands in for the violation of the Christian/Muslim boundary that the wedding between Custaunce and the Sultan plainly invokes but which cannot be explicitly acknowledged. Since the Man of Law cannot disparage the Sultaness for being a Muslim, he turns to her sex in order to condemn the actions that he would presumably celebrate if performed by a Christian prince. Conveniently for the Man of Law, the Sultaness's violation of the sex binary ensures that the Christian/Muslim miscegenation does not happen.[4]

In this light, we may understand the tale's later repetition of the evil mother-in-law plot as a difference set off by a similarity that serves to the underscore the racialization of the Syrians that cannot fully rise to the surface. In this second round of Christian conversions and marriage to Custaunce, the comparably more genuine conversions of the English and, most notably, the consummation of Custaunce and Alla's marriage (eventually followed by the resulting child's accession to the imperial throne) clearly signal, without naming, the racial sameness of the English and Romans. Once again, the plot hinges on a mother's malevolence toward her daughter-in-law, and once again the Man of Law ascribes the mother's evilness to a violation of the sex binary. Turning to address his own character, he laments, "O Donegild, I have noon Englissh digne [i.e., no English words adequate]/Unto thy malice and thy tyranne" (2.778–79). He nonetheless finds those words: "Fy, mannish, fy," he says, declaring that this mannishness is the effect of a "feendlich [fiendly, devlish] spirit" (2.782–83). As with the Sultaness, a woman acting like a man manifests evil in metaphysical terms. Yet unlike the Sultaness, Donegild is not represented as defending, like a Christian would, her people's religious integrity and political autonomy and so thereby signaling a racial difference that cannot be spoken. Rather, she's depicted as herself seeing something like a racial difference where none exists, expressing bigotry toward Custaunce of a vaguely xenophobic, ethnocentric, or racist nature. As the Man of Law tells us, "Hire thoughte a despit [it seemed to her an outrage] that he sholde take/So straunge [alien] a creature unto his make [spouse]" (2.699–700). Her ruse of declaring Custaunce "an elf" and her child a "horrible feednlich creature" (2.751, 754) in her forged letters is hence not coincidental. Donegild wishes to inspire a horror of racial (or species) difference that corresponds in some general manner to the source of her own hatred.

Thus, while the Sultaness's defense of her people uncannily mimics a Christian ruler's defense of his people that we may assume that the Man of Law would endorse, thereby invoking an anti-Muslim bigotry that the Man of Law himself holds but cannot quite name, Donegild's explicitly represented bigotry is depicted as a grave (and eventually fatal) error. On the one hand, the Sultaness's uncanny signaling of racial difference through similarity eventuates not just her own demise but what we may understand as the racial genocide of her people, as the Roman military takes "heigh [that is, both massive and exalted] vengeaunce" on the "Surrians" generally, burning and slaying "Ful many a day" (2.963–65). On the other hand, Donegild's mistake of seeing racial difference where one shouldn't is punished by her solitary execution, thereby implying English racial sameness with the Romans and, accordingly, racial difference with the Syrians. In this way, the Man of Law deploys the tale of Custaunce, with its doubled stories of evil mothers-in-law, as a primer for understanding when religious difference also means racial difference and when it doesn't. Speaking with the forked tongue of colonial mimicry, the Man of Law's celebrative fantasy of a Christian empire reveals his very idea of empire to be riven by contradictions that betray its racist and sexist foundations.

The voice of Custaunce and Father God

Chaucer, of course, did not have the concept of colonial mimicry at his disposal, nor even the terms *racism* and *sexism*. From our twenty-first-century perspective, we're able to see those discourses and structures of oppression in the Man of Law's Tale as such with the benefit of hindsight. It would therefore be inaccurate to credit Chaucer with designing his version of the tale of Custaunce to communicate exactly the sort of anti-imperialist, anti-racist, and anti-sexist message mapped out above. Nonetheless, it would also be inaccurate *not* to credit him with orchestrating the Man of Law's performance in such a manner that it evokes a range of meanings that include those mapped out above, which from our vantage point we are able to characterize in twenty-first-century terms. Chaucer's many strategic alterations to his sources, the metafictional self-questioning of the tale's introduction, and the thematically warping effect of the Man of Law's narrational intrusions all ensure that as a whole, this tale-telling performance makes the underlying mechanisms of empire building and their human costs matters set out for inquiry. These human costs of political structures and social orders are in general a concern that Chaucer clearly shares with us, even if he did not use our set of analytical tools to evaluate them or – what is less clear – arrive at the same conclusions we might hold about them.

In the preceding chapter, we saw how the Knight's Tale foregrounds the subjection of women as one of the human costs of patriarchal social orders, especially by way of Emelye's sole moment of direct speech. In the Man of Law's Tale, consideration of the subjection of women – and especially the suffering women undergo in their function as tokens of exchange between men – is comparatively more pervasive, given that the token of exchange is in this case the tale's protagonist. As with the Man of Law's demonization of mothers-in-law, Chaucer has orchestrated the tale's representation of its idealized suffering female protagonist in a way that makes its ideological underpinnings a matter of inquiry. In particular, the length and detail of Custaunce's moments of direct speech are essentially Chaucer's invention (though he does take a few cues from Gower).

Chaucer allows Custaunce to voice her perspective more than once and initially early on, at the very moment in which she literally embodies the role of token of exchange. About to board the ship to Syria, accompanied by a crowd of "Bisshopes…/Lordes, ladies, knights of renown,/And other folk ynowe [enough]" (2.253–55), she issues a relatively lengthy public farewell to her parents. Far from straightforwardly proclaiming her readiness to perform her father's, the Church's, and the empire's will and thereby to give glory to God, as we might expect, she states the following:

> "Fader," she saide, "thy wrecched child Custaunce,
> Thy yonge doghter, fostered up so softe,
> And ye, my moder, my soverein plesaunce
> Over alle thing, outtaken Crist on lofte,

Custance youre childe hire recomandeth ofte
Unto youre grace, for I shal to Surrye,
Ne shal I never seen you more with eye.

Allas, unto the Barbre nacioun
I moste anon, sin that it is youre wille.
But Crist that starf for oure redempcioun
So yive me grace his heestes to fulfille.
I, wrecche womman, no fors thogh I spille:
Wommen are born to thraldom and penaunce,
And to been under mannes governaunce."
(2.274–87)

Since gauging the tone of these remarks is key to appreciating their implications, here's a full Modern English paraphrase: "Father," she said, "your miserable/worthless/exiled [*wrecched*] child Custaunce, your young daughter, whom you raised so tenderly and comfortably [*so softe*] – and you, my mother, my greatest joy above all (excepting Christ in heaven) – your child Custaunce entrusts herself (again and again) to your good will, for I must go to Syria, and I must never see you again in person. Alas! To a heathen country I must straightaway go, since that is what you demand. But Christ, who died for our redemption, give me the grace to fulfill his commandments. I, a miserable/worthless/exiled woman – it does not matter if I die. Women are born to slavery and suffering, and to be subject to men." Or, as a looser but more succinct paraphrase, Custaunce, for all the crowd to hear, in effect declares to her parents:

Okay, dad (and mom, whom I love), I'm off to do this crappy thing that you, who are supposed to protect your child, are making me do, and I'll never see you again. Who cares if I die, since I'm a woman, and women are born to be enslaved by and suffer at the hands of men. My students have most often identified Custaunce's tone here as precisely one of *passive-aggression*, and, although that term wasn't available to Chaucer, we can readily imagine his winking approval of it. Utter passivity, as we know, is what patriarchy demands of its female tokens of exchange, and Custaunce – who, as the Man of Law tells us, "seeth ther nis noon other ende [i.e., sees no escape from her fate]" (2.266) – complies. But she does so by aggressively proclaiming that what she is exhibiting is exactly passive compliance and that she's profoundly unhappy about this turn of events. In quintessentially passive-aggressive fashion, nothing that she says can be unequivocally taken as critical or even complaining. Yet such implications are readily apparent. She implies, for example, that she expected better treatment from her parents and that if they never see her again

– and, worse, if she dies – that's on them. "I am obeying," she's saying, "because you give me no choice," and she unmistakably insinuates, "you ought to feel shame and guilt about that." If in this regard we recall the framing effect of the Man of Law's introductory comments about Chaucer, Gower, and tales of female suffering, which turns the entire Man of Law's performance into a story about stories, we may recognize that Chaucer here gives Custaunce a chance to talk back not just to her father but to all those who have told her story and indeed to all male authors of stories of female suffering. "We suffer," she is saying, "because that's what you male authors demand; but you should be ashamed."

Strikingly, Custaunce herself makes this generalization of her plight to all women explicit at the end of her speech, and here the religious implications, if not already evident, become unmistakable. She declares, as her final parting words, that she exemplifies the condition of all women and that that condition, subjection to men, is awful. Again, strictly speaking, the remark is neither a critique nor even a complaint. According to one of the official understandings of the medieval Christian Church, it's just a simple statement of fact, as given by Genesis 3:16: "To the woman also God said: I will multiply thy sorrows, and thy conceptions: in sorrow shalt thou bring forth children, and thou shalt be under thy husband's power, and he shall have dominion over thee." In so shrewdly reciting this bit of religious orthodoxy in this context (it in effect takes the place of "goodbye"), she raises the stakes of her passive-aggression in a way that anticipates the Man of Law's later linking of the Sultaness to Eve's disobedience, but with an opposite and rather more profound implication. If the Man of Law's pronouncement equates the Sultaness's acting like man with the fateful moment of Eve's desire and agency, Custaunce's remark equates her father's cruel treatment with the divine curse that entails that even the most virtuous, passive, and feminine women must suffer at the hands of men. If the Man of Law turns to the divinely ordained order of the cosmos to legitimate his strategic deployment of misogyny, Custaunce potentially extends her passive-aggressive accusation from her earthly to her heavenly father, the one ultimately responsible for the abject plight of women generally.

If it seems unlikely that a medieval author would have his virtuous protagonist so complain to God, even if just by implication, we need only recall that there is ample precedent for this in the bible itself – in Job and the Psalms, for example. Nevertheless, as many theologians then and now would affirm, this biblical precedent does not make the spiritual implications of Custaunce's complaint any less vexed. Their theological complications become readily evident later in the more expansive complaint that she voices at a parallel moment in the story. This time another male ruler, her husband, demands (as Donegild makes everyone to believe) that she again board a boat and leave her home forever.

By this point in the story, we have heard much commentary from the Man of Law about God's manner of running the cosmos. In particular, he tells us that everything that happens, everyone's fate for better or worse, is determined by an all-powerful and all-knowing divine male triune God, whose motives are ultimately as unfathomable as they are irresistible. For example, after relating the events in Syria, the Man of Law turns to his audience and rhetorically queries, "Men mighten axen why she [i.e., Custaunce] was noght slain/Eek [i.e., along with the others] at the feeste? Who mighte hir body save?" (2.470–71), and he goes on to explain:

God liste to shewe* his wonderful miracle	It pleases God to show
In hire, for* we sholde seen his mighty werkes.	In her, so that
Crist which that is to every harm triacle*	the cure
By certayn menes* ofte, as knowen clerkes,*	methods; religious authorities
Dooth thing for certayn ende that ful derk is	
To mannes wit, that, for oure ignoraunce,	
Ne conne nat knowe* his prudent purveyaunce.*	we are unable to know; providence, intentions

(2.477–83)

Why doesn't the Sultaness kill Custaunce? Because, says the Man of Law, God wishes to use Custaunce as an example of his miraculous, all-encompassing power. This raises by implication, of course, the more awkward question of why God also allows the Sultaness to slaughter all the new Syrian Christians, which we may understand the rest of the Man of Law's answer to be addressing. Essentially, he says, God works in mysterious ways. All good things come from God, but all suffering also comes from God – both the suffering which is punishment for sin but also that which enables God to "to shewe his wonderful miracle." Hence, as another example of the latter, God allows the virtuous Christian convert Hermengyld to have her throat slit, seemingly so that he can demonstrate his power by blowing out the eyeballs of her murderer when he forswears himself at Custaunce's trial.

In this regard, we may notice an important difference between Custaunce's forced departure from Northumberland and that from Rome. When she leaves for Syria, the stated reason – the "destruccioun of Maumetrye" – is one that we may assume she understood and perhaps even endorsed as a general principle, if not necessarily as applied in her case. In contrast, in this later instance, the cruel abuse and probable murder that she believes her husband is committing against her and their child are to her wholly unfathomable. By all accounts, she has been an exemplary queen and wife, one who has fulfilled the single most important function for a woman within a patrilineal patriarchy, bearing a male heir. At stake in this instance, then, is the human attitude toward the more general, cosmic unfathomability of God's providential justice.

Chaucer, in his rendering of this scene, picks up these implications in his sources and, so to speak, runs with them. He systematically extrapolates from Alla as Custaunce's lord and king, and father of their child, to God as Lord and King of all creation, and Father of us all, including his child Jesus, suffering on the cross. The scene unfolds with the constable, who is agonizingly fulfilling Alla's supposed command, explicitly questioning not just Alla but also God:

> O mighty God, if that it be thy wille,
> Sith* thou art rightful juge, how may it be — Since
> That thou wolt suffren* innocents to spille,* — allow; die
> And wikked folk regnen* in prosperitee? — to reign
> (2.813–16)

"I believe, as I'm supposed to, in the wisdom of your justice," the constable says here to God, "but it sure does seem cruel and unfair in this case." Custaunce, in her subsequent public prayer/farewell, proceeds to raise and complicate these theological stakes by extending the parallel from her and her son's situation to that of Mary and Jesus:

> "Moder," quod* she, "and maiden bright, Marie, — said
> Sooth is* that thurgh wommanes eggement* — It is true; instigation
> Mankinde was lorn* and dampned ay* to die, — lost; forever
> For which thy child was on a crois yrent;* — torn
> Thy blisful eyen sawe al his torment:
> Thanne is ther no comparison bitweene
> Thy wo and any wo man may sustene.
>
> Thou sawe thy child yslain bifore thine eyen,
> And yet now liveth my litel child, parfay.* — by my faith
> [...]
>
> O litel child, allas, what is thy gilt,
> That never wroghtest sinne as yet, pardee?* — by God
> Why wil thyn harde* fader han thee spilt?* — unfeeling, callous, severe, harsh; killed
>
> [...]
>
> Therwith she looketh backward to the londe
> And saide, "Farewel, housbonde routhelees."* — pitiless
> (2.841–63)

Here, Custaunce supplies the essential elements of the Christian theology of the Fall and Atonement, which is to say, the fundamental account of the meaning and significance of human life within a Christian understanding of the cosmos. Because of a woman's agency ("eggement"; although this may also denote, ambiguously, someone's – Satan's – incitement of a woman), Father God demands that all humanity pay the penalty of death. But God subsequently allows that penalty to be paid by his and Mary's "child," whose brutal suffering ("torment") and death Mary must witness. Although Custaunce explicitly disavows comparing herself to Mary, in passive-aggressive fashion the parallels between her situation and Mary's are in fact exactly what she's calling attention to. This she underscores, among other ways, by emphasizing the guiltlessness of her "litel child," seemingly about to be sacrificed, like the guiltless Jesus, by a "harde fader."

The Middle English adjective *harde* had a range of senses, from obviously negative to firmly positive. In my gloss above, I selected the four that seem most likely in this instance. Many Christians, then and now, might understand the word as denoting the sort of severity captured by the advice to "fear God." By itself, therefore, the association of the adjective with Father God is entirely orthodox and perhaps even pious. In this context, however, in which Custaunce must obey the command of a lord and father whom she believes to be cruel and unreasonable, and the constable has just explicitly questioned God, the adjective becomes more theologically dangerous. Pushed to its furthest implication, it asks, who's finally to blame for human suffering and death, including that of Mary's "child"? Is it really Eve in her moment of acting upon her desire? Or is it the "harde fader," creator of the cosmos, who controls everything and everyone within it?

Obviously, this question raises numerous issues (regarding free will etc.) for which Christian theologians, then and now, have provided a host of explanations. Chaucer's aim here is not so much to probe such issues theologically as to reflect on the meaning of human life that these sorts of theological positions establish. Specifically in this case, he seeks to highlight the relation between this particular Christian vision of cosmic order and the patriarchal social order that it justifies, one in which women, as exemplified by Custaunce, must suffer for whatever unfathomable reasons men may have. Indeed, in this respect, "routhelees" is in fact the more dangerous adjective. While God's actions may piously be described as harsh, they cannot as unproblematically be named merciless, at least as applied to the virtuous and innocent. Not coincidentally, therefore, although Custaunce has plainly established a parallel between Alla and Father God, she is careful to attach this latter adjective to "housbonde."

Like Emelye in the Knight's Tale, Custaunce in her moments of direct speech sends the consistent message that what she wants is not to play the role demanded of her. For example, in addition to the lengthy public addresses already considered, we may recall that when she washes up on shore in Northumberland, her first words are a request to the constable that he end her suffering by killing her: "In hir langage mercy she bisoghte/ The lif out of hir body for to twinne [separate, i.e., kill her],/Hire to delivere of wo [free from suffering] that she was inne" (2.516–18). Uniquely in Chaucer's version of the story, Custaunce in effect begs, "Please stop this story now; I've had enough." This sentiment she then repeats in her final moment of direct speech, when she orchestrates the spectacular reunion scene with her father. Again uniquely in Chaucer's version, she pleads, "Sende me namore unto noon hethenesse" (2.1112). In effect, she declares, "I'm done being your token of exchange." And inasmuch as her reference to "hethenesse" recalls the ostensibly spiritual aim of the exchange with Syria, she's asking for "mercy" here not only from her own "goode fader" (2.1111) but also from the heavenly Father for whom her own, as head of the Christian empire, serves as worldly representative.

Chaucer's complicity

What the Man of Law's Tale thus scrutinizes is not just, as with the Knight's Tale, a generalized authoritarian patriarchal social order and its legitimating Neoplatonic metaphysics, which have parallels, albeit vague ones, with Chaucer's present. The Man of Law's Tale delves into the core of Chaucer's present-day Christendom's dream of empire, the patriarchal political, social, and discursive structures through which Christendom's imperial ambitions are pursued, and the human costs of the theology that justifies that dream and those structures. And since for this tale Chaucer fashions a narrator and narratorial performance that call attention to storytelling itself, including this very story, as a participant in these imperial and patriarchal designs, this contribution to the *Canterbury Tales* at once recognizes Chaucer's own complicity in those designs and creates some critical distance from which he can weigh their costs and benefits.

Characteristically, however, if Chaucer arrived at any firm conclusions about those costs and benefits, he did not leave any unequivocal declaration of them in the tale. Given the Man of Law's manifestly irritating ostentation, it seems unlikely that Chaucer, who fashioned the pilgrim to be this way, would've straightforwardly aligned himself with this narrator's views. Nonetheless, Chaucer is, of course, the actual transmitter of this tale of female suffering, and hence in that sense he is as much Custaunce's father as any of those whom she herself mentions. In fact, we might plausibly credit Chaucer with recognizing this very self-incriminating situation – his perhaps inadvertent calling attention to his own complicity – as a kind of richly generative artistic crisis. For whether or not he intended the Wife of Bath to follow the Man of Law, as she does in most editions of the *Tales* – and regardless of which performance he wrote first – we may understand the unprecedented tour de force of the Wife of Bath's performance as a response to this very sort of crisis.

Notes

1 This view is shared by the editors of the most recent scholarly edition of Chaucer as of this writing, *The Oxford Chaucer* (2024), who situate the Man of Law's performance as the terminal one in an initial continuous sequence beginning with the General Prologue.

2 The similarity to the Islamic word for God appears to be a coincidence. Alla, which Chaucer takes from Trevet, was in fact an early medieval English king.

3 In addition to Schibanoff 1996, see, for example, Heng 2018, Whitaker 2017, and Otaño Gracia 2020, all of whose work informs this chapter. This conflation of religion and race, widespread in the Middle Ages, has obviously not vanished in the modern world, as the religious justifications proffered by many racist hate groups make plain.

4 Fascinatingly, in the *King of Tars*, one the several stories similar to the Man of Law's Tale that circulated in medieval England, the racialization of the Sultan figure is much more explicit, even while the marriage with the Custaunce figure is consummated.

4 The Wife of Bath's Tale

If you had heard about any of the Canterbury pilgrims before actually reading the *Canterbury Tales*, chances are that it was the Wife of Bath. Virtually from the moment that Chaucer created this character, she has proven unfailingly provocative and, for many, irresistibly magnetic. Among the pilgrims – or indeed among literary characters in general – she is highly distinctive. Yet at the same time, as scholar Marion Turner has observed, she "is a character whom readers across the centuries have usually seen as accessible, familiar, and, in a strange way, real" (Turner 2023, 2). Indeed, the fact that this remark comes from Turner's popular and critically acclaimed "biography" of the Wife of Bath bears out her very point. Although Turner's book is not (of course) a conventional biography, that it can plausibly apply that label to a wholly fictional character – and garner thereby a wide readership – attests to what many find to be the compelling relatability of a female voice that Chaucer somehow captured, over six centuries ago, in iambic pentameter couplets.

The Wife's voice: authenticity, identity, and representation

One of the Wife of Bath's modern readers whom Turner considers at length is celebrated British author Zadie Smith. In 2021, Smith's play *The Wife of Willesden* made its debut, earning (mostly) rave reviews. Smith recasts the Wife as a present-day woman of Jamaican background living in the London neighborhood where Smith herself grew up, and substitutes a pub setting for the original's road to Canterbury. Within that reframing, though, the play tracks the twists and turns of Chaucer's text fairly closely. In the introduction to the published playscript, Smith describes the sequence of events that led to this seemingly unlikely project. At first, she was unsure and anxious about what she somewhat unwittingly had agreed to take on. But then, revisiting Chaucer's text, she recalls,

DOI: 10.4324/9781003273318-5

> from the moment Alyson [i.e., the Wife of Bath] opens her mouth [Smith quotes the opening lines of the Wife of Bath's Prologue], I knew that she was speaking to me, and that she was a Kilburn girl at heart. What started out as homework soon came to feel like a wonderful case of serendipity. For Alyson's voice – brash, honest, cheeky, salacious, outrageous, unapologetic – is one I've heard and loved all my life: in the flats, at school, in the playgrounds of my childhood and then the pubs of my maturity, at bus stops, in shops, and of course up and down Kilburn High Road, any day of the week. The words may be different but the spirit is the same.
>
> (xiv)

I've quoted Smith's wonderfully unguarded remarks at length not only because they express eloquently the relatability many feel toward the Wife of Bath but also because they raise many of the issues that will occupy us in this chapter.[1] How is it, we might ask, that the Wife of Bath can be "a Kilburn girl at heart," when most basically the Wife consists of just some scraps of text assembled by a cis, white, relatively prosperous fourteenth-century man? (Kilburn, which includes the Willesden parish, is an area of London with many residents of color, emigrants and descendants of emigrants from the United Kingdom's former far-flung empire.) What might "at heart" mean in relation to a fictional character? How can the Wife's "voice" be one that Smith has "heard and loved" all her life, the voice of girls and women in her northwest London neighborhood? What, exactly, is the "spirit" of the "words" that seems effortlessly to span all the historical and linguistic differences between Chaucer's day and her own, somehow remaining "the same"?

I don't mean to suggest that Smith's comments are unusual. Many of us might say much the same thing (perhaps less engagingly) about a literary character from the past whom we find relatable. Rather, my point is that implicit in that very relatability are important considerations of rather fraught complexity, ones that are not just prompted by the Wife of Bath's performance but are in many ways what that performance itself explores. These considerations revolve around two concepts clearly evident in Smith's comments: those of voice and authenticity. Voice in general is tricky to define but in this instance appears to denote a particular category of identity as it is expressed through a characteristic use of language. Authenticity is an even slipperier notion. Here, we may apply it to the deep correspondence, despite surface differences, that Smith finds between Chaucer's fictional Wife and the genuine "heart" of a real, flesh-and-blood "Kilburn girl," or to the "spirit" that for Smith makes a medieval fiction and contemporary reality in some essential way "the same." These two concepts, obviously, are tightly related, as it is specifically the Wife's voice – as illustrated by the lines of Chaucer's Middle English that Smith quotes – that strikes Smith as authentic to her own experience.

What the identity of a "Kilburn girl" consists of is not for me to say. But obviously it rests upon what it means to be "from Kilburn" and what it means to be a "girl." And both of those identities are plainly caught up in larger discursive, geopolitical, and institutional systems – the ones that, say, produce the varying socioeconomic characteristics of different urban neighborhoods and the varying treatment of girls and boys in so many social situations. How much Smith specifically had those systems in mind when writing the above comments I also cannot say, but from the general evidence of her books and essays we know that she has been an acutely perceptive dissector of them. Among what she has recognized is that those systems may be deeply oppressive and, simultaneously, an affirming source of identities that are experienced as authentic – a crucial source for understanding, in a positive way, who we are individually and in relation to others.

It would seem that the historically specific characteristics of those systems are essential in this respect. It would seem, that is, that what it means to be a "Kilburn girl" must have much to do with the status and demographics (racial, class, etc.) of Kilburn and the models of femaleness and opportunities available to girls and women during the time Smith grew up there. Just so, it would seem that whatever the voice of the Wife of Bath represents, it would have much to do with what it meant to be a middle-aged widow residing in the English provincial town of Bath in the late fourteenth century. And yet, what Smith discovers in her project of updating the Wife of Bath's performance is that the identity categories of "Kilburn girl" and "widow from Bath" – despite the massive differences in the systems in place in their respective times – share something that resonates powerfully with Smith's experience. Essential elements of the identity-producing systems in Chaucer's day, we may conclude, must remain congruent with those of the corresponding systems in our own time.

We don't have to scratch our heads about what those elements are. A moment's glance at the Wife's performance tells us that they are plainly those experienced by women in their positions within a patriarchal social order (which is to say, a social order in which men hold the balance of political and economic power). This general condition is unmistakably the explicitly announced and pervasively addressed topic of the Wife of Bath's performance. It's also, as much of this book attests, a very frequent concern of Chaucer's, one that appears to have culminated with his writing of the Wife of Bath's Prologue and Tale. Indeed, as I've suggested, the Wife's performance includes not just representations of female identity within a patriarchal social order but also reflections on the fraught process of, pitfalls in, and potential avenues for coming to affirm an identity in this situation. This chapter will chart some of those reflections, which will eventually provoke a consideration of what the Wife of Bath's performance adds to Chaucer's grappling with the meaning of life more generally. By that admittedly hackneyed phrase, I mean, as I discuss in this book's Introduction, an understanding of the relations between our basic material, corporeal existence and those nonmaterial ideas, ideals, and values that shape our experience of that existence. Not surprisingly, the resources for female identity within a patriarchy turn out to be deeply entangled with assumptions about the nature of human life in this sense. As we will consider, one of the primary challenges in embracing one's 'true' or authentic identity is figuring out what to do with the ideological baggage that accompanies those assumptions about life.

Performance structure

It has been my habit in this book to refer to a pilgrim's *performance* as a way to encompass any introductory remarks by the pilgrim, interactions with other pilgrims, narratorial commentary on the tale, and distinctive narrational stye, along with the actual tale the pilgrim tells. In the case of the Wife of Bath, this term is especially apt, since her introductory remarks – what Chaucer editions label the Wife of Bath's Prologue – are much longer than those of any other pilgrim. Indeed, her prologue, which consists almost entirely of her direct speech, is more than twice as long as the story that it introduces, making for a rather disproportionate "preamble of a tale" (3.831), as the Friar smirkingly observes near the prologue's conclusion. Moreover, that long-deferred tale is best understood, more so than that of any other pilgrim (although those of the Pardoner and the Canon's Yeoman take a close second), as a narrative projection of the concerns, opinions, personality, and psychology of its speaker, which is to say, as an extension of the prologue. This stark prologue/tale imbalance is one of Chaucer's key creative devices for bringing about the effect of voice that readers such as Smith, Turner, and countless others have felt. By giving the Wife such sustained first-person direct speech within the naturalistic setting of the pilgrimage – within the supposedly actual journey that the pilgrim Chaucer is reporting to us – and in having her dwell so much on personal experiences, memories, reflections, and opinions, Chaucer powerfully encourages readers to register her voice as that of a real person, one with wit, psychological depth, and a distinctive personality.

If we keep in mind that two centuries would elapse after Chaucer's day before Shakespeare's plays appeared onstage, and another century before the literary genre that we call the novel fully emerged, we might imagine the impact this innovative rendering of voice had on Chaucer's first readers. We might then further take into account the fact that female literary characters in Chaucer's day were almost wholly limited to queens and princesses (such as Ipolyta and Emelye in the Knight's Tale), holy virgins (such as Custaunce in the Man of Law's Tale), stock lower-class characters (such as Alisoun in the Miller's Tale), allegorical mouthpieces (such as Dame Prudence in Chaucer's Tale of Melibee), or one-dimensional agents of evil (such as Donegild in the Man of Law's Tale). The Wife of Bath, in contrast, is a reasonably prosperous commoner, what we would now call a middle-class small business owner. She is forty-something, a widow, sexually active, salty of speech, and comical but also quick-witted and well informed. Turner declares her "the first ordinary woman in English literature" and notes further, "A woman like this could not speak in texts before Chaucer's; her viewpoint was not seen as interesting. Moreover, she could barely even be spoken" (2, 20). The generous amount of textual space allocated to a woman of this sort to talk about herself is thus a simple but far-reaching structural feature of the performance. It constitutes the bedrock of the voice that so many readers have found so compelling.

Summary: prologue

The Wife's lengthy prologue strikes many (myself included) as convoluted, rambling, and difficult to follow. It may be relatively straightforwardly summarized, however, as it is not so much *what* the Wife covers but – as we will later consider – *how* she covers it that makes it tricky to trace. The Wife begins by introducing the fact of her having been married five times but then quickly digresses to defend her practice of repetitive remarriage against the disapproval of some unspecified religious authority ("But me was told .../That I ne sholde be wedded be but ones [once]" [3.9–13]). She counters apparent biblical injunctions against the practice with her own interpretations of the bible and appeals to common sense. The latter include affirmations of sexuality in general and her own in particular: ("Myn housbonde shal it han [i.e., have access to her sexual organs] both eve and morwe [morning],/Whan that him list [it pleases him to] come forth and paye his dette [i.e., the sex her husband owes her]" [3.152–53]).

This provokes the Pardoner to interrupt and declare that the Wife's revelations have convinced him to abandon his imminent plan to marry. The Wife in effect tells him to shut up and listen, as she has yet even more lurid revelations to relay: "myself hath been the whippe," she announces regarding "tribulacioun in mariage," though adding the winking aside, "taketh nat agrief of that I saye,/For my entente nis but [intention is only] for to playe" (3.173, 175, 192). She then returns to the topic of her husbands, lumping the first three "goode, and riche, and olde" (3.197) ones together. She confides how they gave her control of their land and money and her mocking feelings about their sexual abilities. Then, in a long section of 230 lines or so, she provides numerous, detailed examples and anecdotes to illustrate her strategies of obtaining the upper hand over those husbands.

She begins next to speak of her fourth husband – one of the two "badde" (3.196) ones – but her mention of his adultery and her youth at the time leads her to pause to recall wistfully the revels of bygone days ("But Lord Crist, whan that it remembreth me/Upon my youthe and on my jolitee,/It tikleth me aboute myn herte roote" [3.469–71]). She then admits that his adultery enraged her and reveals that she got back at him by making him think that she was adulterous as well, even though, she says, she never actually crossed the line into sex with another man. She mentions his death, says "God yive [give] his soule reste" (3.501), and then devotes the rest of her prologue – some 350 lines or so – to her fifth husband, the other "badde" one.

The Wife declares that in contrast to her earlier reasons for marrying, she was drawn to this husband – whose name was Jankin and who was twenty years her junior – "for love and no richesse" (3.526). But before that, she discloses a cycle of domestic abuse that remains all too recognizable today. She mentions, first, that he physically beat her and, second, that because he was "so freshe and gay" in their "bed," he always managed to draw her back to him sexually, so "That, though he hadde me bet [beaten me] on every boon [bone],/He coude winne again my love anon [immediately]" (3.508–12). She recalls how she courted him, as it were, mentioning to him while husband number four was still alive that he would make a good number five, and checking out his "paire/Of legges and of feet so clene and faire" (3.597–98) at number four's funeral. After they married, in an apparent reversal of the situation of her first three marriages, we learn that she handed over to him control of the land and wealth that she gained through those earlier marriages. In this context, she introduces the fact that her deafness in one ear (which we initially hear about in the Wife's General Prologue portrait) is due to a blow from Jankin in response to her tearing a page from a book.

This leads to a lengthy, detailed account of Jankin's verbal abuse, which consisted largely of his citation of learned examples of the evilness of women in general. These, the Wife eventually tells us, he read aloud from what she names as "this book of wikked wives" (3.685). Convinced that he would persist forever in this abuse, the Wife finally ripped three pages from the book (up from the single page earlier mentioned) and punched him "on the cheeke" (3.792) so that he fell back into the fire. Leaping up, he struck her hard on the head, sending her to the floor, where, she says, he thought her dead. Still lying on the floor, she accused him of murdering her and asked for one final kiss. He knelt down and issued what we may recognize as an abuser's apology, saying, in effect, I'm sorry but it was your fault ("That I have doon, it is thyself to wite [blame]./Foryif it me, and that

I thee biseeke [beg]" [2.806–7]). In response to this expression of both regret and blame, she once again "hitte him on the cheeke" (2.808).

Eventually, after "muchel care [great distress] and wo" (3.811), they reconciled under the following conditions, as the Wife reports:

He yaf* me al the bridel* in myn hand	gave; bridle, i.e., control
To han governance of hous and land,	
And of his tonge and his hand also;	
And made him brenne* his book anonright tho.*	burn; immediately then
(3.813–16)	

In sum, she demanded from him "al the sovereinetee" (3.817), which is to say, all the agency in regard to their relationship. In return, he demanded, "Keep thyn honour, and keep eek myn estat" (3.821), that is, don't be adulterous and also preserve my public standing among men. The result, she reports, was a happily-ever-after ending. They never again argued, and they were kind and faithful to each other right up until his death. At this point in the Wife's recollections, the Friar interrupts and makes his aforementioned smirking remark. For some reason, this irritates the Summoner, and in their ensuing bickering the Friar and Summoner in turn declare that they'll tell impugning tales about, respectively, a summoner and friar. They in fact go on to do this but not before the Host intervenes and first has the Wife tell her tale.

Summary: tale

The Wife launches her tale with an indication of its romance genre by setting it in "In th'olde days of the King Arthour" (3.857). For Chaucer and his first readers, this was equivalent to something like what the setting of the Star Wars saga is for us: a faraway time and place filled with fantasy but also with clear parallels with the real world. In the Wife's fantasy world, "Al [All] was this land fulfild of faïrye [filled with fairy creatures]:/ The elf-queene with hir joly compaignye/Daunced ful ofte in many a greene mede [meadow]" (3.859–61). This imagined place, that is, with its "elf-queene" and her happily dancing "compaignye," retains traces of what seems to have been an even earlier, pre-Christian, preternatural matriarchy. The Wife then digresses to contrast this fantasy world with her present-day situation in which the elves and fairies have vanished, replaced, she says, by sexually predatory friars.

Returning to her story, she describes, in a chillingly terse and matter-of-fact manner, how a knight of Arthur's court, riding by himself, comes across an unaccompanied maiden and rapes her: "By verray [actual] force he rafte [took with violence] hir maidenheed [virginity]" (3.888). Public outrage at the crime reaches King Arthur, and he sentences the knight to death by decapitation. Queen Guinevere and her court of ladies, however, intervene, and Arthur agrees to let them decide the fate of the knight. Guinevere demands that the knight, within a year's time, discover and report back to the women "What thing it is that wommen most desiren" (3.903). If he succeeds, his punishment will be waived; if he fails, he loses his head.

The knight begrudgingly sets out to fulfill his assigned task, and his problem quickly becomes not too few answers but too many. Wherever he travels, the Wife reports, he couldn't find "Two creatures [i.e., women] according in-fere [i.e., who have the same opinion]" (3.924). The Wife then rehearses a sampling of the answers that he receives, many of which echo sentiments about women that the Wife covered in her prologue. One of these – that women deeply value keeping men's secrets – provokes the Wife's disdainful disbelief, prompting her to relay as a counter-example the story of Midas, the ancient King of Crete, whose ears are those of an ass. As the Wife tells it, only Midas's wife knows about his ears. Unable to hold the secret in, she runs down to a marsh and whispers it to the waters. The Wife of Bath, at the anecdote's beginning and end, tells us that she took the story from Ovid, and it in fact appears in this early first-century Roman poet's *Metamorphoses*. If one bothers to look up Ovid's version, as the Wife urges her listeners to do, one discovers that neither Midas's wife nor any other woman features in the tale. Rather, Midas's male barber discloses the secret, which the marsh reeds then advertise to the world.

Returning to her story, the Wife tells how, near the end of his allotted year, the knight has given up and begins to head back to court. Riding through a forest, he happens upon twenty-four women dancing together. He approaches them, hoping they will finally have the answer he needs. But they suddenly vanish, leaving in their place only a solitary old woman, about whom the Wife remarks, "A fouler [uglier] wight [creature] ther may no man devise [imagine]" (3.999). The knight asks her his question, and she says that she will reveal the answer if he promises to do the next thing she asks of him, whatever it is. He agrees, and she says, don't worry, "Thy lif is sauf [safe]," as "the queene wol saye as I" (3.1015–16). And indeed this is what happens. At court, the knight announces, in a formulation that obviously echoes that of the Wife's reported reconciliation with her fifth husband, "Wommen desire to have sovereinetee/As wel over hir housbonde as hir love,/And for to been in maistrye him above" (3.1038–40).

All the women in the court affirm the correctness of this answer, and the old woman then publicly demands that the knight fulfill his promise to her – by marrying her. The knight, acknowledging the promise, expresses horrified dismay at her choice, urging the old woman, "Tak al my good [wealth] and lat my body go" (3.1061). But the old woman does not budge, and so they marry and head to bed on their wedding night. The knight is deeply disturbed by the prospect of sex: "Greet was the wo the knight hadde in his thoght:/.../He walweth [tosses] and he turneth to and fro" (3.1083–85). The old woman – with no small amount of knowing irony – says to him, "O deere housbonde, benedicite [bless me],/Fareth [Behaves] every knight thus with his wif as ye?/Is this the lawe of King Arthures hous?" (3.1087–89). She asks him (disingenuously, as from the conclusion of the tale we know that she knows the answer) what it is that bothers him about her. He answers bluntly that she's lowborn, old, and ugly.

The old woman proceeds to address each of these objections in what Chaucer scholars have nicknamed her "pillow lecture," given that the academic tone and length of her explanations, which occupy about a quarter of the tale's lines, are ostentatiously ill fitting to the situation. Most of this lecture focuses on the knight's class objection, in regard to which the old woman systematically and definitively deconstructs the knight's ideology of natural-born class superiority. She explains that the positive qualities associated with upper-class individuals – encompassed by the medieval term *gentilesse* – reflect their virtuous actions. Hence, she says, anyone who characteristically performs such actions, regardless of their heritage or wealth, possesses *gentilesse*, and for this she cites no less authority than Dante Alighieri – the celebrated early fourteenth-century Italian author of the *Divine Comedy*. Conversely, anyone who performs vicious deeds, no matter what their class status, has no claim to *gentilesse*. Pointedly, she says to this rapist knight, "men may wel often finde/A lordes sone do shame and vileinye" (3.1150–51). Such a man, who "nil [will not] himselven do no gentil deedes/.../... is nat [not] gentil, be he duc or erl [duke or earl]" (3.1155–57). Adjacently, then, she declares about her poverty that it likens her to Christ, who "In wilful poverte chees [chose] to live his lif" (3.1179), that the happy poor are in fact rich because they do not desire more than they have, and that the poor are easily able to discern who are their true friends.

She has much less to say about his objections to her age and appearance. For the former, she merely points out that everyone knows the rule about respecting one's elders; and for the latter, she suggests that the fact that men find her ugly means she's unlikely to be adulterous. Jarringly, then, immediately following the latter argument – which is dubiously misogynistic – she abruptly ceases her lecture and makes her new husband this offer:

"But nathelees, sin* I knowe your delit, since
I shal fulfille youre worldly appetit.
Chese now," quod she, "oon of thise thinges tweye:* two

To han me foul and old til that I deye* — die
And be to you a trewe humble wif,
And never you displese in al my lif;
Or ells* ye wol han me yong and fair, — else
And take youre aventure* of the repair* — chance; i.e., frequent visits by men
That shal be to youre hous bycause of me –
Or in som other place, wel may be.
Now chese* youreselven wheither that you liketh."* — choose; whichever you want

(3.1218–27)

In essence, she says, "Have me as I am and you can count on me being humble and faithful, but if you'd rather have me young and beautiful, well, don't so much count on that." After some hesitation, the knight makes the following answer, in language that once again notably echoes that of the Wife of Bath's reconciliation with her fifth husband:

My lady and my love, and wif so dere,
I putte me in youre wise governaunce:
Cheseth* youreself which may be most pleasaunce* — Choose; pleasure
And most honour to you and me also.
I do no fors the wheither* of the two, — don't care which
For as you liketh* it suffiseth* me. — it pleases you; is satisfactory to

(3.1230–35)

In effect, the knight throws up his hands, shrugs his shoulders, and says, "Whatever you like is fine."

After verifying that the knight is indeed giving her full agency in this matter of determining the fundamental nature of their relationship ("Thanne have I gete of you maistrye?" [3.1236]), the old woman announces that in fact she will be "bothe faire and good" (3.1241) – young and beautiful as well as humble and faithful. She transforms herself immediately. In response, "For joye he [the knight] hente [seized] her in his armes two," and "she obeyed him in everything/That mighte do him pleasance or liking" (3.1252, 1255–56). A happily-ever-after concludes the tale proper, but the Wife of Bath has the final word. She petitions Christ to send "us" – that is, women in general – "Housbondes meeke, younge, and fresshe abedde [in bed]/And grace t'overbide hem [outlive them] that we wedde," and urges the plague on husbands who "wol not be governed by hir [their] wives" (3.1258–62). In other words, for real wives in the late fourteenth-century world, the Wife reminds her listeners, happiness depends on husbands who listen to them and understand at least something about female sexuality. Those without such husbands may hope for early widowhood.

Sources

In other chapters, I typically consider Chaucer's sources in the course of the summary, but I have not done so here because in this case his use of sources is considerably more complex than anywhere else in the *Tales*. In contrast with the Knight's and the Man of Law's Tales, for example, no principal source guided Chaucer's composition. For the Wife of Bath's Prologue, Chaucer has deftly woven together snippets from numerous sources, and, crucially, the general character of these texts creates enormously uncomfortable dissonance for those who, like Turner, Smith, and many others, hear in the prologue an authentic female voice. As Turner and Smith are well aware, almost all of the prologue's sources were in Chaucer's day considered authoritative digests of the reasons why men shouldn't get married and even why they should generally avoid women altogether. The bulk of his sources, that is, represents a sort of greatest hits collection of misogynist and misogamist (anti-marriage) writings by medieval churchman. Notably, the Wife of Bath herself explicitly identifies several of these sources when she names the texts that have been compiled into Jankin's "book of wikked wives." The sheer irony of this moment, in which a fictional character condemns the very sources from which much of what she has been saying – indeed, much of what constitutes her as a character – has been drawn, suggests well the level of complexity involved. Much of the scholarship on the Wife's prologue in one way or another tackles this complexity and not surprisingly arrives at a variety of different (and sometimes polar opposite) conclusions about it. We'll return to this complexity shortly.

For the tale that the Wife tells, there also does not appear to be a single guiding source, although its two main folklore motifs were widespread. Those motifs are that of the so-called loathly lady stories (perhaps most familiar to modern audiences from the film *Shrek*) and that of stories that feature a man on a quest to discover what women really want (a permutation of which is evident in, say, the film *Groundhog Day*). A few other Middle English narrative poems combine these two motifs in roughly similar fashion as the Wife of Bath's Tale. One of these, known as "The Tale of Florent," was written by Chaucer's friend and literary competitor John Gower for inclusion in his *Confessio Amantis* (*Lover's Confession* – a collection of short narratives in verse) just before, just after, or at roughly the same time as Chaucer wrote his version. The others were most likely written later. The differences between Gower's and Chaucer's versions have led most scholars to doubt that either was the source for the other, although they could well have had a common inspiration, whether a written source that has not yet been discovered or just some conversation between the two poets. In this respect, then, Gower's and the other Middle English versions of the story serve to underscore what's so unusual about Chaucer's – for example, the nature of the knight's crime, the nature of the offer the old woman eventually makes to the knight, and the tale's abundant commentary, much of it learned, including the entirety of the "pillow lecture" (most of Chaucer's minor sources, such as Ovid and Dante, contribute to this commentary). These distinctive features of the tale, as well as others unique to Chaucer's version, are what most compel further inquiry.

Identity and its discontents

The questions about voice and authenticity that I raised at the outset of this chapter necessarily rest upon the complex concept of identity. As an initial approach to that concept, I'll start with myself. These days, when I'm in the situation of needing to identify myself explicitly, I might supply something along the lines of "Asian/white mixed-race (or, in some situations, just Asian or just Chinese), middle class, more or less non-disabled, straight cis man." I'm also a husband, father, and college professor. You no doubt have at hand your own list of labels for when the occasion calls for them. The aim of these labels, obviously, is to help communicate to others who we are in relation to a range of categories, and we may also have embraced one or more of them as especially central to our own sense of who we are. Yet if you're like me, you've sometimes felt that what's odd and perhaps uncomfortable about these labels is that we have little control over their meaning and implications. In an essential way, they are external to us, even while they inescapably organize how we understand ourselves and how others understand us. As I earlier suggested, they each mark a position within larger social, cultural, and ideological systems, the collection of which overlapping systems shape much if not all of our experience of ourselves and the world.[2] To the extent that I'm aware of the unearned privileges and accompanying injustices deriving from my positions in some of those systems, I might wish to disassociate myself from those respective labels. Yet I cannot do so without disavowing an identity through which I continue to understand myself. I cannot do so, that is, without being to some degree *inauthentic*, which is to say, at some level I continue to affirm, however ambivalently, that those labels 'truly' denote who I am.

One of the systems evident in my list of labels is that of sex/gender. As gender theorists such as Judith Butler have well established, we are each born into a world that already has defined and organized sex and gender differences in some fashion. Most of us had little or no agency in regard to the labels assigned to us in this system, often indeed being assigned a label by, say, an ultrasound technician well before our birth. Consequently, from our very origins, we are treated and come to understand ourselves in some essential way in relation to sex/gender categories that come preloaded with systemic implications and imperatives (e.g., the imperative sometimes directed at those carrying a male label to "be a man"). While nonbinary and trans identities have become increasingly available, in most places the system still divides primarily between male and female, masculine and feminine, and is typically organized to some degree hierarchically. Indeed, such a hierarchy is evident in the very way (tellingly, the most typical way) that I just phrased that division, with men coming first. It's precisely through such common discursive habits – and, to many (especially men), largely invisible habits – that a sex/gender system most subtly functions and thereby serves to support the social order of which it is a part.

As a general rule, social orders seek stability and perpetuation, and this tendency, as a *general* rule, is not in itself oppressive. I'm not unhappy when I can count on, say, my recycling being picked up, even if I'm aware of inequities in the systems that enable that to happen. Obviously, however, some inequities are more severe than others, and those individuals who are slotted in a lower position in a hierarchy generally suffer most from a social order's means of stabilization and perpetuation. We might therefore be moved to resist an oppressive aspect of a social order, whether for ourselves or for others. But one of the most vexing challenges in this effort can be the deeply entrenched relation between our identities and the systems that produce and maintain that social order. Within a patriarchy specifically, simply to be a woman or a man is to embody sex/gender categories in a way that potentially perpetuates the sex/gender system and its attendant hierarchy.

The term *internalized misogyny* is often used to designate the manner in which girls and women understand themselves and treat other girls and women according to sexist stereotypes that, through early and constant exposure, have come deeply to inform their values and beliefs. This is an insidious but relatively palpable way that a patriarchal order reproduces itself by way of identities. More troubling because more far-reaching and invisible is the possibility, as theorists such as Luce Irigaray have argued, that the very structures of language and thought are organized patriarchally. This view begins with the understanding that all individuals come to possess consciousness itself by psychologically taking up residence within prestructured linguistic formulations along the lines of "I am X." Irigaray and other feminist theorists, reworking ideas developed by psychoanalytic philosopher Jacques Lacan, emphasize that within a patriarchal social order, all these prestructured formulations at their most essential level function something like my phrase "male and female," though less self-evidently. The structures of the formulations reflect an assumed hierarchy, and that hierarchy is then enacted in the real world through the formulations' *enunciation* – that is, through their repeated writing, speaking, and thinking. Insofar as we all can know ourselves to be selves per se only by being able to think "I am," we are ceaselessly performing these acts of enunciation that serve to reproduce the social order.

This situation seems quite grim, in which simply to have consciousness is to be entrapped within a patriarchy that one cannot help but to perpetuate, even when one consciously seeks not to do so. This entrapment holds, moreover, even for the less radical version of this situation, in which we just recognize that all ideas about femaleness and femininity come from somewhere. If one lives within a patriarchy, it's likely that the ideas that are most available and prominent are those that somehow reinforce men's position in the hierarchy, regardless of the sex/gender of whoever happens to be transmitting them. This entails that in living out a female/feminine identity, in which one is necessarily embodying some ideas about femaleness/femininity, the possibility of internalized misogyny always lurks, even, perhaps, when one is explicitly resisting or countering that misogyny. As the next section explores, the Wife of Bath's Prologue confronts precisely this grim situation as one of its central projects, albeit doing so with strikingly incongruent joviality.

The Wife of Bath's Prologue: entrapment and mimicry

Shortly after the Wife of Bath describes Jankin's "book of wikked wives," she explicitly charges it and all such writings with what we today would term representational bias. "For trusteth wel," she says, "it is an impossible [logical impossibility]/That any clerk [churchman, scholar] wol speke good of wives/But if [Unless] it be of holy saintes lives/.../Who paintede the leaoun, tel me who?" (3.388–92). With the rhetorical question of that last line, the Wife alludes to an Aesopian fable in which a lion and a man view an artist's depiction of a man killing a lion. The lion points out that if lions were able to create such depictions, it would show the reverse. In brilliantly compact fashion, therefore, the Wife has made two key critiques: that the supposedly objective, authentic representations of women in Jankin's book are in fact ideologically freighted fabrications, which perpetuate male domination precisely by pretending to be simply true; and that this strategy of domination has worked so well because women have been almost wholly barred from producing their own written representations (e.g., by greatly limiting women's access to education).

In this chapter's terms, the Wife here is calling out her entrapment within patriarchal representations of women – the fact that her society's definitions of femaleness and femininity (at least the most authoritative ones) are inherently denigrating. Moreover, by plain implication, she's casting her eye outside her fictional world and calling out her own author, who is, of course, the painter of this particular lion. In this way, Chaucer makes more or less explicit his own complicity in the discursive perpetuation of patriarchy, and this has a double logic. On the one hand, the Wife's rhetorical question *impugns* Chaucer along with Jankin as a male disseminator of misogynist representations of women. On the other hand, in its self-consciousness it *aligns* Chaucer with the Wife, as it suggests that, just like the Wife, Chaucer understands that he cannot escape patriarchal representations of women.

It's clear that the vast majority – if not simply all – of the existing textual precedents available to Chaucer for fashioning female literary characters reinforced patriarchy. Above I described a range of these textual precedents when contrasting them with the character of the Wife of Bath. They include, for instance, female objects of noble men's erotic desire (e.g., the princess) and virginal female saints, both of which character types Chaucer does indeed recapitulate in his writings. While in some respects these particular character types may seem positive depictions of femininity, they reinforce patriarchy in more or less readily discernible ways. The first type, for example, confines women to the role of sexualized object of exchange between men, while the second demonizes female sexual desire by equating female holiness with virginity. And along with these supposedly positive kinds of female representations, there were a host of straightforwardly negative kinds, such as that of the shrewish wife, which obviously reinforce male domination quite directly. The question that this situation then raises is, if one wishes to fashion a truly positive literary representation of a woman, what words and phrases are at hand to accomplish this aim that aren't already somehow infected by the discursive machinations of patriarchy?[3]

Working through this problem in general, Irigaray and other feminist theorists have urged the adoption of *formal* interventions: adjustments not so much to words and phrases themselves but to the way that patriarchal discourse is performed. Irigaray in particular proposes the technique of *mimicry* or assuming "the feminine role deliberately." By this she means the conscious occupation of the "feminine role" as patriarchal discourse defines it but in a winking sort of way, so as to "convert a form of subordination into an affirmation, and thus to begin to thwart it." With this technique, a woman seeks "to recover the place of her exploitation by discourse, without allowing herself to be simply reduced to it." Through mimicry, she may "make 'visible,' by an effect of playful repetition, what was supposed to remain invisible: the cover-up of a possible operation of the feminine in language" (76).

Chaucer scholars such as Carolyn Dinshaw (1989) and Susan Crane (1994) have powerfully demonstrated the relevance of these ideas for the Wife of Bath's Prologue. Here, we may recall the irony of the Wife's explicitly naming several of the very misogynist sources out of which most of her prologue – which is to say, most of her own characterization – has been drawn and condemning them as "wikked" and false representations of women. With Irigaray's aid, we see that this naming serves to signal the Wife's consciousness of her role-playing. The Wife's strategy (which is necessarily also that of Chaucer, her lion-painting author) is not to attempt to leave patriarchal discourse behind in favor of some yet-unconceived feminist discourse. It is rather to dive headfirst into some of the most virulent, negative representations of women, *mimicking* them in both her character and speech, while simultaneously calling attention to their nature and her own entrapment. Somehow, what emerges from this winking reproduction of misogyny is, for readers such as Smith, Turner, and many others, "a possible operation of the feminine in language," or exactly that elusive authentic female representation, the "voice" that Smith hears speaking in the Wife of Bath's Prologue that is also that of the real girls and women of her modern-day London.

Irigaray also helps us to see, however, that while the Wife's explicitly naming and condemning of her misogynist sources effect an essential signaling function, they are perhaps not as far-reaching contributors to that sense of voice as some of the prologue's other, less obvious techniques. What's needed is not just to mark the several stereotypes that the Wife embodies in the prologue as indeed the stock clichés of misogynist discourse (she appears, for example, as the nagging wife, gold-digging wife, sexually promiscuous wife, jealous wife, gossiping wife, etc.). More crucially, the very manner in which the Wife performs – or mimics – these stereotypes must point back at the otherwise unrepresented and unknowable performer herself. She must "try," as Irigaray says, "to recover the place of her exploitation by discourse, without allowing herself to be simply reduced to it."

As an analogue, we might think of a viscerally convincing cinematic depiction of a horrendously evil villain that nonetheless compels us to admire the actor portraying that villain, whom we may otherwise know nothing about. By some sort of verbal sleights of hand, the Wife's words must ultimately represent not the manifest content of the stereotypes but the mystery of what lurks behind, the agency of the performer of those stereotypes, thereby conveying a sense that everything is delivered with a knowing wink. While exactly what that wink knows will necessarily remain elusive within a patriarchy, it's that distinctive sense of "a person who knows" that the peculiarities of the form of the Wife of Bath's Prologue achieve. They convey to us that the Wife is joking (in the profoundly serious way that Irigaray describes) and make us feel as though we're in on that joke, even if we're not actually sure what the joke is.

I'll describe two of the specific techniques involved. First, there's what I mentioned above as the prologue's "convoluted, rambling, and difficult to follow" organization. The prologue's unexpected digressions, logical U-turns, and grandstanding confessional set pieces, among other characteristics, greatly unsettle what is otherwise a linear, chronological account of the Wife's five husbands. Their destabilizing effect comes across as something like (to use an astrophysics metaphor) the warping of the fabric of time and space by the force of gravity. Thus, for example, the Wife begins by declaring that she will "speke of *wo* that is in marriage" (3.3) but then speaks instead in *favor* of marriage, in particular by supplying sermon-like arguments defending her practice of serial marriage and her embrace of the sexual activity that it enables. She eventually does return to "wo that is in marriage," however, and indeed her own woe with her fifth husband is the prologue's aptly positioned narrative and thematic climax. A modern-day college writing instructor, we might imagine, would praise that final move but encourage the Wife to be more systematic in the rest of her presentation and to provide more reader-friendly logical transitions. And in fact from Chaucer's other writings we know that he would be perfectly capable of rendering her speech in that fashion. Her discrepancies in these respects thus serve as markers of her performative agency. Another, particularly compact instance of such a marker is the otherwise wholly superfluous couplet that, in its very excrescence, functions as a wink: "But now sire – lat me see, what shal I sayn?/Aha, by God, I have my tale again" (3.585–86). "Wait, where was I?," the Wife asks no one in particular, and answers herself, "Ah, yes, there." Whether or not the Wife has truly lost the thread of her comments – that is, whether Chaucer means to dramatize her as actually doing so or as feigning to do so for rhetorical effect – is a question that we could generalize to the whole collection of the prologue's organizational peculiarities. We have no certain way of knowing the answer, but the very prompting of the question registers the effect of the gravitational force of the Wife's performative agency.

The second technique is the head-spinningly nested manner in which material from Chaucer's misogynist and misogamist sources is in several stretches of the prologue incorporated virtually verbatim. Across hundreds of lines, this material appears as the Wife's quoting of her own earlier quoting of her husbands' quoting of those denigrating sources. For example, to her pilgrim audience, she quotes herself as having said to one of her first three husbands, "Thou saist we wives wil oure vices hide/Til we be fast [i.e., securely married], and thanne we wol hem shewe [reveal them] – /Wel may that be a proverbe of a shrewe!" (3.282–84). Here, the Wife attributes to her husband the words from after "saist" up through "shewe," and scholars have identified this specific remark as originating in the source that the Wife herself later names as "Theofraste" (3.671). In effect, then, she's quoting him quoting this material. And as the entire comment is framed by her earlier speech tag "But herkeneth how I saide" (3.234), she's quoting herself quoting her husband quoting "Theofraste." The resulting dizzying series of nested speech boxes foregrounds the activity of quotation over and above whatever is actually being quoted, thereby marking misogynist and misogamist discourse as instrumentalized discourse per se. It indicates that supposedly truthful descriptions of the world are in fact verbal weapons wielded by specific speakers for specific reasons – here, as the Wife puts it, as "a proverbe of a shrewe." The technique is even more complicated than this, however, since we must factor in that it's Chaucer who's ultimately quoting "Theofraste" here, putting those words into the mouth of a fictional woman who in turn puts them into the mouth of her fictional (to Chaucer and us) husband. In this way, the husband becomes Chaucer's double, as an example of a man who, like him, rehearses misogynist texts. But between himself and his own double, Chaucer has positioned the Wife as a mediating agent who speaks Theofrastus's words for the man who stands in for Chaucer and, in the process, names all three men "a shrewe."

When the Wife subsequently confesses to the pilgrim audience that her husbands never spoke the words that she accused them of speaking ("al was fals" [3.382], she declares), she explodes this whole structure of nested boxes. But she does so in a way that underscores her agency and mimics, at a deeper level, the operation of patriarchal discourse. She has falsely put Theofrastus's words into her husbands' mouths in the same way that Chaucer has put misogynist stereotypes into her character, and she does this to men, just as patriarchy does to women, as a means of domination. "They [i.e., her husbands] were ful glad to excusen hem ful blive [to apologize very quickly]/Of thing of which they never agilte hir live [were guilty in their lives]," she reveals, and so, "Attte ende [In the end] I hadde the bet [better of them] in ech degree [every way]" (3.404). Just so, patriarchy, through internalized misogyny, in effect prompts women to apologize for being the kind of women that patriarchy says they are and to accept the domination of men. The Wife's mimicry ostentatiously flip-flops the gender positions of this operation. It thereby achieves a repetition with a winking difference, laying bare the discursive operations of patriarchy in a way that also calls attention to her agency and voice.

Or does it achieve this? Some skeptical readers (e.g., Hansen 1992) have noticed that when the smoke of all these verbal pyrotechnics has cleared, the character of the Wife remains firmly tied to misogynist stereotypes. Her gravitational warping of the prologue's organization might be readily assimilated, for example, to the stereotype of the flighty, irrational feminine mind. Her fabrications of her husband's speech might be taken as simply what she admits that they are, the sort of manipulative deception that might be readily assimilated to the stereotype of the shrewish (and possibly adulterous) wife. But in fact the stubborn persistence of these stereotypes is exactly what Irigaray and other theorists would predict. The all-encompassing nature of patriarchal discourse means that even resistance to it, as in turning it upside down, winds up just reiterating it. In this view, we cannot really expect that the Wife will escape the stereotypes that constitute her or that Chaucer, in painting this lion, will manage to show how a lion instead of a man would render the scene. Nonetheless, for many readers, the prologue's way of reiterating patriarchal discourse – the Wife's mimicry – leaves a residue or a surplus beyond that repetition, perhaps that which is felt by Smith to be the "spirit" of her words that somehow reaches from medieval to modern England and from fiction to reality.

The Wife of Bath's Prologue: female experience and male authority

With this general technique of mimicry in mind, we may revisit the initial portion of the prologue, in which the Wife takes up religious questions with what seems a strikingly irreverent emphasis on matters of the flesh. She indicates the nature of the opposition at stake in her very first words, when she declares that "Experience, though noon [no] auctoritee/Were in this world, is right ynough [good enough] for me/To speke of wo that is in mariage" (3.1–3). The word "auctoritee" here refers specifically to textual authority, the truths about the human condition preserved and transmitted in authoritative writings, especially those by eminent churchmen that provide official interpretations of what the bible says about those truths. "Experience," in contrast, means here knowledge about the human condition gained directly through the senses, that is, via the physical body. We may recognize this opening statement, at its simplest level, as a cutting witticism, given what we (and the Wife) know about the sources of her prologue, which constitute the specific "auctoritee" she has mind. Since the male clergymen of these misogynist and misogamist sources were supposed to be celibate, they lacked (or were supposed to have lacked) experience about the very subject of their writings, in stark contrast with the Wife, whose body has endured, through five husbands, thirty-plus years of "wo that is in marriage": "Of five housbondes scoleying [schooling] am I" (3.44f), the Wife later points out. "If you want to know about golf," a modern Wife might ask as an analogy, "do you seek someone who's never played but has written books about it, or someone who's played – successfully – for decades?"

Much deeper layers of significance underlie this lighthearted jab at churchmen, however. Ultimately, the remark raises the question of the relative importance of different sources of human knowledge, along with the life-guiding values that lead to and from those sources. On the one hand is experience of the physical world, and on the other hand are books that explain that world. The Wife's quip invokes a long history of writings by male Christian authorities about one specific aspect of that world: the sexualized human body. As is still familiar to many today, those authorities in one manner or another declared, to boil their message down to its simplest formulation, that ever since the Fall, the sexualized body is the sign and vehicle of sin. One of the most crucial biblical texts in this regard is Paul's first letter to the Corinthians, chapter 7, which begins, "Now concerning the thing whereof you wrote to me: It is good for a man not to touch a woman." Fusing the degradation of the sexualized body with the denigration of women, this verse supplies the basic prompt for and capsule message of all the misogynist and misogamist sources of the Wife's prologue.

Not at all coincidentally, then, the Wife directly engages with 1 Corinthians 7 in her prologue. Or, rather, she mimics the direct engagement with 1 Corinthians 7 found in *Adversus Jovinianum* (*Against Jovinianus*), a treatise written by eminent fourth-century Christian authority Jerome, creator of what was in Chaucer's day the official Latin text of the bible (the English translation of which I quote in this book). As its title indicates, in this treatise Jerome refutes the arguments of a monk named Jovinianus, who among other claims insisted that sex within marriage and sexual abstinence were equally holy. The Wife names both author and title of the treatise when listing out the contents of Jankin's "book of wikked wives": "And eek [also] ther was sometime a clerk [scholar] at Rome,/A cardinal, that highte [was called] Saint Jerome,/That made a book again Jovinian" (3.673–75). By this point in the prologue, however, she has herself long been drawing upon the treatise, beginning with her defense of her serial marriages that directly follows her opening contrast of "experience" and "auctoritee."

At part of this defense, for example, the Wife remarks,

Th'Apostle,* whan he speketh of maidenhede,*	i.e., Paul in 1 Cor. 7; virginity
He saide that precept* therof hadde he noon:*	commandment; none, i.e., he wasn't commanding it
Men may conseile a womman to be oon,*	i.e., a virgin
But conseiling nis no comandement.	
He putte it in oure owene juggement.	
(3.64–68)	

The Wife here reproduces a passage in *Against Jovinianus* fairly closely. Jerome's aim in this section is to counter the implication that Jovinianus draws from 1 Corinthians 7.25, which reads, "Now concerning virgins, I have no commandment of the Lord; but I give counsel, as having obtained mercy of the Lord, to be faithful." Acknowledging that this verse does have the effect of permitting sexuality within marriage, Jerome nonetheless insists that it establishes a clear spiritual hierarchy:

> Do not marvel then if, placed as we are, amid temptations of the flesh and incentives to vice, the angelic life be not exacted of us, but merely recommended ... The great Creator and Fashioner, knowing the weakness of the vessel which he made, left virginity open to those whom He addressed ... And therefore Christ loves virgins more than others, because they willingly give what was not commanded them. And it indicates greater grace to offer what you are not bound to give, than to render what is exacted of you.[4]

Those able to resist the "temptations of the flesh," Jerome argues, earn more of Christ's love. The fact that marriage is left as a choice to human beings is therefore not an endorsement of sexuality but rather a sort of holiness placement exam. Those who score low should aspire to a better grade, to be obtained through remediation. As Jerome puts it (imagining how Paul might've spoken to the Gentiles), "Let them begin with short periods of release from the marriage bond, and give themselves unto prayer, that when they have tasted the sweets of chastity they may desire the perpetual possession of that wherewith they were temporarily delighted." The Wife does not repeat this particular suggestion, but she also does not suppress the general assertion of a spiritual hierarchy. "Al were it [Although it would be] good no woman for to touche," she says, quoting the first line of 1 Corinthians 7, "This is al and som: he [Paul] heeld virginitee/More parfit [perfect, i.e., holier] than wedding in freletee [frailty, i.e., in weakness of the flesh]" (3.87, 91–92). Following Jerome's suggestion that virgins are favored by Christ, she observes, "He [Christ] spak to hem [spoke to them] that wolde live parfitly [i.e., in upmost holiness]." But then in her own words, she declares to her pilgrim audience, "And lordinges, by youre leve, that [i.e., one who wishes to 'live parfitly'] am nat I" (3.112). Instead, she says, "I wol bistowe the flour of al myn age [i.e., prime of my life]/In th'actes and in fruit of marriage [i.e., in marital sexual activity]" (3.113–14).

With this aside, she offers a verbal wink that signals the way in which her mimicry has been operating throughout this portion of the prologue. She reproduces Jerome's meaning more or less accurately, but her selection and organization of his comments create an emphasis that is wholly her own, namely an emphasis on her agency in regard to her sexualized body, as evident above in "He putte it in *oure* owene juggement" and "*I* wol bistowe." This is yet another example of how the form of the prologue disrupts its manifest content. But here we see also how that disruption, and the agency and voice that it evokes, overturns the spirit/flesh binary that informs the broad understanding of the human condition evident in Jerome's treatise and that was widely, though not universally, held in Chaucer's day. In this understanding, not just marriage but corporeal existence generally is a sort of spiritual test, in which those who score highest are those who most resist material, physical desires. The basic aim of human life, in this view, is to score high enough on this test to free the soul from what Pope Innocent III, writing in the year 1195, characterized as the prison of the body.

In this book, I have been regularly considering the way in which Chaucer contemplates the question of the meaning of life as I defined that phrase above: an understanding of the relations between our basic material existence and those nonmaterial ideas, ideals, and values that shape our experience of that existence. Such understandings are at some level always operative as we go about our activities, though we tend to become conscious of them only when the relations become in some way conflictual. Say, for example, I want to purchase an expensive cone of gourmet dark chocolate salted caramel ice cream but happen to be reminded of the billions of people barely surviving on subsistence diets. I might hesitate, unsure of how to weigh the corporeal pleasure of the ice cream against whatever monetary contribution I might make toward global economic equity. Jerome, we may imagine, would tell me to fast and give any money thereby saved to a church-run charitable organization. The Wife would declare that God gives us the choice, and she'll take a double scoop in a waffle cone.

What this ice cream analogy leaves out, of course, is the deep connection between the spirit/flesh binary and Western Christian patriarchy. Prominent among the latter's justification of women's subjugation has been women's allegedly greater susceptibility to carnality, as exemplified and inaugurated by Eve's fateful desire in Paradise: "And the woman saw that the tree was good to eat, and fair to the eyes, and delightful to behold: and she took of the fruit thereof, and did eat, and gave to her husband who did eat" (Genesis 3.6). The Wife's mimicry of Jerome reproduces exactly this view of female carnality but celebrates rather than condemns it. She proclaims, for example, "In wifhode wol I use myn instrument [i.e., her genitals]/As freely [generously] as my Makere hath it sent" (3.149–50). Again, we see here a link between an assertion of female agency ("wol I") and an embrace of female carnality, as if each is the necessary corollary of the other. And again, we may notice that along with what we might hear as her voice in that couplet, the Wife in this way remains trapped in misogynist stereotypes, in which the stereotypically willful woman is also the stereotypically sexually voracious woman.

In the same way, however, that the Wife's voice, in its very over-the-top performance of such stereotypes, seems to register a conscious roleplaying that points at something beyond those stereotypes, this ostentatious embrace of female carnality may point at something beyond just confirmation of misogynist expectations. For example, immediately after the Wife declares "I wol bistowe the flour of al myn age/In th'actes and in fruit of marriage," she asks rhetorically about the purpose of genitalia: "Telle me also, to what conclusioun [purpose]/Were membres maad of generacioun [reproductive organs created]/And of so parfit wis a wrighte ywroght? [made by a so perfectly wise maker]?" (3.115–17). Here, the Wife insists that the sexualized body is part of God's necessarily perfect plan for creation.[5] The implication at hand, which she doesn't quite voice, is that the body, rather than being the soul's prison, partakes of the divine, and indeed its very corporeality, including sexuality, may supply access to the divine with a singular immediacy. An alternative metaphysics is hinted at, one in which the spirit/flesh binary is leveled, inverted, or just eliminated altogether.

In Irigaray's terms, this binary corresponds to that between the *sensible* and *intelligible*, a distinction made throughout Western philosophy between body/matter and mind/soul/form. Patriarchy has aligned the essence of the female sex with the former and that of the male with the latter and established a clear hierarchy between them. Irigaray's alternative feminist metaphysics, like that hinted at by the Wife, seeks to point to what this binary has occluded, which cannot quite be expressed in the discourse that patriarchy has provided. While the complex machinery of Irigaray's theoretical framework is obviously not something we can straightforwardly attribute to the Wife, we can readily imagine the Wife's wholehearted agreement with that framework's centering of female sexual enjoyment. "What remains the most completely prohibited to woman," writes Irigaray about patriarchal entrapment, "is that she should express something of her own sexual pleasure" (1985, 157). Inasmuch as the Wife seeks to express exactly that within the misogynist discourse available to her, we might understand her as pushing that basic patriarchal prohibition to its breaking point – even while, inevitably, reiterating that very discourse.

The Wife of Bath's Tale: rape

In this regard, that male sexual violence constitutes the inaugurating event of the tale that the Wife tells is wholly apt, if deeply disturbing. With that event, the Wife recognizes that underneath its discursive strategies, a patriarchal social order's most fundamental level of enforcement is physical. Female threats to that order, such as the one that the Wife's prologue may represent, have almost always in the final resort been countered, across the long history of patriarchy, by a regime of systemic physical violence and very often sexual violence. With cruel irony, patriarchy has written what it insists is women's inherent carnality on women's bodies themselves, in the process denying women's agency and erasing their desire. This ultimate enforcement mechanism is unmistakably evident in the Wife's prologue, when the Wife's demonstration of her agency and desire, in the form of rending pages out of the very textual sources from which Chaucer has made her, is met by an act of domestic violence – specifically a blow to her head that deafens her. Her refusal to listen to misogynist discourse is, again with cruel irony, countered symbolically as well as corporeally, through her husband's permanent damage to her hearing.

The supposedly happy ending of the Wife of Bath's Prologue is haunted by this act of domestic violence, perhaps making that ending for her a conscious bit of wishful thinking that prompts her to return in her tale to the problem of violence and to do so more directly and severely. Crucially, moreover, it's of course the lion-painting Chaucer who ultimately has staged this bit of wishful thinking and the subsequent return of the violence that it cannot evade. That the specific form of this renewed violence, the knight's crime of rape, is unique to Chaucer's version of the story therefore urges us to take into account an incident in Chaucer's life that was first recovered from the historical archives in the late nineteenth century and has ever since vexed Chaucer scholars, albeit different scholars in different ways. The most vexing of the documents pertaining to this incident reads as follows:

> Let all know that I, Cecily Chaumpaigne, daughter of the late William Chaumpaigne and his wife Agnes, have remitted, released, and entirely quitclaimed on behalf of myself and my heirs in perpetuity to Geoffrey Chaucer, esq., all manner of actions related to my *raptus*, or to whatever other situation or cause, and of whatever condition they are, that I ever had, have, or could have, from the beginning of the world down to the day of making these presents.
>
> (Roger. 445)

The translation that I have quoted leaves the word *raptus* in its original Latin, because precisely how to render it has been a subject of great contention, swinging pendulum-like from one meaning to another. At first, scholars – male scholars in an academic field in which there were then very few women – were keen to point out that *raptus* did not necessarily mean *rape* but could instead mean *abduction*. This might seem only somewhat less damning, but these scholars were quick to add that among the prosperous classes in Chaucer's day, abduction for the purpose of, say, compelling marriage was not uncommon – it happened to Chaucer's own father, for example. Eventually, however, the evidence of the legal archives led most Chaucer scholars to agree that, in this instance, *raptus* denotes sexual assault. They then had to determine how to respond to an official legal document in which a woman named Cecily Chaumpaigne releases Chaucer from "all manner of actions" related to her rape.

Predictably, male scholars in the then mostly male field of literary studies often played defense attorney for Chaucer. They assured readers, for example, that this document's *release* of Chaucer meant that the original charge was false. Sometimes, they imagined exculpatory scenarios that reprised the very misogyny that links the rape cultures of Chaucer's day with our own. More recently, a number of female Chaucer scholars have brought our attention to the toxicity of this critical tradition and have, moreover, urged us to contemplate what it would mean – for our understanding of Chaucer's texts and for the whole enterprise of Chaucer study – if Chaucer was in fact a rapist (e.g., Baechle and Harris 2021). Then in 2022, in a rare moment of popular press interest in Chaucer, the world learned from scholars Euan Roger and Sebastian Sobecki about newly unearthed documents that seem to swing the pendulum of the meaning of *raptus* back to abduction and in a way that actually makes Chaumpaigne and Chaucer legal allies rather than opponents in a case involving labor obligations rather than sexual assault. Specifically, these documents record that Chaumpaigne, at her own initiative, left her job as domestic servant in the household of a man named Thomas Staundon and took a job in Chaucer's household. The aim of the release quoted above, then, seems to have been to protect Chaucer and herself against Staundon's legal suit against them both, with Staundon claiming that Chaucer compelled her to leave his employment before the end of her agreed-upon term.

As of this writing, most (though not all) Chaucer scholars have accepted Roger and Sobecki's new interpretation of Chaumpaigne's *raptus*. Only time will tell whether the pendulum might eventually swing back the other way. Yet, even if it does not, as much as Chaucer fans might be relieved to put aside the likelihood of Chaucer's guilt in this case, it would be deeply short-sighted (as Roger and Sobecki would agree) also to put aside the topic of rape and, more generally, systemic violence against women, as irrelevant to Chaucer. Everything that this chapter has so far covered – not to mention the many sexual assaults, or threats thereof, that appear elsewhere in Chaucer's writings – argues otherwise. Regardless of what in his own experience might have prompted him to foreground this topic (and, of course, most of that experience, despite a wealth of historical documents, remains irrecoverable), the fact remains that he does indeed foreground it – albeit, as we will see, in a characteristically ambiguous way.

The Wife of Bath's Tale: the pillow lecture and the finale

Some aspects of the Wife of Bath's Tale seem more or less to reprise the prologue's strategies of mimicry. For example, the initial range of answers to the question of what women most desire might be understood as another round of the Wife's winking rehearsal of misogynist stereotypes. And her extended exemplum about Midas might be understood as mimicking misogynistic scholarly commentary on such classical texts as Ovid's *Metamorphoses*. Among other aspects of the tale, however, two in particular – the pillow lecture and the tale's conclusion – stand out as requiring additional explanation, which will take us as far this chapter will be able to go into the implications of the Wife's overall performance.

The most immediate question prompted by the sixty-eight lines that Chaucer devotes to the topic of *gentilesse*, in a tale totaling a mere 408 lines, is: what the heck are they doing here? The knight's preceding complaint that his just-wedded wife is "comen of so lowe a kinde [i.e., has a lower-class heritage]" (3.1100) would not appear to justify such a dramatic shift of focus from gender/sex to class. It seems that the knight just tosses out this complaint along with several others, and little in the tale before this tends toward this topic. The very ostentation of this non sequitur, then, suggests a bit of characteristic Chaucerian trickery, and in this case Chaucer likely had his initial inner circle of readers especially in mind, those who would've been aware of Chaucer's interest in the subject of *gentilesse*. Modern readers know about that interest because one of Chaucer's short poems, in which he directly addresses the reader in his authorial voice, is wholly dedicated to this subject. Indeed, its three stanzas express precisely the same sentiment about *gentilesse* as does the old woman. For example, the poem's first stanza declares,

The firste stok, fader* of gentilesse –	first ancestor, father
What man* desireth gentil for to be	Whoever
Must folowe his trace,* and alle his wittes dresse*	footsteps; apply
Vertu to sewe* and vices for to flee.	follow
For unto vertu longeth dignitee*	comes nobleness, high social rank
And nought the revers,* saufly* dar I deme,*	reverse; confidently; judge
Al were* he myter, croune, or diademe*	Although wear; i.e. the headdress of bishop, king, or emperor

As in the old woman's remarks, the positive qualities associated with the upper classes, termed *gentilesse*, have been severed from so-called good birth. One does not inherit *gentilesse* from one's ancestors but gains it only by emulating those ancestors' virtuous deeds, regardless of the lofty social position one may hold, up to and including emperor.

Let's assume, therefore, that Chaucer wants his readers to know that the old woman's remarks about *gentilesse* are ones that he shares. Then, to use a stage metaphor, this most extended portion of the pillow lecture represents an odd, gender-bending moment in which Chaucer, dressed up as the old woman, breaks the fourth wall and addresses his audience directly. (Notably, in theatrical performances in Chaucer's day, women's parts were all played by men, and so this metaphor is not merely fanciful.) What's more, Chaucer's remarks are – unusually for the *Canterbury Tales* – apparently wholly in earnest, and what they boil down to is a kind of class egalitarianism, in which so-called good breeding in fact depends not on breeding in the literal sense but rather on moral action. Chaucer in effect peeks over the top of his mask and says to the audience, "This, truly, is the message I want you to take from this story."

And yet, at the same time, that mask remains on his face. Although he stretches the fictional scenario of the wedding night to its limit, he doesn't wholly break it but remains to some degree still in character. This doubleness – in which the passage simultaneously has Chaucer speaking as his real self to his real audience and the old woman speaking to her rapist husband – is the trick, I believe, that Chaucer was after, as it brings to fore what is in fact a ready parallel between class and sex/gender egalitarianism. Both seek to demystify claims to superiority based on biology – claims that insist that one group of people deserves special privileges because of something intrinsic about their bodies. In declaring his views about class, Chaucer was transmitting arguments that were circulating in his day that would've appealed to many in his immediate circle of readers, who, like Chaucer himself, had climbed some number of rungs up the social ladder. For these readers, the argument that merit rather than blood is what ought to determine social rewards would've been met by immediate nods of approval. In delivering this message while in effect wearing a dress, Chaucer thereby brings the parallel notion of sex/gender egalitarianism into view, if not into actual words. If, as Irigaray argues, all the resources of language are tainted by patriarchy, perhaps tricks such as this are what are required, ones in which the doubleness of author/character expresses what neither has the words to say.

The partial abandonment of the tale's fictional situation upon which this trick depends, however, makes the return to that situation with the tale's conclusion all the more jarring. Suddenly, as if the old woman realizes that the implications of her lecture on *gentilesse* were beyond her listener's mental capacity (which is not hard to imagine for the knight), she breaks off without waiting for a response. She makes brief comments about her ugliness and then offers him a choice between two physical conditions of her body, which seems to reprise the very misogynist stereotypes that the implications of her lecture aimed to overcome. The particular nature of the two choices – either ugly and faithful or beautiful and adulterous – is another of the unique features of Chaucer's version of the story (the *Shrek* formula, fair by night and foul by day, or vice versa, is the more typical). Both choices imply that men's possession of women's sexualized bodies is paramount and that whether or not a woman is sexually desirable to other men determines the relative security of that possession. We may presume that neither choice is particularly appealing to the knight, and it's hard to imagine the old woman being happy either bound to a man who finds her disgusting or, alternatively, suffering the fate of a promiscuous woman in patriarchal society. By itself, this dilemma, with its promise of starkly unhappy endings for everyone involved, might seem to supply yet another sideways critique of misogynist stereotypes, a sort of pillow lecture redone by the old woman in an ironic, fairy tale key. But any such critique seems quickly withdrawn in the supposedly happy resolution of the dilemma that immediately follows.

That resolution – in which the knight is treated to both/and rather than either/or – has for many readers provoked no small amount of outrage, especially in recent years. As Carissa Harris succinctly summarizes, the tale "often offends readers' sense of justice" by focusing on the perpetrator of a rape rather than the victim-survivor; while the latter never speaks and "disappears entirely from the tale after her assault," the former "avoids legal punishment, and is ultimately rewarded with a youthful, fair, obedient, and faithful wife" (Harris 2024). From this perspective, the tale's supposedly happy ending seems not just a reiteration of the prologue's wishful thinking but a wholesale abandonment of whatever has been gained, in respect to the prison house of patriarchal discourse, by all that has preceded. In place of the Wife's winking mimicry of stereotypes, the tale's finale – in which a "fair" and "yong" woman "obeyed him [the knight] in everything/That mighte do him plesance or liking" (3.1251, 1255–56) – seems to many to be a straightforward, even bland reprise of a toxic male sexual fantasy.

Not surprisingly, many Chaucer scholars – including no few feminist ones (e.g., Lipton 2019) – have sought to explain how this finale might be squared with the several levels of complexities that lead up to it. For example, we might recall that the reason that the knight "avoids legal punishment" is initially because of the intervention of the women in Arthur's court. We might understand that intervention as their recognition that chopping off the knight's head will not alter the toxic patriarchal social order. What the women demand, rather, is a public proclamation of precisely what that social order denies: the sovereignty of women's agency and existence of women's desire. This proclamation the women receive from the knight. We might then understand the knight's response to the choice the old woman offers him – his giving the choice back to her – as his internalization of the truth that he was compelled to proclaim. In giving the choice back to the old woman and thereby submitting himself to her agency and waiting for her to act on her desire, the knight, we might conclude, has finally understood something that his social order has hidden from him. We might even suppose that through that understanding he has been reformed, and in that way he represents the possibility of systemic reform more broadly.

Such a prospect of systemic reform would be a happy ending indeed. Yet it's precisely in imagining what such a reform, or such a happy ending, would look like that the tale falters, or, rather, that it relapses back into the prison house of patriarchal discourse. The problem is that because the terms of the choice that the old woman offers are so wholly determined by that discourse, any resolution will likewise be so determined, even if, in the brief moment of transit from choice to resolution, we catch a glimpse of what may lie beyond that discourse. In the same way that there are no words for the gender egalitarianism that is otherwise the obvious parallel to the class egalitarianism that the old woman urges in her pillow lecture, there seem to be no words for describing a social order, represented in miniature by the marriage between the old woman and knight, that honors women's agency and recognizes their desire.

Indeed, any glimpse of what may lie behind patriarchal discourse is grimly overshadowed by the finale's recollection of the sexual violence that initiated the story. Not only does the old woman cede all her agency back to the knight virtually the very instant that she has confirmed his recognition of it, but she also does so excessively, even granting him the power to kill her on the spot if he finds her anything less than the most beautiful and perfectly faithful woman in the world: "Do with my lif and deeth right as you lest [however you please]" (3.1248), she says. In this way, she grants him the absolute power over her body that King Arthur granted Guinevere over the knight's, in punishment for the knight having presumed to possess that power over the body of the woman he raped – and so, in a sense, we're back where we started. Moreover, the physical action that the knight takes upon first seeing the old woman's transformation, described as "For joye he hente hire in his armes two" (3.1252), is at best uncomfortable and more likely deeply disturbing. David Lawton, in the Chaucer edition that I've been quoting, glosses the verb "hente" here relatively benignly as "took," which was certainly one of its possible meanings. But Chaucer's more common use of this word, by far, is in the sense of "to seize," and the action that it denotes is usually an aggressive and often violent one. If Chaucer's more typical use applies here, he would seem to be signaling that far from pointing to systemic reform, at the end the knight represents reassertion of the physical coercion that undergirds the patriarchal status quo.

Admittedly, this interpretation of the tale's happy ending, while it perhaps honors the levels of complexities that lead up to the finale, is a bleak one. If in the Wife's prologue Chaucer points the Wife's finger back at himself as a painter of lions, and so recognizes his own entrapment in patriarchal discourse, the conclusion of the Wife's tale remorselessly restages that entrapment. It invokes the possibility of transcendence of that discourse seemingly for the ultimate purpose of confirming its inescapability. This is why, perhaps, Chaucer does not in fact end the Wife of Bath's performance with this conclusion. Instead, he has the Wife leave her story behind and speak directly to her listeners one final time, in the jolly, combative, winking voice of the prologue. He appears to have recognized that with that voice he has unleashed something not wholly containable, even if, paradoxically, everything the voice actually says remains contained. It seems indeed to have been the fashioning of this voice, rather than anything that can be paraphrased as insights or arguments, that stands as the culmination of Chaucer's career-long meditation upon the ramifications of women's abjection within patriarchal social orders. That readers – and rewriters – such as Zadie Smith continue to hear this voice's reverberations is the best measure of its accomplishment.

Notes

1 Crocker 2024 similarly takes these comments as a point of departure.
2 In this account of how our identities are at once internal and external, I'm loosely drawing upon the theorist Louis Althusser's concept of *interpellation*.
3 One measuring stick for how much progress has been made in this respect among today's storytellers might be the famous Bechdel test for evaluating representations of women in films. From the results of that test, the ready conclusion is: not near as much progress as one might have thought.
4 From Book 1, section 12; here and elsewhere, I quote the translation freely available at https://www.newadvent.org/fathers/30091.htm.
5 Line 3.117 appears with various wordings in the manuscripts, and so exactly what Chaucer wrote is uncertain. But its basic point about the divine source of human genitalia is evident in all versions. The Wife here is mimicking a question that Jerome attributes to Jovinianus (Book 1, section 36).

5 The Pardoner's Tale

The literary critic Harold Bloom has called Chaucer's Pardoner the "ancestor of all Western literary characters condemned to nihilism" (1994, 119). This claim, of course, is unproveable and perhaps a bit irritatingly self-assured. Nonetheless, its association of the idea of "condemned to nihilism" with the Pardoner may indeed anchor an exploration of those distinctive qualities of the Pardoner's tale-telling performance that so many readers have found mesmerizingly profound. While the term *nihilism* may be defined in a variety of ways, most simply it designates the view that human life has no meaning, good or bad, or, more generally, that the universe itself is empty of meaning (*nihil* in Latin means "nothing"). Chaucer's Pardoner thus potentially supplies an especially unnerving answer to the question of the meaning of life, one that threatens to become a kind of black hole at the center of the *Canterbury Tales*' vision of humanity, sucking the light from all alternative, more positive answers.

Other chapters of this book consider several of those alternative answers. These emerge by formulating the question of the meaning of life in a way that, I hope, sloughs off its surface banality: taking "life" to denote our physical, corporeal existence, the material realities of birth, hunger, pleasure, suffering, sensation, death, etc., and taking "meaning" to denote the incorporeal or, more generally, nonmaterial ideas, ideals, and values that we cannot touch and yet which altogether seem comprehensively to shape our experience of "life." With the Pardoner's nihilism, if that's what it is, Chaucer would seem to arrive at a view that makes all answers to the question mere delusions and, indeed, the very voicing of the question nonsensical.

But *is* the Pardoner's supposed nihilism really that? A ready objection is that the idea of nihilism was simply not available to Chaucer, as it is a product of nineteenth-century Europe, articulated with particular force by German philosopher Friedrich Nietzsche (d. 1900) and developed further in response to the unprecedented human self-destruction of the twentieth

DOI: 10.4324/9781003273318-6

century's World Wars. Chaucer, in contrast, lived in the so-called Age of Faith. In his day, the religion that we now call Roman Catholicism suffused all aspects of the everyday life of most inhabitants of Western Europe and the British Isles, albeit in a vast range of different manners and degrees. One might suppose, therefore, that this historical difference preemptively precludes naming the Pardoner a nihilist. Yet as is evident throughout this book, many other modern ideas that were not strictly speaking available to Chaucer, such as feminism, are plainly applicable to his work, if we are careful to track the continuities and disjunctions between past and present thinking. This chapter will attempt another such tracking effort in respect to the idea of nihilism. It seeks to show how something like this idea emerges in the Pardoner's performance in a way that is both deeply embedded in the contradictions of the reigning ideologies of Chaucer's day and that remains acutely resonant with some of our present-day concerns.

Fourteenth-century nihilism: theological paradox, bad jobs, queer theory

One of those late fourteenth-century reigning ideologies, which still possesses some currency today, was an understanding of the material world as hostile to the spiritual and, more specifically, of the body as a threat to the soul. This view is succinctly expressed by one of the Pardoner's fellow pilgrims, the Second Nun, in her prayerful plea to the Virgin Mary: "And of thy [Mary's] light my soule in prison lighte,/That troubled is by the contagioun/Of my body" (8.71–73). In this common medieval theological imagery, the body both incarcerates the soul and poisons it. Another then-reigning and still-current ideology, however, took an apparently opposite position, holding that all creation – and thus the physical body as well as the entire material world – since it comes from God, must be good. As many readers of this book will know, what holds these seemingly disparate views together were (and are) some of the basic tenets of Christianity, especially the original sin of Adam and Eve's disobedience and the atonement for that sin accomplished by the incarnation and crucifixion of Christ. For the Second Nun and the view that she epitomizes, inasmuch as the body's threat to the soul manifests these basic Christian tenets, corporeality paradoxically becomes central to spirituality. Because individuals directly experience the problem of the body – which is to say, the problem of corporeal desire, understood as the sin of concupiscence – they have palpable access to spirituality in the form of the demand to overcome, and the actual practice of overcoming, that problem. The physical reality of the body in this way becomes, through its negation, confirmation of the spiritual truths that, unlike the body, we cannot see or touch. Insofar as today we still find physical corroboration of some of our abstract values through some form of physical self-denial (say, the decision not to eat meat despite really wanting a juicy hamburger), we are making use of a version of this paradox, however distant our commitment may seem from traditional modes of Christian piety.

What many readers have found so uncanny about the Pardoner's performance is that from his introduction through his prologue and tale, he forges something like a personal credo out of the darker possibilities of this paradox of body and spirit, in which negation of the physical manifests not the presence of the spiritual but its absence. He accomplishes this, most explicitly, simply by doing his job as broker of spiritual commodities. Or more exactly, he forges this credo by wholeheartedly embracing the fact that in engaging with great gusto in the particularities of this job, he has necessarily become wholly corrupt. This chapter will dig into these particularities, exploring how something that we might label nihilism emerges by way of them. At stake in this exploration will be how, in general, one's job may become personally corrupting by its very nature and, much more troublingly, how simply doing one's job well may seem to disclose that what one's world holds to be true and good is the very source of that corruption. With that revelation, the Pardoner's performance grimly suggests, there may be no way back to one's former state of innocence. Salvation, in whatever form one desires it, may be out of reach.

Although we all hope, of course, never to hold a job that has these consequences, I think it's safe assumption that if you've not experienced such a job yourself, you're aware of the possibility and perhaps know individuals in this situation. What has made Chaucer's Pardoner especially evocative in this respect, however, is not only this sort of wary relatability. Over the centuries, readers have also been unable to take their eyes off the Pardoner's striking physical appearance, as depicted in his General Prologue portrait. In this way, Chaucer has made the physicality of the Pardoner himself, his body, central to our understanding of the overall meaning of his performance, although the exact relationship between body and meaning has been a topic of much debate. Indeed, according to several Chaucer scholars, the very indeterminacy of this relationship is essential to its significance (see, for example, Dinshaw 1995). This chapter will follow the lead of these scholars and in particular emphasize the utility of the modern collection of ideas that's come to be known as queer theory. Although, like nihilism, queer identity as a named concept postdates Chaucer by centuries, it will nonetheless help us to grasp the challenges that the Pardoner posed for Chaucer's time and continues to pose for ours.

Summary

Like the Wife of Bath's performance, the Pardoner's begins with a prologue in which he shares details about his life and then continues with a tale that we are clearly to understand as an extension of the concerns of the prologue. In contrast with the Wife's performance, however, the prologue's 134 lines are more in proportion to the tale's 505, and, more importantly, the very distinction between prologue and tale is murkier. The Pardoner fills so much of both prologue and tale with illustrations of his professional speech as a pardoner that most of his performance comprises an extended example of what he does for a living. It is, in that sense, a performance of a performance.

Prior to the prologue is a short linking passage. Here, the Host expresses his acute emotional response to the "pitous [pity-inducing, sad] tale" (6.302) just told by the Physician. Wishing to be cheered up, he asks the Pardoner for "som mirthe or japes [a jokey tale] right anon [away]" (6.319). The Pardoner agrees but says that he first must have a drink and snack at a pub. Other pilgrims object to the Host's request, and, instead of "ribaudye" or an obscene story, they demand "som moral thing" from the Pardoner. Again the Pardoner agrees, saying that he'll think about some "honeste thing" or moral tale while he has his drink. This brief exchange contains much of thematic importance. Here, I'll just note the Pardoner's ready ability to tell either an immoral or a moral story and his indifference as to which, and the winking irony of his determination to think of some morally affirming matter while having a drink in a pub.

It's not clear whether we're to understand the Pardoner's ensuing performance as occurring during or after his proposed digression into a tavern, but, as we'll see, it fits well with the aforementioned winking irony if we assume a tavern setting. The Pardoner devotes his prologue to confiding in his fellow pilgrims about his practices as a broker of spiritual commodities, detailing his various stratagems and providing several illustrative mock performances of his sales pitches. He thus brags about how successfully he takes people's money to a group of individuals who, in a different context, would be his targets rather than his confidantes. He declares repeatedly that he is wholly motivated by greed and that, ironically, the sin of greed is also his favorite topic for the preaching that he performs as part of his sales pitches. Taking "radix malorum est cupiditas" (Latin for "greed is the root of evils," from the bible, 1 Timothy 6:10) as both the theme of his sermons and his personal theme, he observes, "Thus can I preche again [against] that same vice/Which that I use" (6.427–28), and, indeed, "though myself be gilty in that sinne,/Yet can I make other folk to twinne [depart, i.e., repent]/From avarice, and sore [painfully eager] to repente" (6.429–31). He creates genuine remorse among his listeners for their committing of the very sin that he himself is committing at that very moment. Accordingly, his work, he acknowledges, can be spiritually beneficial for his targets. Yet, as soon as he calls attention to this, he declares his total indifference to their spiritual welfare:

For myn entente* is nat but* for to winne,*	intention; only; earn money
And nothing for correccioun of sinne:	
I rekke* never whan that they been beried*	care; buried, i.e., when they die
Though that hir soules goon a-blackeberied.*	go blackberry picking, i.e., go to hell

(6.403–6)

He concludes this bit of confessional irony by circling back to the request to supply "som moral thing" for his contribution to the tale-telling contest. But now he puts that request in the context of his habitual, ironic utilization of moral speech to further his own corruption: "For though myself be a ful vicious [wholly corrupt] man," he remarks, "A moral tale yet I yow telle kan,/ Which I am wont [it is my practice] to preche for to winne" (6.459–61).

He begins his tale by establishing its setting in a tavern in present-day Flanders and indicating its main characters: a group of morally dissipated "yonge folk that haunteden folye [habitually engaged in vices]" (6.463). This brief exposition doesn't lead directly into a narrative, however, but rather serves as a cue for the Pardoner to segue into a sermon condemning the several sins these "yonge folk" commit. He addresses drunkenness, gluttony, lechery, gambling, and swearing – the very sins, then and now, associated with the tavern setting of the story and, perhaps, the setting of the Pardoner's own tale-telling performance (in which case, the Pardoner tells a tale that condemns sinning in a tavern while he is sinning in tavern). The length and heightened rhetoric of the sermon (e.g., he laments at one point, "O glotonye, ful of cursednesse!/O cause first of oure confusioun! [ruin, i.e., the Fall]" [6.499–500]) make plain that the Pardoner's "moral tale" is in fact just another illustrative example of his sales pitches, albeit a fuller and more intricate one than those he supplied in his prologue. When he returns to the story of the "yonge folk" after nearly 180 lines, then, we understand it to be part of the encompassing sermon, which is to say, part of the pitch. In particular, it supplies a vivid narrative illustration of the deadly consequences of the sin of greed.

The dissipated youth or "riotoures," drinking in a tavern well before 9:00 am, notice a corpse being carted to its burial. One of them asks his servant to find out the dead man's identity, and the servant says he was "an olde felawe of yours" who was slain, while drunk, by a "privee [stealthy] thief men clepeth [call] Deeth," an obvious personification who, the servant continues, has "a thousand slain this pestilence [bout of plague]" (6.672–79). Continuing to speak figuratively, the servant then provides the good advice "to be war [beware] of swich [such] an adversarye;/Beth redy for to meete him [i.e., Death] evermore" (6.682–83). The rioters, however, take the servant to be speaking literally. The three of them determine to go on the offensive against this "adversarye" and "sleen this false traitour Deeth" (6.699). On their way to find him, they meet a very old man, of whom one of them inquires, "Why livestou [do you live] so longe in so greet age?" (6.719). The man tells them, figuratively, "Deeth, allas, ne wol nat [will not] have my lif," and he therefore walks the earth, "lik a restelees caitiff [wretch]" (6.727–28), longing to die. The rioters – taking the old man, too, to be speaking literally – accuse him of being Death's spy and insist that he tell them where they may find "thilke [that same] traitour Deeth/That in this contree alle oure frendes sleeth" (6.753–54). The old man directs them toward a "croked way [crooked path]" (7.761) where, he says, he left Death under an oak tree. Arriving there, the rioters discover to their great delight eight bushels of gold coins. One of the rioters, observing that they need to carry the treasure out by night, advises that they draw straws to see which of them should go to town to bring back provisions ("breed and win" [6.797]) while the others guard the gold. The youngest rioter is chosen for the task, and, once he leaves, the other two conspire to kill him upon his return, thereby leaving more gold for them. Meanwhile, the youngest, likewise motivated, determines to kill the others by poisoning their wine. When he returns, the other two murder him, drink the wine he brought, and die themselves.

With this expertly delivered narrative denouement, the Pardoner, having now reached the peroration of the encompassing sample sermon (the moment when preachers, at sermon's end, sum up and apply their theme), bewails the rioters' sins. Turning then to address an imagined audience of "goode men," he advises them to "ware you [preserve yourself] fro the sinne of avarice" and declares that his "holy pardoun may you alle warice [save]/So that ye offre nobles [gold coins] or sterlinges [silver coins]" (6.904–907). The Pardoner, that is, having reached the end of his sample sales pitch, completes the illustrative performance exactly as if it were an actual one: by offering his pardons for purchase. By this point, however, we may fairly suppose the pilgrims to have been caught up in the vividly told tale of the rioters and so occupying, in their absorption, the very place of the Pardoner's imagined audience. Hence, when the Pardoner suddenly announces, "And lo, sires, *thus* I preche" (6.915), the remark functions as a jarring reminder to the pilgrims that he hadn't really been offering *them* his pardons for purchase – that he wasn't attempting to dupe them but rather showing them how he dupes others.

What has been so perplexing to centuries of readers, then, is that immediately following this reminder to his fellow pilgrims, the Pardoner does in fact attempt to dupe them, and in exactly the same fashion as he just disclosed in his sample performance. Observing, "But sires, oo [one] word forgat I in my tale" (6.919), he proceeds to say precisely what he hadn't forgotten, what he had indeed just said: that he has "relikes and pardoun in [his] male [bag]" (6.920) for which they should "offre always newe and newe [over and over]/Nobles [gold coins] or pens [pence] whiche that be goode and trewe" (6.929–30). And lest we think that he is merely addressing an imaginary audience once again, he singles out one of the flesh-and-blood pilgrims, the Host, for his initial customer, adding the rationale that the Host "is most envoluped [enveloped] in sinne" (6.942). The Host refuses, uttering perhaps the most violent speech in all of Chaucer's writings. Saying that the Pardoner would have him kiss, not a saint's relic, but the Pardoner's shit-stained breeches, the Host threatens to castrate him. The Pardoner is so furious that he cannot speak. The Host says he won't "playe" (as if that were what he was doing) with such an "angry man" (6.958–59). When the rest of the pilgrims laugh, something prompts the Knight, the individual of highest social rank, to intervene. He has the Host and the Pardoner perform a kiss of peace, and the Pardoner's Tale comes to end with the Knight insisting that everyone return to the festive spirit that has presumably been lost: "as we diden lat us laughe and playe" (9.967).

Sources

For the Pardoner's performance, Chaucer does not make use of a principal guiding source, as he does, say, with the Knight's and Man of Law's Tales. Instead, as with the Wife of Bath's performance, he has drawn upon a variety of different sources to stitch together something altogether novel. Yet also as with the Wife of Bath, a basic inspiration for his tale-teller comes from the *Romance of the Rose*. This thirteenth-century French poem was immensely popular across late medieval Europe, judging from its many surviving manuscripts, countless allusions, and several translations into other languages – including one into English by Chaucer himself. Its long, complex narrative takes the form of a personification allegory, in which a dizzying array of concepts (Fair Welcome and Nature, to name just two) appear as characters in the story. (The 2015 animated film *Inside Out* and its 2024 sequel are modern instances of personification allegory.) The characterization of Chaucer's Pardoner plainly owes a debt to one of these personifications, *Faux Semblant* (False Seeming), and another, *La Vielle* (Old Woman), forms the basis for the Wife of Bath. In both cases, Chaucer's great inspiration was to lift these personifications out of the allegory and drop them into the naturalistic setting of the pilgrimage, where they appear as a prosperous five-time widow from Bath and an industrious pardoner associated with the Hospital of St. Mary of Rouncivale at Charing Cross. The resulting effect is to redirect the considerable conceptual and expressive energies of the original personifications into the voices, and the imagined psychological interiors, of these supposedly historically actual (though of course fictional) individuals. In the Pardoner's case, this creative strategy deepens and darkens the boisterous irony of the *Romance of the Rose*'s False Seeming into something like nihilism.

Among the other sources for the Pardoner's performance are those that Chaucer draws upon for the Pardoner's sermon on tavern sins. These most likely include some Latin religious treatises that we know he uses elsewhere, such as Pope Innocent III's 1195 *De Miseria Condicionis Humane* (*On the Wretchedness of the Human Condition*) and Saint Jerome's fourth-century *Adversus Jovinianum (Against Jovinianus)*. As these are sources that an actual pardoner might very well draw upon in composing a sermon, Chaucer oddly functions here as a kind of proxy for his own character, encouraging us to attribute the sermon's expert selection and reshaping of homiletic material to the Pardoner – to see this as evidence of the Pardoner's professional accomplishment. In this way, Chaucer's use of sources in this section becomes part of the characterization of the Pardoner's enthusiasm for his own spiritual emptiness.

The basic plot of the story of the three rioters is quite an ancient one, with deep and widespread folktale roots. Versions of it have been identified across the centuries and around the world, with a recent iteration appearing in Spike Lee's 2020 film *Da 5 Bloods* (and, as my students remind me, with "The Tale of the Three Brothers" in the Harry Potter saga.) As the story is exactly the sort of short narrative that a preacher would supply as a captivating illustration of his message (and in fact versions survive in medieval preachers' handbooks), it functions in many respects like the Latin treatises used earlier. We are encouraged, that is, to ascribe to the Pardoner the ways in which the story is cleverly and distinctively delivered, as further illustration of his professional expertise and, consequently, spiritual emptiness. This is perhaps most evocatively rendered in the speech of the old man who directs the rioters to Death. Notably, Chaucer draws upon a rather different kind of source for this speech (a poem by sixth-century Roman author Maximianus), creating a figure whose combination of pathos, vividness, and mystery has no parallel in other versions of the story. Indeed, the very evocative excess of this speech – which goes well beyond the needs of the otherwise economically told narrative – has led no few Chaucer scholars to suppose that here the Pardoner, in some enigmatic, perhaps unfathomable way, has projected the mystery of his own character into the story (see, e.g., Patterson 1991).

The job of a pardoner

In what we've covered so far, I've been regularly referring to various aspects of the Pardoner's profession (e.g., his preaching), and I've suggested that the profession itself has profound and troubling implications. To get at those implications, let's now dig a little deeper into the details of the Pardoner's job. In Chaucer's day, a pardoner was a retailer of indulgences, which were also called pardons. If you have a religious background that includes one of the Protestant denominations, the term *indulgence* may feel synonymous with the institutional corruption of the Church that was assailed by such sixteenth-century reformers as Martin Luther. In fact, there's no doubt that whatever merits it may have held in principle, the indulgence – which was most basically a fundraising instrument for charitable causes – was subject to widespread and inevitable abuse. Indeed, its problems were no secret from the time of its emergence centuries before Chaucer's day.[1] What's crucial to recognize, however, is that the indulgence was not invented by, say, some greedy evil genius lurking within Church hierarchy to dupe gullible ordinary Christians out of their money. Rather, it evolved over the centuries to fill a long-standing religious-social-economic need, developing into a complex system that performed a valuable – and what must have seemed irreplaceable – pair of interlocking functions in Chaucer's world. In this sense, it had become one of those manifestly broken systems that are widely recognized as such but which nonetheless persist because of the needs they fill – akin to how many on both sides of today's partisan divide feel about the US healthcare system, for example.

One of those interlocking functions of the indulgence was to raise funds for organizations such as the historically actual one with which the Pardoner is affiliated, the Hospital of St. Mary of Rouncivale at Charing Cross. In Chaucer's day, this organization was something like a blend of hostel, hospice care facility, homeless shelter, hospital, and church. Unlike those sorts of organizations today, however, it was financed wholly by gifts of some kind from individuals. It did not charge the people whom it served, nor did it receive regular funding from the government or the Church. Like many of today's charitable organizations that are similarly dependent on donations, the hospital employed for its fiscal sustenance professional fundraisers who not only sought out contributions but also used various tactics to inspire the good will of potential donors. These fundraisers were pardoners. Thus, insofar as we understand such an organization in Chaucer's day to provide an essential public good, we may also conclude that pardoners were key contributors to that public good.

The other interlocking function of the indulgence pertains to the manner in which it served as an instrument of fundraising. The indulgence possessed a specific place in the penitential system, the set of beliefs and practices that the Church developed over the centuries for individuals' management of the accumulation of sins that, according to its doctrines, human corporeal existence after Adam and Eve's Fall inevitably incurs. For Christians in the Middle Ages, this system provided the only viable route toward salvation and heaven. By Chaucer's day, the individual sinner's participation in this system, or penance, had three distinct, ordered stages. First is *contrition*, in which the individual feels genuine sorrow and regret for sinning. Second is *confession*, in which the individual admits to the specific sins committed and expresses sorrow and regret for them to a priest. If the latter judges the confession to be complete and sincere, he bestows *absolution* or forgiveness of the *guilt* of those sins. Third, then, is *satisfaction*, in which the individual somehow pays the *penalty* for the sins, thereby making restitution to God and restoring the divine relationship that was broken by sinning.

In penance's early formulation, well before Chaucer's time, all these stages needed to be completed, for all serious sins, prior to the individual's moment of the death to avoid an eternity in hell. The deathbed confession was therefore crucially important, so as to receive absolution before it was too late. But having received absolution on the point of death, how does one then manage the satisfaction stage? What if there's not enough lifetime left to complete all the actions required? The development of the doctrine of purgatory in the twelfth century helped greatly in this regard, as it created the possibility of completing restitution to God *after* death. There was now viable hope for heaven, even for sinners with a heavy debt to pay. Nevertheless, the torments of purgatory – as preached from the pulpit and envisioned in treatises, paintings, and imaginative literature – although not eternal, were likely to be just as hellish as those in hell. The indulgence, by supplying a kind of shortcut toward completing the requirements of satisfaction, was thus profoundly comforting to those who longed for unity with God or, less selflessly, simply feared purgatory or damnation.

In theory, an indulgence worked as follows. An authority in the upper echelons of Church hierarchy – say, the pope or a bishop – may issue indulgences or grant the power to issue indulgences to an organization such as the Hospital of St. Mary of Rouncivale at Charing Cross. If a truly contrite sinner has gained absolution from a priest, and that sinner, out of sorrow for their sins and desire to make amends with God, makes a charitable gift to an indulgence-issuing organization, the indulgence documents the wiping-away of some or all of the debt of satisfaction for those sins (often measured by time in purgatory). The indulgence formally recognizes the virtuous deed of making a charitable gift, performed out of devotion to God and regret for past misdeeds, as a legitimate substitute for other sorts of repayment to God.

On the one hand, then, the charitable gift redirects money that may have been spent on worldly things toward the ultimately spiritual ends of an organization like the Hospital at Charing Cross, serving thereby the glory of God as well as a social need. On the other hand, the virtuous action of so redirecting one's money benefits the giver's soul, nudging them closer to God and heaven. These interlocking functions of the indulgence were, in theory, win-win and must have felt to many individuals close enough to that in practice for the system to persist for centuries.

Nonetheless, history plainly records that the practice of the indulgence system was rife with problems. The reasons aren't difficult to spot. On the institutional side, as is all too common for charitable organizations today, fundraising may easily take on a life of its own. Then and now, it is difficult to draw a hard line between the amount of money a nonprofit organization needs to perform its service well and income in excess of that. Questions about, say, the size of the salary of the organization's leader or the lavishness of its buildings may have endlessly contestable answers. All too easily, the public service of a charitable organization may become a means for making money rather than the reason for which money is raised. For the indulgence system, this slippery slope gave great impetus to the expansion and marketing of indulgences, inspiring innovations in their nature, advertisement, and distribution that made them attractive and readily available. On the individual contributor's side, the basic difficulty lay in the utterly imperative necessity to maintain a clearcut distinction between giving and purchasing, activities which in practice might be quite difficult to disentangle. This distinction was essential because the purchase of a spiritual good – of, say, years off purgatory – was then (and remains now, at least for Catholics) a sin, that of simony. If an individual experiences the obtaining of an indulgence as the exchange of money for a pardon, rather than as a virtuous gift of money to a charitable organization that the obtained pardon merely documents, that individual, far from receiving the indulgence's spiritual benefits, is committing a sin. And as this sin is likely to go unrepented and unconfessed, it will send that supposedly pardoned individual straight to hell.

The two sides of this problem obviously exacerbate each other, since a desire to purchase increases a desire to sell, and vice versa. Pardoners, as direct retailers of indulgences, were positioned at the very center of the system, at the interface between selling organizations and buying individuals. Consequently, the nature of their work was intensively subject to, or itself encapsulated, all the problems to which the system was vulnerable. In theory – and according to rule – a pardoner was licensed to carry indulgences to a certain region, provide evidence of his authorization, explain the nature of his indulgences, and receive contributions. This is, indeed, the superficial sheen of the activities of Chaucer's Pardoner, as he recounts them to his fellow pilgrims. In practice, pardoners operated like traveling salesmen. Like the latter, they often earned their income by commission, quite frequently in the form of a kind of reselling. An organization, rather than selling indulgences directly, would sell licenses to distribute them to pardoners (or to middlemen, who in turn would sell them to pardoners) and in that way obtain an immediate, guaranteed income. The pardoners, with then no obligation to transmit money back to the organization, would endeavor to earn as much over their costs as possible, as that went directly into their pockets.

As most of us who have worked in sales on commission will admit, the situation inherently induces the temptation to overstate the desirability of the product or to become somehow chummy with potential buyers, if not simply just to lie to them in some fashion. Your economic survival depends upon your customers wanting to buy your product, and to thrive beyond mere survival, you must be able to evoke that desire consistently and broadly. Chaucer's Pardoner's compelling powers of oratorical persuasion, along with his bag of tricks, his unlawful preaching, and his usurpation of the absolving role of the priest, all plainly serve this purpose. They have made him – if we are to believe his own claims and the observations of the General Prologue narrator – an expert, accomplished, and well-remunerated salesman. Like most of the other pilgrims, as that narrator tells us, he excels at his trade. But this very accomplishment must also, according to the beliefs of the time, send him to hell, since selling a spiritual good is the other side of the coin of purchasing it and so commits the sin of simony.

In theory, a pardoner might do his job without sinning, and, correspondingly, the recipient of an indulgence might also do so without sinning. On both sides, this possibility depends upon intent. If the pardoner intends not to sell an indulgence but just collect a contribution from a penitent individual, and if the individual intends not to purchase the indulgence but just make a charitable contribution to the organization associated with it, then neither has sinned. In fact, both have performed a virtuous action that glorifies God. But only God can perfectly judge intent, and, what's more, no one can hide one's true intent from God. In this situation, any slight discrepancy between what one appears to do or be, and what one knows one actually is doing or being, kicks the salvational beam the wrong direction.

The Pardoner doing his job

Against the backdrop of the nature of his profession, then, we can see how something like nihilism arises for the Pardoner. Everything that was broken in the indulgence system was drawn into and magnified in that profession, in that the structuring conditions of his work made it virtually impossible for him to harbor absolutely zero intent to sell pardons, rather than just collect the contributions that they document. In comparison, the organizations that employ pardoners and even the individuals who receive indulgences are one or more steps removed from the worst pressures of the system's brokenness. The former, in selling licenses to pardoners, can believe themselves to be not selling salvation per se but just paying for labor. The latter, as the Chaucer's Pardoner himself observes in his prologue, might truly be moved by a pardoner's persuasive speech to contribute to an organization out of remorse for sin. But the pardoners' position within the broken system of penitence, in which their material survival depended upon successful retailing of pardons, all but ensured that the only way that they could believe that they are not selling pardons is if they lied to themselves. And this Chaucer's Pardoner, a consummate liar otherwise, refuses to do. Instead, he repeatedly – we might say obsessively – insists that his "entente" is precisely "nat but for [only] to winne [make money]/And nothing for correccioun of sinne" (6.403–4).

In being honest with himself, he's being honest with God, and so he's avoiding the sin of divine deception. But, of course, in this case that means he's embracing the sin of simony. Hence, he's damned either way, whether by pretending (to himself and to God as well as to his customers) not to be selling indulgences when he knows he is or, conversely, by honestly embracing the structural requirements of his livelihood. We might imagine that, aware of this dilemma, he could just find another line of work. Yet in Chaucer's day, as we have seen, the long-standing indulgence system was believed to be a necessary and even desirable part of the way Church and society functioned. The world needed someone to be pardoners, but in filling that need, pardoners in effect sacrificed their souls. Facing this double bind and its inevitably damning absurdities, a pardoner might readily conclude that he's the only honest thing within the whole system. Because this system in its fullest extent included penitence, salvation, heaven, hell, and God, and since there was no alternative to it in Chaucer's England, this meant embracing nihilism.

Within the Pardoner's performance, this embrace may at times seem similar to what we saw in Chapter 2 with the Miller's leveling of the difference between sex and spirituality in, for example, his quip about "Goddes privetee" (1.3163). But the Miller's (and, likewise, the Wife of Bath's) topsy-turvy celebration of corporeality, while it ascribes value to physical life in a way counter to a more orthodox position like that voiced by the Second Nun, stops short of the Pardoner's nihilism. For the Pardoner, it's not just that the spiritual is put aside or deprioritized in favor of the corporeal. Rather, the spiritual is emptied out from the inside, while leaving its husk in place. This is evident, for example, in the sermon that the Pardoner delivers in the first part of his tale, condemning the sins associated with the tavern. Here, he draws from sources such as *De Miseria Condicionis*

Humane that foreground the spiritual problem of corporeal desire and so see negation of the body as a mode of holiness. The Pardoner expertly reproduces this message virtually verbatim, but as we have seen he does so for the purpose not of spiritual edification but of furthering his greed, that is, his own corporeal desire (and perhaps also while having a drink in a tavern). In contrast with the Miller's and Wife's turning upside down of the priorities of the corporeal and spiritual, the Pardoner must leave them in place, since that's what the performance of his job requires, and yet that very performance leads to a denial of those priorities. In the Pardoner's self-cancelling sermon, the value of the corporeal and the value of the spiritual yield a zero sum.

The story of the three rioters reiterates this self-cancelling effect but in a cleverer and more disturbingly profound fashion. In comparison with other medieval versions, the Pardoner has deftly deepened the theological resonance of this oft-told anecdote. The three rioters, as a trio who take on the task to slay Death, form a ready parallel with the Christian Trinity – the Father, the Son, and the Holy Ghost – who, by collectively effecting the Atonement, supply an escape from the curse of death and a route to eternal life. Ensuring that his listeners do not miss this parallel, the Pardoner has one rioter declare their unified purpose with the Trinitarian formula of "we three been alle ones" (6.696). And with the phrase "Deeth shal be deed" (6.710), the Pardoner uses near-biblical phrasing (specifically that of Hosea 13:14) to describe their aim. That the rioters do not themselves understand that they are enacting a spiritual allegory thus underscores the nature of the sin that they instead illustrate. Taking the servant's figurative speech about death literally, they also take themselves literally, and so they are trapped within the category of the literal – that is, the earthbound, the non-spiritual, the bodily. As their story is part of a sermon intended to help its auditors recognize sin and urge them to repent, that story's lesson is clear: we must not be earthbound like the rioters but rather strive for the eternal life made possible by the Trinity, which the rioters themselves signify in a sort of reverse polarity. The Pardoner delivers all this expertly but in a way that re-reverses that polarity. He tells a story that urges its listeners to turn away from the literal/earthbound toward the figural/spiritual, but he does so for his own literal, earthbound motive, not coincidentally exactly the same motive as illustrated by the literal rioters.

With the story's figural and literal meanings thus both right and wrong at the same time, the Pardoner's performance once again produces a zero sum. In this case, however, the self-cancellation includes the Atonement, Christianity's most central theological concept, in which the death of one man's physical body creates the possibility of eternal spiritual life. Here, in refusing to lie to himself – in wholly embracing the structural conditions of his job, which demand the use of spiritual edification as an instrument for material gain – the Pardoner conveys a nihilism that understands the zero sum of literal/figural, or rioters/Atonement, as the human condition.

The Pardoner's queerness

These self-cancellations of the Pardoner's performance therefore have the effect of emptying out the significance of the binary oppositions of literal/ figural and material/spiritual, the very binaries upon which so much of the then-orthodox understanding of self and cosmos – of the meaning of life – depended. To use a term from our own time, we might say that the Pardoner thereby *queers* medieval culture. At first glance, however, this might seem to overgeneralize the notion of *queer*, to extend it outside of its proper domain. As initially developed by late twentieth-century scholars who became known as queer theorists, *queer* most immediately pertains to the sex, gender, and sexuality binaries of, respectively, male/female, masculine/feminine, and heterosexual/homosexual, all of which individually and in relation to each other are governed by an overall binary of normal/abnormal (see Corber and Valocchi 2003). Queer theory argues that the supposition that these identities arise from nature, and hence in the 'normal' situation are stable in themselves and in their relations to each other, serves to maintain a patriarchal, heteronormative status quo. Calling attention to the enormous amount of ideological energy that is in fact directed toward producing and maintaining this supposition, queer theory explains that, notwithstanding underlying physical differences, this series of identities is social rather than natural. Queer theory seeks to expose these identities' social fabrication and their embeddedness within the reigning social, economic, and political systems they serve. In that way, queer theory also emphasizes the actual range and fluidity of sex, gender, and sexuality identities and practices that the supposition of stable binaries obscures or marginalizes. The success of these efforts is evident in, for example, the now-widespread acknowledgment of nonbinary gender identity and the corresponding social protocol of inquiring about the pronouns that individuals use to refer to themselves. Conversely, the success is evident, too, in the considerable pushback that these trends have received in some quarters.

By this point in the history of Chaucer studies, the suspicion that queer theory is somehow relevant to the figure of the Pardoner seems almost inescapable (see, for example, Dinshaw 1995; Minnis 2003). Urging this conclusion above all is a famous set of descriptive lines in the Pardoner's General Prologue's portrait:

This Pardoner hadde heer* as yellow as wex,*	hair; wax
But smoothe it heeng* as dooth a strike of flex;*	hung; bundle of flax

By ounces henge* his lokkes that he hadde,	strands hung
And therwith he his shuldres overspradde,	
But thinne it lay, by colpons,* oon by oon;	clusters
...	
Swiche glaring eyen* hadde he as an hare.	eyes
...	
A vois* he hadde as smal* as hath a goot;*	voice; high-pitched; goat
No berd* hadde he, ne never sholde have;	beard
As smoothe it was as it were late yshave:	
I trowe* he were a gelding or a mare.	believe
(6.675–91)	

We might imagine the speaker of these lines, the General Prologue narrator (Chaucer in his "gee whiz" persona), furrowing his brows as he scrutinizes what is plainly to him the Pardoner's strikingly odd physical appearance. Making note of the Pardoner's long, thin, yellow hair, glaring eyes, high voice, and permanently whiskerless chin, the narrator seems driven by the unspoken question of "what exactly *are* you?" And he finally ventures a guess: the Pardoner is, metaphorically, "a gelding or a mare," that is, a castrated male horse or female horse.

Generations of Chaucer scholars have sought to determine the precise condition that the narrator's guess denotes. Some have focused on "gelding," arguing that the Pardoner is a eunuch, whether born or made that way. Others have focused on "mare," claiming that the Pardoner is a gay man who, the narrator supposes, occupies the role of female in sexual relations with men. Still others have explored various alternative possibilities, such as that the Pardoner is intersex, a straight but feminine man, or a woman. These views have been proffered with carefully assembled historical and textual evidence. Yet what they all must confront is the sheer indeterminacy of the narrator's guess. He offers not one metaphor but two, each of which possesses various possibilities for its precise literal meaning and which are joined by an "or" that may or may not signal mutual exclusivity. His entire statement, moreover, is qualified by the verb "trowe," which like its modern gloss "believe" could express absolute certainty ("I believe that Frodo lives!"), marked uncertainty ("I believe that there was one cookie left, but I'm not sure"), or some ambiguous position between certainty and uncertainty. Amid all this, what the narrator does make entirely clear is that *something* seems to him 'off' about the Pardoner, which is to say not 'normal,' which is to say *queer*. We thus have plenty of reasons to conclude that these lines collectively signify a category that we now term *queerness*, which, in the very range of different and shifting identities that that term encompasses, neatly also captures the description's indeterminacy.

Queer theorists have called attention to the way in which normative identities demand the very non-normative identities that they marginalize. What counts as 'normal' in any given time and place is always in process, contested, and relative. To be perceived by yourself and others as a 'real man,' for example, requires behaviors that vary with time and place and is always subject to self-doubt or others' skepticism. Most crucially, it depends upon there being men who aren't 'real men' in order to shore up normative identity through defining contrast – hence the frequent (though not universal) use of homophobia as an expression of heteronormative masculinity. As theorist Robert McRuer writes, heteronormativity's "casting of some identities as alternatives ironically buttresses the ideological notion that dominant identities are not really alternatives but rather the natural order of things" (2002, 89). A dominant ideology works by consolidating a 'natural order' that requires some individuals to attest to it by failing to fit into it.

In any given society, therefore, individuals who are labeled queer (by whatever actual term carries that meaning) function to define by contrast what counts as normal. For those individuals so labeled, the result may be a suffocating double bind. On the one hand, they might disavow that label, directing their energy toward an achievement of normality within a society intent on refusing that recognition, and so spending their days neither comfortable with themselves nor wholly accepted by others. On the other hand, they might embrace that label, as the very name *queer theory* has done, and perhaps thereby achieve a level of comfort with themselves, but doing so at the cost of structural marginalization and often outright persecution. In a logic analogous to the double bind of the Pardoner's job, in which he's (literally) damned whether he embraces his inevitable fraud or not, a queer identity can mean trouble for the individuals so labeled, whether they embrace that identity or not. And just as someone had to perform the job of pardoner in Chaucer's day, normative identities demand that some people must be queer.

This parallel logic between the Pardoner's queerness and the double bind of his job seems integral to Chaucer's artistic design for the Pardoner's character and performance. Considerably less obvious, however, is the significance of this parallel, which Chaucer characteristically doesn't spell out for us. Most straightforwardly, we might see in it the tendency for a moralistic, intolerant late medieval English society to associate spiritual corruption with sexual 'perversity' or physical 'deformity.' This would follow from the ideology of a body/spirit dichotomy, in which the corporeal signifies the spiritual through negation (e.g., by sexual abstinence). In this view, the Pardoner's non-normative corporeality, whatever it might consist of, serves as the physical attestation of his self-admitted spiritual corruption.

Over the years and in various ways, no few Chaucer scholars, sometimes with nuance and sophistication and sometimes not, have understood the meaning of the Pardoner's performance along these lines and so see it as rearticulating and hence reinforcing an ideological status quo. Other scholars have suggested that that view underappreciates the implications of the performance's defining complexities. Among the latter is, as we've seen, the paradox that the Pardoner, by embracing his spiritual corruption, is being truthful and authentic in the only way a pardoner could be. The Pardoner's queerness, with its parallel double bind, is part of this truth. If the Pardoner's performance explores the way in which the broken indulgence system demands the destruction of the souls of those retail laborers who make it work, the Pardoner's queerness, by consolidating normativity, extends this scapegoating of him to his personhood, thereby justifying it. In effect, this extension of scapegoating says, "It's okay that the Pardoner is going to hell, because he's a weirdo, and so he was going to hell anyhow." Rather than merely signifying the Pardoner's spiritual corruption, the Pardoner's queerness serves as a means to maintain a broken system by blaming its brokenness on its victims.

The Pardoner's ending gamble and the Host's rejection

This view has the advantage of supplying a possible explanation for that so very puzzling moment near the end of the Pardoner's performance. As summarized above, the Pardoner, after having so thoroughly disclosed his deceptive practices and bad motives, nonetheless goes on to attempt to sell indulgences to the very people to whom he's just confessed. Whatever psychological or dramatic explanations might be offered for this seemingly inexplicable action (and there have been many), we can also see this moment as serving thematically as the Pardoner's last-ditch effort to circumvent nihilism, even while continuing to be a pardoner who refuses to lie to himself. If his fellow pilgrims in full knowledge of his debased motives were nonetheless authentically spiritually moved to acquire his indulgences, they would in effect be recognizing the Pardoner's sacrifice of his soul for their own spiritual welfare. Their awareness that the Pardoner's action is damning him while leading them toward salvation would simultaneously be a recognition of their scapegoating of him. And if *they* are able to recognize the Pardoner's sacrifice, then surely so can God, whose mercy might then be understood to extend to those individuals who shoulder the burden of the broken indulgence system. A possible way out of the Pardoner's double bind is thus to be embraced by his fellow pilgrims as he is, in the full glory of his throughgoing corruption and associated queerness. While this may seem a highly unlikely gamble, it's perhaps the only one he has.

In this light, the Host's response to the Pardoner's concluding sales pitch is as bleak as it is brutal. With this response, Chaucer gives voice to precisely the intolerant collocation of spiritual corruption and corporeal non-normativity that some readers have taken to be Chaucer's principal aim with the Pardoner's performance. For this reason, it's crucial that we recall that, throughout the *Canterbury Tales*, almost without fail, the Host's responses to pilgrim performances are quite obviously to be taken as somehow wrongheaded. With the Host, Chaucer typically conveys the viewpoint of a misogynist, middle-aged man, whose patently unsophisticated responses to preceding tales imply that those tales instead call for more complex responses. In this instance, the Host responds not to the tale told by the Pardoner but to the Pardoner himself, and the deep offense that the Host expresses is squarely directed simultaneously at the Pardoner's spiritual corruptness and queerness. Here's the final exchange between the two:

"Com forth, sire Host, and offre first anon,*	right away
And thou shalt kisse the relikes everichon,	
Ye, for a grote:* unbokele* anon thy purs."	a coin; unbuckle
"Nay, nay," quod he, "thanne have I Cristes curs!*	i.e., I will be damned
Lat be," quod he, "it shal nat be, so theech!*	as I thrive
Thou woldest make me kisse thyn olde breech*	underpants
And swere it were a relik of a saint,	
Though it were with thy fundement depeint.*	i.e., shit-stained
But, by the crois which that Sainte Elaine fond,	
I wolde* I hadde thy coilons* in myn hond,	wish; testicles
In stede of relikes or of saintuarye.*	reliquary
Lat cutte hem of:* I wol thee helpe hem carye.*	Have them cut off; carry them
They shal be shrined* in an hogges tord."* (6.943–55)	enshrined; hog's turd

In the Pardoner's initiating entreaty, he invites the host to "offre" – to make a charitable contribution – in a way that emphasizes the physicality, even intimacy, of the exchange. He invites the Host to kiss his relics, which are in the same sack as his indulgences (6.920), and this sack, at least in the General Prologue description, sits on his lap (1.686). Moments earlier calling the pilgrims to kneel before him (6.925), here he suggestively urges the Host to approach and "unbokele anon [his] purs." While it remains ambiguous how rife with homoerotic double entendres these lines may be, they clearly have the effect of coupling the Pardoner's request to embrace his retailing activity with an embrace of his person. Consequently, the Host quite unequivocally voices simultaneous refusal of both, emphasizing the spiritually corrupt and corrupting nature of the Pardoner's professional activity by way of a proposed vicious assault on the Pardoner's body, one that seems calibrated to call attention to his queerness. Far from granting the Pardoner efficacious spiritual agency, the Host insists that acquiring indulgences from this particular pardoner would earn him the same "Cristes curs" that by implication will be sending the Pardoner to hell. Then, by pointedly interpreting the Pardoner's invitation to kiss his relics as an invitation to kiss his shit-stained underwear – which is to say, by this envisioned proximity of mouth to anus – the Host conflates the Pardoner's professional activity with scatological homoeroticism. Finally, when the Host expresses a desire to seize hold of and sever the Pardoner's testicles, he threatens a brutal act of queer bashing as a means to construct a relic as fraudulent as those carried by the Pardoner, carving up the Pardoner's body in the process. Even if we suppose that the Host is aware that the Pardoner is already in fact a eunuch and so his threat is knowingly ironic, the cruelty of the 'joke' (that the imagined hog-turd reliquary would be empty) would be just as severe and perhaps even more so. Either way, by his imagined transformation of the Pardoner's body into a false relic, the Host makes the Pardoner's queerness and his spiritual corruption literally one and the same.

Strikingly, this literal corporealization of the spiritual has the same logic as that which we saw illustrated by the three rioters in the Pardoner's Tale, which is also more generally the logic that underlies the Pardoner's queer nihilism. The very form of the Host's rejection of the Pardoner's entreaty thus mirrors the threat posed by the Pardoner's performance to the religious and metaphysical status quo. But it does so, presumably, in order to limit the threat's applicability to just this particular pardoner. The Host's rejection seeks to figure the Pardoner as the bad apple that ensures that other apples can be good ones, as long as we cast him out of the basket.

This sort of scapegoating, however, leaves the actual threat of the Pardoner's performance unanswered. As we have seen, that threat ultimately derives from the brokenness of an indulgence system that nonetheless seemed necessary in order to make penance – which is to say, late medieval Christian culture – functional. What's queer about this Pardoner is that he's honest about what he does and who he is. In rejecting that honesty, the Host is tacitly continuing to embrace instead an indulgence system in which buyers and sellers continue to lie to themselves, to each other, and to God about what they're actually doing. In this regard, the Pardoner's last-ditch effort to escape nihilism and find grace is in fact also a last-ditch effort to make the broken indulgence system work and open a way for *everyone* to find grace. The Host's brutal rejection of this effort, presumably unbeknownst to him, not only happily sends the Pardoner to hell but also nudges himself and everyone else toward that same destination. It ushers in a prospect of a collective metaphysical tragedy, in which the nihilism unleashed by the Pardoner's performance threatens to engulf everyone.

It is for this reason, I believe, that Chaucer does not give the Host the last word. When the Host says, "I wol no lenger playe/With thee, ne with noon [no] other angry man" (6.958–59), after his sheer verbal assault has rendered the Pardoner speechless, he disavows that assault by saying, in effect, he was only joking. This is the familiar sort of disingenuous disavowal that, say, tellers of sexist jokes weaponize when they declare that feminists have no sense of humor. It makes an appeal to the rest of the group in order to consolidate the marginalization of the victim. It encourages the group to understand the victim's failure to see the humor in their own marginalization as yet another sign of their abnormality. Since the Host is the agreed-upon leader of the pilgrims and orchestrator of the tale-telling contest, his response has sway, and the rest of the pilgrims laugh. At this critical juncture, then, Chaucer has the Knight intervene precisely because of the pilgrims' laughter, in one of only two places that the Knight speaks outside of the General Prologue and his own tale:

> But right anon the worthy Knight bigan,
> Whan that he saugh* that al the peple lough,*   saw; laugh
> "Namore* of this, for it is right ynough.   No more
> Sire Pardoner, be glad and murye of cheere,*   i.e., put on a happy face
> And ye, sire Host, that been to me so deere,*   dear
> I praye you that ye kisse the Pardoner;
> And Pardoner, I praye thee, draw thee neer,
> And as we diden lat us laughe and playe."
> Anon they kiste and riden forth hir waye.
> (6.960–69)

Chaucer, characteristically, leaves unspecified exactly why the Knight decides to reverse the trajectory of the group's treatment of the Pardoner. Whatever reasons we might imagine, however, it's evident that he feels that the situation calls for him to assert the authority that he possesses outside the liminal space of the pilgrimage to Canterbury. Since outside that space he far outranks the innkeeper, the group's nominal leader, he can force the Host to perform a version of the very act of physical intimacy to which the Pardoner entreated the Host and which the Host scatologically refigured in his rejection of that entreaty. Instead of the kissing of relics or underpants, what we get here in the final lines of the Pardoner's performance is a kiss of peace: a formal signification of reconciliation and Christian brotherhood. The Pardoner's person – his queer body – thus receives at the end at least superficial embrace by the community.

We may readily suppose, though, that the Host merely bows to the Knight's authority and so his embrace of the Pardoner is likewise merely proforma, likely to vanish the moment the Knight turns his back. Notably, no one offers the Pardoner any money for his indulgences, leaving his final entreaty to the group unanswered. As a result, the nihilism unleashed by the Pardoner's performance is not at the end dissipated but just put on hold. The Knight urges them to reenter the liminal social space in which they "laughe and playe" *together*, rather than direct that laughter and 'play' toward a single member of the group, thereby deferring more serious matters during the festive occasion of their journey. Yet when they "riden forth," they are as we know headed toward Canterbury Cathedral in an act of pilgrimage, which is to say, as an act of penance – "The holy blisful martyr for to seeke" (1.17), as the first sentence of the General Prologue puts it. The final words of the Pardoner's performance thus remind us that the problems posed by that performance for the penitential system reach into the thematic heart of the entire work, casting a shadow over its most spiritually hopeful trajectory. Chaucer, by ending the entire work not with the pilgrims reaching Canterbury but rather with a quite serious and quite unfestive penitential treatise, apparently recited by the Parson a couple miles away, seems to leave the final resolution of those problems in our hands.

Note

1 This chapter's account of the history of the indulgence, the practices of its retailing, and the controversies it engendered relies upon Swanson 2007 and Minnis 2008.

6 The Prioress's Tale

For a book like this one that emphasizes the present-day relevance of some of Chaucer's better-known compositions, one might suppose that the brief, brutally antisemitic tale told by the Prioress would be best passed over. Why give the tale's medieval hate speech any more airspace than the considerable amount it has already occupied by virtue of existing within a foundational work of British literature? In fact, precisely because of this book's emphasis, the nature and implications of this hate speech demand examination – for nothing in all of Chaucer's writings, alas, remains more urgently relevant to the present day.[1] The Prioress's Tale, in justifying horrific, murderous actions toward an already persecuted minority on the basis of that minority's imagined crime of murdering children, contributes to a very long, continuous history of weaponizing the accusation of "they're harming our children" to demonize whoever happens to be one's opponent. To mention just a single example from recent years, in 2018 then Kentucky Governor Matt Bevin claimed that because schoolteachers in the state were on strike, "somewhere in Kentucky today a child was sexually assaulted," in effect accusing schoolteachers of being indirect pedophiles.[2] The Prioress's Tale supplies an iteration of medieval England's distinctive innovation upon this general trope: the blood libel, which casts Jews as ritual murderers of Christian children. Emerging in England in the twelfth century, various versions of this conspiracy theory were quickly taken up throughout Europe, with devastating consequences for Jewish communities. And, as several Chaucer scholars have observed, it persists in more or less recognizable ways into the present, underwriting such antisemitic movements as QAnon, which imagines Christian children to be victims of a global conspiracy featuring prominent Jews (see, for example, Lampert-Weissig 2021; Norako 2024; Wilson 2024).

This present-day relevance of the Prioress's Tale extends, moreover, beyond antisemitism specifically to a more general logic of socially exclusionary hatred, of which racism is a predominant form. Indeed, this

DOI: 10.4324/9781003273318-7

connection between the tale's medieval antisemitism and modern-day racism has been the subject of important scholarship not just on Chaucer but also in critical race theory, helping to expand that theory's reach by extending it back in time. To study the Prioress's Tale, therefore, is to investigate the mechanisms and ramifications of antisemitism, racism, and – as we'll also see – sexism.

The question of Chaucer's culpability

In respect to all those -isms, what will inevitably haunt this chapter from beginning to end is the question of to what degree, in what way, and to what end does the Prioress Tale, in its context as a fictional pilgrim's contribution to the *Canterbury Tales*, itself pursue this investigation. That is, how much is Chaucer here *scrutinizing* the mechanisms and ramifications of antisemitism, racism, and sexism instead of (or in addition to) simply *reproducing* them? We have some basis for supposing the former, since as other chapters in this book attest, Chaucer is a habitually self-interrogating writer. But even so, because he also characteristically doesn't make plain the results of this self-interrogation, we may wish to hold him responsible for what he doesn't say as well as for what he does, especially in such instances of egregiously problematic subject matter. Simply put, we are urged to wonder, how culpable is Chaucer for all that's objectionable about the Prioress's Tale?

Not surprisingly, this question has vexed generations of Chaucer scholars, so much so that an entire book has recently been devoted not so much to this question but to the nature and implications of the scholarly vexation about it. As Heather Blurton and Hannah Johnson, the book's authors, observe, "Between the story's high ethical stakes and its ambiguities, arguments about this tiny piece of the Chaucerian canon are more than usually fraught" (2017, 3). Among the ambiguities to which they refer, the most intractable derive from what I describe in Chapter 1 as one of the affordances of the *Canterbury Tales*' overall form: because Chaucer represents himself as a nonjudgmental verbatim reporter of tales told by others, each tale-telling performance involves a possible distinction between its point of view and Chaucer's, with the nature and amount of that distinction never entirely clear and often quite opaque. For Chaucer, this affordance almost nonchalantly opens up for scrutiny his culture's most cherished and socially structuring values and beliefs. It enables a surprisingly capacious meditation upon, in the corny old phrase I've repurposed, the meaning of life. In the case of the Prioress's Tale, as we will see, the values and beliefs under scrutiny include those that comprised the particular form of late medieval Christian devotion now referred to as affective spirituality as well as the implications of this form of devotion for Christian identity more generally.

As laudable as such self-scrutiny may be, we remain confronted by the fact that Chaucer rarely supplies his readers with a clear sense (or any sense at all) of what we are to take as the results of such critical self-reflection. With what I've labeled his habit of laconic profundity, he often takes us on a journey into the abysses of our governing ideologies far deeper than we realize, points at the exposed veins of our values and beliefs, and heads back to the surface without comment. Obviously, such silence is especially unnerving in the face of the Prioress's Tale's unmitigated antisemitism. It feels akin to someone announcing to an audience, "I overheard this horribly racist joke today," and proceeding to repeat the joke verbatim, without irony or rejoinder. Therefore, howsoever much it may be said that within the context of the *Canterbury Tales*, the tale that the Prioress tells becomes a meditative scrutiny of antisemitism (and this remains hotly contested), its ambiguity in this effort makes it, in one sense, morally inexcusable. Insofar as the tale's antisemitism may be perceived as lacking any certain authorial condemnation, the tale serves to perpetuate antisemitic discourse. It thus may help to bring about in reality the violence against Jewish bodies that it imagines in fiction. Indeed, as scholar J. R. Mattison has pointed out, this is exactly what happened when Édouard Adolphe Drumont lifted the tale out of its *Canterbury Tales* context and incorporated a French translation of it into his 1886 book *La France juive* (*Jewish France*), doing so to fill in the supposed long history of evil committed by Jews against Christians. In this way, the Prioress's Tale supplied a building block for one of the founding documents of modern antisemitism, a book that has had horrific repercussions that extend through the Holocaust up to the present.

This is the weightiest reason why, as I mentioned at the outset, I'm tempted to deny the Prioress's Tale any further airspace. Yet surely to pretend in this way that it's not part of the *Canterbury Tales* – to try to sweep it under the rug – would not really remedy anything. That would let Chaucer too easily off the hook and, much more worryingly, leave the tale too readily available to be coopted by the next Édouard Adolphe Drumont. It's better, then, to tackle the tale head on and consider how, in its scrutiny of affective spirituality and Christian identity, it winds up exploring the relations among what we now recognize as antisemitism, racism, and sexism – to consider how, despite its moral failure, the Prioress's Tale has great bearing on topics that urgently matter to us.

The Prioress's portrait

Most often at this point in other chapters, I supply a summary of the work under discussion. I depart from that pattern in this instance, and consider first the tale-teller's General Prologue portrait, because the bearing of this particular pilgrim portrait on the tale that the pilgrim later tells has been – as Blurton and Johnson detail at length – an especially vexatious question.

The portrait begins with the narrator announcing, "There was also a Nonne [nun], a Prioresse,/That of hir smiling was ful [very] simple and coy" (1.118–19). Those latter two adjectives held a range of senses in Middle English, with "simple" most likely meaning here "sincere and modest," and "coy" meaning "demure," in contrast with its more pejorative modern sense. With these initial two lines, therefore, we learn, first, that this nun is not just any nun: she is also a prioress, who, as head of a convent, held a position of considerable social prominence and, with its managerial responsibilities for the convent's landholdings and other wealth, substantial institutional power. Second, we learn that with the character of her "smiling," she conveys the sort of outward impression that her fellow pilgrims would expect from someone in her position and of her gender.

The next twenty-two lines supply detail that elaborates on these ideas. Noting that she was called by the rather refined name "Madame Eglentine" (1.121), the narrator proceeds to inventory her behavioral characteristics, which on the whole accord with societal expectations for a woman of her social dignity. She sings the liturgical service "ful semely" (1.123) or very adeptly. She speaks French (albeit the sort of French taught in England) "ful faire and fetisly" (1.124) or very eloquently. When she dines, no crumbs fall from her mouth, her fingers do not wind up stained with sauce, no grease appears on her upper lip, and she was pleasant company (1.127–38). Because "In curteisye was set ful muchel her lest [i.e., she took great delight in refined manners]" (1.133), she "pained hire [took pains] to countrefete cheere [the manners]/of court" (1.139–40), with "countrefete" meaning here not the modern pejorative "counterfeit" but the more neutral "imitate." The whole latter phrase thus has the sense of "she conscientiously exhibited the demeanor and behaviors of a noble woman."

The narrator next comments on what he believes to be her "conscience" (1.142) based upon her weeping when she sees a mouse caught in a trap or a man beat one of her small pet dogs (to which she feeds roasted meat and fine white bread) (1.144–49). She is, the narrator says, "charitable" and "pitous" (1.143) or full of pity, possessing a "tendre herte [tender heart]" (1.150). He concludes by describing her wimple, nose, eyes, mouth, forehead, cloak, rosary, and brooch, the last of these carrying the Latin inscription *Amor vincit omnia* (Love conquers all) (1.151–62). All these features are quite elegant, with many of their descriptions similar to conventional ones for romance heroines, although the narrator also inserts the ambiguously snarky remark, "For hardily [assuredly], she was nat undergrowe [not undersized]" (1.156).

Notwithstanding that enigmatic dig, the narrator describes the Prioress, as he does for most other pilgrims, with a general attitude of approval.

Nonetheless, while the Prioress over the years has had a handful of readers in her corner, the vast majority have understood the narrator's attitude as somehow ironic and hence the portrait to be in fact disapproving of the Prioress, albeit in widely varying degrees. At one extreme, some see the portrait as sharply satirical, a description of a vain, failed social aspirant and morally and emotionally shallow religious hypocrite. Such readers often then extend this perceived authorial condemnation from portrait to tale. Connecting the social and spiritual failings of the pilgrim to the antisemitism that she goes on to express, they thereby understand the portrait as the basis of Chaucer's critique of antisemitic discourse. Notably, as Blurton and Johnson show, some of these scholarly condemnations of the Prioress cross the line into misogyny by seeing the Prioress's failings as those to which her sex in general is fallible. Other readers have argued, in contrast, that virtually everything in the Prioress's description was in Chaucer's day typical or at least not surprising for a woman of such social stature and institutional role. They hence see the narrator's implied attitude as far less severely judgmental. In this view, the element of critique is considerably more subtle, with its precise moral valence vague. For that reason, it's less (or just not) available as a rationale for accounting for the tale's antisemitism.

In general, Chaucer scholars over the years have tended to sort the pilgrim portraits into groups of goodies and baddies, which is to say, to separate them according to whether we are to believe that Chaucer the author actually deems them virtuous or actually deems them corrupt. The sheer amount of disagreement that this effort has generated, however, suggests that in many – perhaps most – cases, Chaucer's aim with a portrait is not in fact to provoke this sort of binary judgment. His aim, rather, is to prompt a moral response of more nuance, complexity, and reflection (on this topic, see Mann 1973). It's also important to keep in mind that Chaucer is not attempting with any of the portraits to create characters with a fully coherent, wholly developed psychology, and thereby present their tales as reflecting whatever virtue or corruption resides within the deepest recesses of their psyches. The assumption that this is his aim – once widespread in Chaucer scholarship and still influential if waning – misleadingly projects the conventions of modern naturalistic fiction backward upon Chaucer's writing in a way that the text cannot actually sustain. Instead, it's better to think of each portrait as assembling an individualized set of values that derive from and reflect back on a pilgrim's specific social identity or, more simply, on their 'job,' if that term is understood to encompass more than just work. For each of these social identities, Chaucer inherits a set of literary stereotypes, often satirical. But in most instances, he complicates these stereotypes significantly, most prominently by way of his narrator's sympathetic reporting, which in effect sees the world from a given pilgrim's point of view.

In this light, we may return to what most readers in some way notice about the Prioress's portrait: that the individualized set of values that it assembles, pertaining to the job of prioress, emphasizes a proper performance of a gendered social identity in the *material* world. Spiritual values, in contrast, are scarcely even acknowledged. For example, charity, in the sense of love of one's fellow humans, is among the most essential of spiritual values, according to most Christian denominations. Here, that value pertains to mice and pet dogs, and hence the Prioress, as scholar Karl Steel puts it, seems to be "fawning over the wrong love objects" (2019, 34). There is in particular an overriding emphasis on physicality in the portrait, with much of this focusing in some way on the Prioress's own body. The possible significance of this is a topic that we'll explore later, after considering the tale that the Prioress tells. At this point, let's just keep in mind the fact that in Chaucer's assembly of the Prioress's contribution to the tale-telling contest, one of two scenarios must have held: he wrote either the portrait before the tale or the tale before the portrait. While we have no firm basis for deciding between these scenarios, we nevertheless may fairly suppose that he wrote the later composition with the earlier one in mind. His association of portrait and tale is therefore certainly meaningful in some fashion, although how it is so remains difficult to ascertain, even while ethically urgent.

The tale: summary, genre, and sources

The tale that immediately precedes the Prioress's is a fabliau, a genre of short comic narratives that, as I describe in Chapter 2, emphasizes the corporeal realities of human life. This fabliau is told by the Shipman (although, as many scholars suppose, Chaucer may have originally written it for the Wife of Bath, since in its opening lines the pilgrim narrator refers to wives generally using first-person plural pronouns). Its main characters are a merchant, his wife, and his best friend, who is a monk, and the story involves the circulation of money and sex among the three. The wife sleeps with the monk in order to secure from him 100 francs for a dress that she wants to purchase, the monk borrows the 100 francs from the merchant and later tells him that he paid it back to his wife, and the story concludes with the wife promising her husband – who remains ignorant of the adultery – that she'll repay those 100 francs in bed. The merchant is a little put out, but not so much, as he has just arrived home after earning a huge business windfall.

I've supplied this much detail about the Shipman's Tale to emphasize its stark contrast with the one that the Prioress tells, the possible significance of which I'll return to later. Following the Shipman's performance, the Host expresses hearty approval and then for the next tale turns rather mischievously to the Prioress, one of the pilgrims most likely to have been offended by the Shipman. Notably, he makes his request with exceptional politeness, to a degree that likely becomes obsequious, referring to the Prioress five times in five lines of speech with the polite plural form of the second-person pronoun (a convention that Middle English then followed, as in modern French).

The Prioress begins not with her story but instead with a prologue of five stanzas that comprises a prayerful invocation – a request for divine aid, in this case from the Virgin Mary. These stanzas, as well as the rest of the Prioress's performance, take the seven-line form that we now call rhyme royal, which Chaucer seems to have invented. He uses this form in compositions that, at least on the surface, lay claim to high cultural authority (such as *Troilus and Criseyde*) or high moral/spiritual seriousness (such as the Man of Law's Tale). In comparison, he writes most of the *Canterbury Tales* – including the preceding Shipman's Tale – in rhymed iambic pentameter couplets, a simpler form that he also seems to have brought to English poetry and which later became ubiquitous. Among the few opinions that most Chaucer scholars share is that in the Prioress's Prologue he wields rhyme royal masterfully, weaving together elements of the medieval Christian liturgy and material from the climactic ending of Dante Alighieri's *Divine Comedy* to fashion an exquisitely lyrical hymn in praise of Mary. This hymn could readily be lifted from its context and appreciated, without irony, as is. Yet it also expertly suits its context. It's plainly a fitting opening for a nun and also possesses several thematic connections to the story that follows, in particular to the childlike devotion to Mary that the story's protagonist embodies. Chaucer's defenders have sought to relate such thematic connections back to what they perceive to be the thoroughgoing satire of the portrait, but, as Blurton and Johnson discuss, this effort has been troubled by the invocation's very artistic mastery and deeply felt piety.

The tale that the Prioress proceeds to tell is of the genre that scholars name Miracles of the Virgin, which are "brief religious folk tales of wonders wrought by Mary as a reward for faithful devotion to her" (Chaucer 2000, 438). Such stories were popular throughout Christian Western Europe, serving as a kind of semi-official Church discourse that audiences presumably found both edifying and entertaining. They are precisely the sort of story that we might imagine a medieval English nun, outside her convent, turning to when called upon to speak to a group of mostly layfolk. No specific source for this instance of the genre has been identified, although numerous very similar stories circulated before, during, and after Chaucer's day, possessing the same basic plot and characters and even many particular details. Most likely, the tale that the Prioress relates is Chaucer's innovation upon a story he encountered in one or more versions.

We may assume, then, that the tale's antisemitism was present in whatever materials Chaucer drew upon, as it's an integral part of the other extant versions and in general a relatively common element of the genre.

The Prioress begins by setting her story in Asia, which is to say, somewhere outside medieval Christendom proper, in a city where, she goes on to tell us, both Christians and Jews reside. She locates a school for Christian children at one end of the city's Jewish quarter and introduces the story's protagonist, "A litel clergeon [schoolboy] seven yeer of age" (7.503), explaining how he walks through that quarter to and from school. This little boy is precociously worshipful of Mary. Hearing the Latin anthemic hymn *Alma Redemptoris Mater* (*Gracious Mother of the Redeemer*), he's instantly and instinctively drawn to it, even though he doesn't understand its Latin. He subsequently learns from an older schoolmate the anthem's basic gist and memorizes its entirety. From then on, "Twies a day it passed thurgh his throte –/To scoleward and homward whan he wente./On Cristes moder [mother] set was his entente" (7.548–50).

Satan here enters the picture, who, according to the Prioress, "hath in Jewes herte his waspes nest" (7.559) – a remark that, like its whole encompassing stanza, is often noticed for its onomatopoeic hissing sounds. The devil proclaims to the Jews that the boy performs his twice-daily singing in praise of Mary as he walks through their quarter in "despit" or contempt of them, against the "reverence" of their "laws" (7.563–64). So incited, the Jews hire an assassin, who hides in an alley and when the boy walks by, cuts his throat and throws his body into the pit of a public latrine.

After some pointed narratorial commentary on this moment in the story, the Prioress turns to the boy's mother, whom she describes as becoming increasingly desperate when her son does not return from school and she cannot find him in any "place wheras she hath supposed/By likihede hir litel child to finde" (7.595–96). Searching the Jewish quarter, she asks about the boy. When the Jews deny seeing him, his corpse miraculously begins to sing *Alma Redemptoris Mater*. The Christians immediately send for the city's "provost" or chief magistrate, who proceeds to bind, torture, and finally execute all the Jews "That of this mordre wiste [murder knew]" (7.630) by the grisly method of first dragging them by horse and then hanging them.

Meanwhile, the boy is taken to a nearby abbey and laid before an altar. When the abbot sprinkles him with holy water, he begins singing again, prompting the abbot to ask, "what is thy cause for to singe,/Sith [since] that thy throte is cut, to my seeming?" (7.647–48). The boy explains that when he was killed, Mary came to him and requested that he sing *Alma Redemptoris Mater*, laying a "grain" or seed upon his tongue when he did so, and that he must continue to sing until the grain is removed. The abbot pulls out the boy's tongue and removes the grain, and the boy dies (again).

The abbot and all the rest of the gathered monks fall onto abbey's floor and weep, and then they go off to bury the boy.

Rather than end the story there, at the conclusion of its plot, the Prioress – egregiously to our ears – calls the audience's attention to what would have been in Chaucer's day a real-world historical parallel. She recalls the story of "Yonge Hugh of Lincoln, slain also/With cursed Jewes, as it is notable –/For it is but a litel while ago" (6.684–86). In fact, the boy known as Hugh of Lincoln died not "a litel while ago" but one hundred forty years or so before the setting of the Canterbury pilgrimage. When his body was found in a well, the local community of Jews was accused of ritual murder. This led to riots and, eventually, the execution of nineteen Jews at the command of King Henry III. The Prioress's narrative postscript therefore attests, in a deeply disturbing commemorative manner, to the real-world consequences of antisemitic discourse such as the fiction that she has just supplied. To us, her reference to Hugh of Lincoln underscores how the dissemination of stories of harm supposedly done to 'our' children leads to the brutal persecution of an already oppressed minority. Indeed, having suffered for centuries under the rule of the Christian majority, all English Jews were finally expelled from the kingdom by King Edward I in 1290, roughly one hundred years before the setting of the *Canterbury Tales*. The Prioress's postscript thus makes acutely evident that even in the actual absence of the demonized other – even without a physically proximate target – the ideology that justifies dominance must keep that demonized other in circulation, through fiction if not in fact.

Passion

That last point, I would suggest, is what we might generally take away from the Prioress's performance, although the specifics of that performance naturally develop that lesson in a narrower fashion, which has the effect of making it even more fraught as a general principle. Among the most prominent of these specifics is the performance's emphasis upon powerful emotion, making the story in some ways most essentially about *passion* in both its modern sense of especially strong feeling and its older sense of suffering. To some extent, this emphasis was built into the genre as Chaucer received it, as Miracles of the Virgin stories tend to depict passion in both senses in order to arouse the emotions of their audiences (see Steiner 2017). But Chaucer accentuates this emphasis in several ways, which extend from the Prioress's opening invocation through her tale and its concluding postscript.

The invocation, which is unique to Chaucer's version of the story, makes use of profoundly emotive language. Addressing Mary, for example, the Prioress declaims,

O moder* maide, O maide moder free!* — mother; bounteous, noble
O bussh unbrent,* brenning in Moises* sighte! — Unburned; Moses's
That ravisshedest* doun fro the deitee,* — ravished; deity, God
Thurgh thyn humblesse, the gost* that in th'alighte, — Holy Spirit
Of whos vertu* whan he thyn herte lighte,* — power; illuminated
Conceived was the Fadres sapience.* — Father's wisdom, i.e., Christ

(7.467–72)

Notably, what this impassioned praise of Mary describes is specifically her impregnation, the conception in her womb of "the Fadres sapience." It makes elegant, figurative use of an allusion to Moses's encounter with God, in the form of a burning bush that remains unburnt (Exodus 3:2), to convey the heat of a passionate sexual encounter with the "deitee" that isn't, literally, sexual. While every element of this passage has precedents among the standard tropes of Marian devotion, the dramatized first-person context individualizes their inherent emotionality, making that emotionality characteristic of the Prioress's distinct voice. At the same time, the passage relates that emotionality and voice to the body, in this instance a female body that achieves holiness precisely through a sexuality that isn't. Subsequently, and somewhat atypically for *Canterbury Tales* performances, the distinctiveness of this voice regularly and significantly reappears in the tale's narration. (The Knight's Tale, for example, contains very few moments that remind us that it is the Knight specifically who is speaking.)

Strikingly – and revealingly – when the Prioress next uses this very highest register of impassioned speech, she does so in response to the Jews' murder of the schoolboy, and so there the register expresses hatred rather than adoration. But prior to that point, she seeds the emotional atmosphere to establish this contrast in more subtle ways. In the tale's first stanza, we do not merely learn about the presence of Jews, but we also hear of their "foul usure" (6.492), that is, their usury or moneylending, which was forbidden to Christians (which in turn often made the economies of Christian communities to some degree reliant upon Jews). For the Prioress, this usury makes Jews categorically "Hateful to Crist" (6.493). Jarringly contrasting with the emotional valence of the prologue, the negative emotional charge of such adjectives as "foul" and "Hateful" is then immediately followed by a prominently repetitive set of word choices that turns the valence back the other direction. We're next introduced to the "*litel* scole [school] of Cristen folk.../... in which ther were/*Children* an heep [i.e., a lot of children]," who learned "to singen and to rede,/As *smale* [small] *children* doon [do] in her *childhede* [their childhood]" (7.495–501). The obsessive emphasis on children's diminutiveness evident in these lines quickly becomes focused on the protagonist, the "*litel* clergeon" who at seven years old is made younger than in any of the story's other extant versions. Over and over in the stanzas that follow, we hear about the schoolboy in ways that underscore his youthful vulnerability and so are calibrated to evoke a feeling of maternal protectiveness and love.

These abrupt juxtapositions of opposite emotional charges reach a peak of intensity with the Prioress's response to the boy's murder. Immediately following her description of the assassin's throwing the body "in a pit" (7.571), she supplies a sequence of three emotionally stirring stanzas. The first directs hatred toward the Jews, the second celebrates the martyrdom of the boy, and the third describes the increasing anxiousness of the mother:

I saye that in a wardrobe* they him threwe,	public latrine
Wheras thise Jewes purgen hir entraile.*	empty their bowels
O cursed folk of Herodes al newe,*	once again
What may youre yvel* entente you availe?	evil
Mordre* wol out, certayn it wol nat faile,	Murder
And namely* ther th'honour of God shal sprede:	especially
The blood out cryeth on youre cursed deede.	
O martyr souded* to virginitee,	bonded
Now maistou singen,* folwing ever in oon*	may you sing; constantly
The White Lamb* celestial – quod she –	i.e., Christ
Of which the grete* Evangelist Saint John	great
In Pathmos wroot, which saith that they that gon	
Biforn this Lamb, and singe a song al newe,	
That never fleshly womman they ne knewe.*	i.e., they were virgins
This povre widwe* awaiteth al that night	poor widow
After hir litel child, but he cam noght;	
For which, as soone as it was dayes light,	
With face pale of drede and bisy* thoght,	anxious
She hath at scole*and elleswhere him soght,	school
Til finally she gan so fer espye*	i.e., discovered
That he last sein was* in the Jewerye.	was seen
(7.572–99)	

The first stanza begins by doubling down on the scatological conclusion of the boy's murder, supplying gratuitous elaboration ("I saye") as if concerned that the audience missed this element of filth. The stanza then links the murder to the New Testament story of King Herod's command, upon hearing of the birth of the next king of the Jews, to kill all infant boys in and around Bethlehem (Matthew 2:16). In this context, because of the inevitable association of Herod's failed attempt to kill Christ with Christ's later crucifixion, this allusion figures the schoolboy's murder as a repetition of the latter. In this way, the Prioress relates the boy's murder to what is for Christian antisemitism the foundational crime of the Jews: their responsibility for Christ's death, the archetypical Passion. And indeed, this chain of association has been present from the start, as from her invocation on the Prioress has incorporated elements of the Christian liturgy of the Mass of the Holy Innocents, the Church's official commemoration of Herod's attempt to kill Christ.

The second stanza then swerves from this expression of hatred to a passionate celebration of the murdered schoolboy. Oddly, however, it does so not as we might expect, by recalling the boy's precocious adoration of Mary. Instead, it praises him for dying while still a virgin – which of course for a seven-year-old would not seem to require any special virtue. This apparent non sequitur is a consequence of the effort to amplify the connection to the Mass of the Holy Innocents by a further New Testament allusion, this one to a passage in Revelations (the book written by "Evangelist Saint John/In Pathmos") that was read during that mass. The liturgy's use of this passage (Revelations 14:1–5) equates its account of 144,000 male virgins who follow Christ in heaven ("they who were not defiled with women") with the infant boys killed by Herod's command. Hence, by a kind of transitive logic, since virginity is what is celebrated about those 144,000, and since those thousands are the same as those killed by Herod, and since the murder of the clergeon has just been equated with Herod's murders, then it is the seven-year-old's virginity that must be praised here.

This praise of the schoolboy, although apparently unrelated to his initial characterization, therefore follows seamlessly from the tale's network of allusive association. At the same time, it reaches back to the Prioress's emphasis on virginity in her prologue, albeit it does so, notably, in a way that explicitly derogates the sexualized female body, in contrast with the prologue's celebration of Mary's holy impregnation. And amid all this, pointedly and yet inscrutably, Chaucer inserts the narratorial speech tag "quod she" in an intrusive fashion that he avoids in other pilgrim performances, except when he needs to distinguish the voices of different pilgrims. This unusual speech marker, whatever might be its larger significance, serves as a reminder that the allusive gymnastics of this stanza, and of the whole narration, are part and parcel of the emotive voice of the Prioress.

The third stanza then abruptly turns back to the plot of the story and the plight of the poor widow who is the boy's mother. All the details supplied here are calibrated to amplify the situation's inherent pathos – to evoke the deeply anxious feeling that most parents, then and now, have experienced at some point when a child cannot be found or a child's well-being is otherwise potentially but uncertainly threatened. Indeed, from the Romantic poet William Wordsworth's comment about the tale's "tender-hearted sympathies with Mother and Child," we may suppose that it was this specific emotive power that led him, over four hundred years after Chaucer, to single out the Prioress's Tale for one of his two efforts at *Canterbury Tales* modernization. Wordsworth no doubt recognized the similarities between this maternal pathos and that which filled much of his own poetry of the 1790s (compare, for example, "The Female Vagrant," "The Thorn," "The Mad Mother," "The Complaint of the Forsaken Indian Woman," and "The Idiot Boy"). Eventually, he also noticed the tale's antisemitism, and so he prefaced that same comment by acknowledging the "fierce bigotry of the Prioress" (see Page 2000). Plainly, though, his belated awareness of this element of the tale did not sway his decision to publish his modernization. In this way, Wordsworth exemplifies those readers who have found that the emotive power of the Prioress's Tale, no matter what its baggage, conveys an authenticity that is worth admiring, in his case by reproducing it.

Pity and rage

If the twentieth-century philosopher Hannah Arendt had ever heard of Wordsworth's decision in this regard, she would no doubt have remarked upon its grim irony, given the time that Wordsworth spent in Revolutionary France in the years before his modernization of Chaucer. In her book *On Revolution*, Arendt famously considers the emotive conditions that led the French Revolution of 1789 to devolve into the Reign of Terror of the 1790s, during which tens of thousands of individuals were publicly executed. Arendt understands the revolutionaries as having broadcast a sentiment of pity toward an undifferentiated mass of miserable French poor, which entailed that "the course of the Revolution depended upon the release of the force inherent in suffering, upon the force of delirious rage" (1965, 111). In general, she argues, pity, when directed toward the suffering as an ideological strategy, very often generates such "delirious rage," which is conversely directed toward the perceived agents of that suffering. Hence, as Arendt remarks in a well-known aphorism, "Pity, taken as the spring of virtue, has proved to possess a greater capacity for cruelty than cruelty itself" (1965, 89).

This generative relation between pity and rage is, among other things, what Wordsworth seems to have discounted in the Prioress's Tale, despite himself witnessing it in France. Most likely, simple prejudice – manifesting as his relative lack of concern about the Jewish victims of rage – explains this oversight, which in turn suggests the more general and deeply troubling implications of the way that Arendt's ideas are applicable to the story. The pity that the tale both represents and asks its audience to feel is obviously directed toward the Christian mother and child, and so the "delirious rage" that accompanies pity, which is also both represented in and beckoned by the tale, just as obviously is to be directed toward the agents of their suffering, the Jews (see Hines 2022 and Spector 1991). In respect to Arendt's formulation, Christians play the role of the miserable oppressed, while Jews play the role of the powerful oppressors – which is to say, the two roles are precisely the inverse of what was virtually always the actual situation in medieval Europe. Such an inversion realizes a longstanding discursive strategy of the socially and politically dominant: the claim that they cannot be oppressors because they themselves are the oppressed. With this disavowal of their oppression, they thereby perpetuate the status quo of their dominance.

Racialization

As the Prioress's Tale further illustrates, this same discursive strategy almost always incorporates a justification for dominance involving an intrinsic, unalterable superiority. It conveys some version of the assurance that we, who are not oppressors because we're oppressed, will overcome our oppression because we're intrinsically righteous, pure, and good, whereas our oppressors – those culpable for our suffering – are corrupt, polluted, and evil. In other words, the discursive strategy of depicting the dominant as the persecuted almost inevitably relies upon and produces distinctive, opposing, mutually defining identities for the dominant and dominated.

In providing a vivid example of this strategy, the Prioress's Tale thus illustrates not only the mechanics of antisemitism but also, as I mentioned above, a more general logic of socially exclusionary hatred. This has led scholars such as Geraldine Heng to consider the tale through the lens of critical race theory, notwithstanding that theory's original formulation with regard to the systemic racism that accompanied the rise, more than a century after Chaucer's death, of the global trade in enslaved Africans, and which continues to structure modern societies. Generalizing from the more specific features of today's racism, Heng defines race as

> one of the primary names we have…that is attached to a repeating tendency, of the gravest import, to demarcate human beings through differences among humans that are selectively essentialized as absolute and fundamental, in order to distribute positions and powers differentially to human groups.
>
> (Heng 2019, 4–5)

In respect to this definition, epidermal shade – so often designated by the binary black/white – is just one of the many possible vectors of "differences among humans" that have been used to characterize individuals' bodies as having categorical, unchanging implications for how they are sorted socially. In Heng's expansion of critical race theory, what constitutes racism is not the operation of any specific vector of difference but an ideology of a difference's "absolute and fundamental" nature as the principle for organizing a society hierarchically, that is, "in order to distribute positions and powers differentially to human groups."

The ideology that differentiated Christians from Jews in the Middle Ages (and which, alas, persists in many circles today) quite clearly held this character and function. Summarizing the historical scholarship on the topic, Heng observes that far from Jews being seen simply as worshippers of a different religion, "Across Europe, scientific, medical, and theological treatises argued that the bodies of Jews differed in nature from the bodies of Western Europeans who were Christian" (2019, 11). The religious prejudices that understood Christians as spiritually superior to Jews were corroborated by racial prejudices that understood that superiority as biological as well, and in practice the spiritual and biological were deeply entangled, with one reciprocally confirming the truth of the other. We see this entanglement in the Prioress's Tale, as Heng points out, when the children who attend the clergeon's school are described as "ycomen of Cristen blood" (7.497), that is, Christian by "blood" rather than just conviction, and in how Jews' bodies are the dwelling place of Satan, who "hath in Jewes herte his waspes nest" (7.559). Heng concludes, "The two populations – one a blood-race, the other an infernal race – are *embodied* races" (2019, 83; emphasis in original).

Medieval England was ahead of its time (so to speak) with respect to the several ways that this ideology was instrumentalized in the administrative systems of the kingdom. The country was an early instance of the kind of racial state that has typified modernity, as in, for example, the former apartheid regime of South Africa. In this way, not only was Christian identity through its racialization defined and legitimated as a principle of superiority but so was the identity denominated "English." The official, bureaucratic character of Jewish oppression helped to define the distinctive identity of the community for whom that official bureaucracy was a mouthpiece. As Heng writes,

> In England, the Jewish badge, expulsion order, legislative enforcements, surveillance and segregation, ritualized iterations of homicidal fables, and the legal murder of Jews are all constitutive acts in the consolidation of a community of Christian English – otherwise internally fragmented and ranged along numerous divides – against a minority population.
> (2019, 20)

The persecution and eventual expulsion of Jews helped to consolidate the unified English identity of the country performing that persecution and expulsion. It follows, then, that in order to maintain and perpetuate that identity, more than one hundred years following the expulsion, "ritualized iterations of homicidal fables" such as the Prioress's Tale continued to circulate. That tale's evocations of deep feelings of love and hatred, its depiction of the generative relationship between pity and rage, and its rooting of all this in the bodies of Christians and Jews thus constitute a set of interlocking mechanisms for representing and transmitting a racial ideology that shores up the Christian, English identity of the dominant and legitimates the status quo.

And yet what ruffles the feathers of this relatively straightforward ideological function is, as we've noticed, the painstaking manner in which the tale links these features to the distinctive voice of its narrator, evident in its prologue, the "quod she" tag, and other devices. With the advantage of historical hindsight and the additional perspective gained by critical race theory, modern readers of any religious affiliation can see through the narrator's piety and expose the operations of racialized antisemitic discourse that pervade the sometimes lofty poetry of her performance. But we still then face the question of what that performance means in its literary context: what it means for *this* pilgrim to supply *this* story at *this* moment in the dramatized journey toward Canterbury. In the way that the *Canterbury Tales'* structure works, a tale's literary context always gets the last word about the tale's meaning, even if we're never exactly sure what that word is.

The generic gymnastics of Fragment VII

One important component of the literary context of the Prioress's Tale is its placement within the continuous, dramatically linked sequence of six pilgrim performances that most *Canterbury Tales* editions title Fragment VII. I've already called attention to the several contrasts between the Prioress's Tale and the immediately preceding Shipman's Tale, which launches the sequence. Immediately following the Prioress's Tale is the Tale of Sir Thopas, which Chaucer himself tells in his pilgrim persona. Here, Chaucer the author burlesques the conventions of popular Middle English romance, which in Chaucer's view seems to have had the cultural status of something like today's low-budget action movies. He characterizes his pilgrim alter-ego as an ingenuous but feeble hack, who's so incompetent that the Host interrupts his performance midsentence, unable to stomach any more of Chaucer's "drasty speche" (7.923), with "drasty" roughly equivalent, if less scatological, to our "crappy." The Host tells Chaucer to start over with something different, and Chaucer obliges, supplying the Tale of Melibee. This moral allegory in prose is serious, learned, and dense. Based upon a Latin original (though mostly by way of French translation), it's also very long, dry, and repetitive. However we might imagine Chaucer means his actual audience to respond, it's clear that nothing could contrast more starkly with Sir Thopas. Afterward, the Host, commenting approvingly, transforms the Melibee's ethical meditations into crude, misogynist remarks about his wife. Then, continuing this crudeness in a more sexualized vein, he asks the Monk to tell a tale.

The Monk supplies what he names "tragedies" (6.1971), a collection of short verse narratives with each telling a story of the bad end of some famous personage. These stories are drawn from a set of sources that in Chaucer's day held great esteem, among them Dante's *Inferno*. The whole effort is modeled upon a remarkably ambitious work by Giovanni Boccaccio, one of Dante's Italian successors and Chaucer's go-to author for such compositions as the Knight's Tale and *Troilus and Criseyde*. But the Monk's rather repetitive performance is poorly received by the pilgrim audience, or at least by the Knight and Host. The Knight interrupts the Monk, and the Host, boisterously amplifying the Knight's disparagement, declares that the Monk "clappeth loude [blabs nosily]" (7.2781). The Host then turns to the Nun's Priest (i.e., the priest who accompanies the Prioress) and rather rudely requests from him the next tale. This "sweete Preest" (7.2820), as the narrator calls him here – and about whom we learn nothing in the General Prologue other than that he (along with apparently two others) is present – goes on to tell a dizzyingly erudite and trenchantly witty beast fable. Scholars generally agree that this is one of the *Tales'* bravura performances. Some even suggest that if any performance is actually in something like Chaucer's own voice, this may be it. For most readers, therefore, the Nun's Priest's Tale serves as a satisfying culmination of the narratively continuous sequence of tale-telling performances that begins with the Shipman's Tale.

I hope this longish summary makes plain this sequence's single most prominent feature: its breathtaking diversity of literary genres, with the abrupt segues between them having the effect of the old Monty Python sketch transition tag, "And now for something completely different." Chaucer seems to be experimenting here, trying his hand at this and that genre.[3] From the joking meta-literary commentary within the links between tales, we can be sure, further, that Chaucer is exercising his characteristic literary self-consciousness, his habit of including in his writing some sort of reflection upon that writing, directed in this instance toward genre. Specifically, we may conclude that this sequence is as much about its genres – their nature and implications, including nonliterary implications – as it is about the content of its stories. And for most of the tales in this sequence, a significant portion of their genre's implications resides within its association with the individualized set of values embodied by its corresponding pilgrim narrator.

Affective spirituality and its discontents

With the Prioress's Tale, then, we may understand Chaucer as exploring the nature and implications of, specifically, the genre of Miracles of the

Virgin and doing so in relation to a set of values embodied by the Prioress. Chaucer appears especially interested, as have seen, in the genre's capacity for emotive power, which he links to the Prioress through her prologue and other devices. As several scholars have noted, among the important nonliterary implications of this emphasis are the religious disposition and devotional practice that have come to be labeled *affective spirituality*. Evolving across the three centuries before Chaucer, affective spirituality prioritizes emotional identification with the humanity of Christ and especially Christ's suffering. By association, this emotional identification extends to Mary's suffering (in enduring the suffering of her son) as well as that of any Christian martyr. It also includes identifications with joyful emotions of the same personages, such as that felt by Mary upon learning that she will give birth to Christ. Affective spirituality was popular in England in Chaucer's day, especially – though by no means exclusively – among women. In the generation after Chaucer, another of England's famous Middle English writers, Margery Kempe, hailed as the author of the first autobiography in English, founded much of her self-understanding upon this mode of spirituality.

The hymn in praise of Mary that the Prioress delivers as her prologue is an expression *par excellence* of affective spirituality. Indeed, in the view of many scholars, it is one of the more literarily accomplished of such expressions. In its role as a preface to a Miracles of the Virgin story (which, again, is one of Chaucer's innovations), this prologue thus yokes affective spirituality to the emotive power typically carried by that genre. At the same time, with its first-person voicing, the prologue also takes us back to the Prioress's General Prologue portrait. Putting all this together, some scholars, understanding that portrait as satirical, have in turn understood the antisemitism of the Prioress's Tale as Chaucer's searing critique of affective spirituality. And since for Chaucer affective spirituality would've been associated with women, his critique also encompasses gender. Consequently, for scholar Karma Lochrie, the effect of the Prioress's performance is both antiracist and misogynist: "By inflating the affective register of the Tale along with the violence of the narrator's rhetoric against the Jews, Chaucer is perhaps making one of the first attempts to understand racio-religious prejudice in terms of a gendered religious sensibility" (2005, 67).

This view, although diminishing the reputation that Chaucer has in some quarters as a proto-feminist, understands him as criticizing antisemitism, as we hope anyone would do. Yet, in the absence of any explicit indicator of this criticism, is this wishful thinking? The comments about Jews that appear elsewhere in Chaucer's writings, such as some antisemitic ones in the Parson's Tale, are all couched within some equivocal literary context. We do know that, in general, late medieval Western European Christians exhibited a broad spectrum of attitudes toward Jews, ranging from the unmitigated racist hatred expressed by the Prioress to something close to tolerance. As Chaucer's recent biographer Marion Turner has emphasized, Chaucer, in his travels abroad, would've encountered a variety of these attitudes as well as actual Jewish communities (Turner 2019). Nevertheless, inasmuch as my analogy holds of someone prefacing an unapologetically racist joke with initial acknowledgement that it's racist, I don't find that the possibility that Chaucer's attitude toward the Jews was different from the Prioress's necessarily entails that the Prioress's performance is his critique of antisemitism.

Some sort of critique of affective spirituality, however, seems likely. In particular, with the collocation of portrait, prologue, and Miracle of the Virgin that constitutes the Prioress's performance, Chaucer appears to have placed under the microscope the potential for affective spirituality to manifest the generative relation between pity and rage so evident in tale. Rather than supposing that he did so to condemn antisemitism, we may more confidently see him as investigating the implications of the way that affective spirituality configures the relation between the corporeal and the spiritual, given the emphasis on that relation we have traced across the performance. This topic, as other chapters in this book attest, is one that Chaucer returns to throughout the *Canterbury Tales*, from its first sentence through its concluding Retraction. For Chaucer, the topic is integral to the basic question of the meaning of life, by which I mean, as I explain in this book's Introduction, an inquiry into the relation between our physical, biological existence and the nonmaterial ideas, ideals, and values that determine our experience of that existence. In pursuing this inquiry across his writings, Chaucer turns from one ideological formula to another, exploring the various possibilities available in his Christian culture as well as some he imagines as available outside that culture. In this case, the formula under inspection is the one offered by affective spirituality.

With its emphasis on the suffering body and on emotional identification with that suffering (emotions, too, being at some level corporeal), affective spirituality makes the human body a vessel for experiencing holiness. It achieves in this way a harmonious configuration of the corporeal and the spiritual that contrasts with the more typical medieval Christian configuration. The latter understands the body as hostile to the spiritual element of humanity, the soul, with the "flesh" constituting one of the soul's three principal enemies, along with the world and the devil. The other nun among the pilgrims, whom *Canterbury Tales* editions name the Second Nun, succinctly expresses this configuration in her own introductory prayer to Mary: "And of thy [Mary's] light my soule in prison lighte,/That troubled is by the contagioun/Of my body" (8.71–73). This configuration was particularly troublesome for women, since the female sex was understood as categorically more carnal than the male, an essentialized difference that justified male supremacy following a logic akin to that which Heng defines for racism. It's not surprising, then, that women would be drawn to the alternative configuration of affective spirituality or that men such as Chaucer would associate it with the category of female, regardless of its actual cross-gender appeal. As we have seen, the Prioress's passionate celebration of Mary centers the holiness of Mary's pregnant body. Insofar as we may assume that Chaucer/the Prioress associated the capacity to become pregnant, regardless of whether it's realized, with the category of female, the Prioress's hymn to Mary also makes her own body holy.

In the Prioress's performance, this corporeal sanctification exacts the cost of a binary division of bodies into pure/holy and polluted/evil. This division pervades the performance, starting with the way it's underscored in the contrastive segue between the Shipman's and Prioress's Tales. The Prioress, in response to a fabliau about the circulation of sex and money, supplies a Miracle of the Virgin that insists that the most holy and pure bodies are virginal and the most polluted and evil bodies are those infamous (to her) for circulating money, the Jews guilty of "foule usure."[4] The question that arises, then, is whether Chaucer, in so vividly charting this cost of corporeal sanctification, is suggesting that the effort of affective spirituality to undo the rigid binary between body and soul *inevitably* just generates, in whack-a-mole fashion, a different but equally rigid binary, this one wholly corporeal and therefore with grave implications in the physical world.

In this regard, consideration of the overall tenor of the Prioress's General Prologue portrait becomes important. In the interpretation that I followed above, the portrait may not so much straightforwardly satirize the Prioress as a bad nun as depict less judgmentally one version of the result of the inevitable confrontation between material and spiritual values involved in her social identity. Outside of moralizing contexts such as the sort of satires that Chaucer's portrait innovates upon, late fourteenth-century English society generally expected someone in such an institutionally prestigious position as that of a prioress to be classy, as we would put it informally. In practice, therefore, the impression that a prioress is a woman of genteel social background wouldn't have been in itself a reason for negative judgment. In many situations, the impression would've helped to maintain her authority and fulfill her considerable responsibilities, which involved dealings in the secular world as well as the religiously cloistered one. Those many prioresses who in fact did come from genteel backgrounds were likely able to create this impression as a matter of course. For others – such as perhaps Chaucer's Prioress – more conscious adoption of the 'correct' presentation would've been required. In all cases, a prioress's performance of this aspect of her social identity required an embrace to some degree of the sort of material values that performances of class status necessarily demand, involving her clothing, speech, manners, education, etc. This aspect, in turn, would have been at odds with the more general social identity of nun, which emphasizes the categorical rejection of material values in favor of spiritual ones. In this respect, we may understand Chaucer's portrait of the Prioress as depicting one side of the negotiation of this inherent conflict between values. In this instance, a prioress grooms her physical presence with the aim of creating the expected impression of social dignity, which potentially decenters the spiritual values that are also demanded by her social identity.

With the assembly of the Prioress's portrait, prologue, and tale, therefore, Chaucer presents us with an example of affective spirituality that on the one hand is channeled through the shaping force of the genre of Miracles of the Virgin and on the other hand is through its speaker linked to a set of values that represent compromises with the demands of spiritual perfection that life in the physical world makes to some degree inescapable. In thereby considering the answer to the question of the meaning of life that affective spirituality supplies, in which the corporeal and the spiritual might in theory be harmonized, Chaucer's conclusion appears to be one of skeptical concern. He suggests that in practice, if not inevitably, the necessary compromises required by life in the physical world, as exhibited by the Prioress's portrait, incur this harmonization's aforementioned cost, in which a physical distinction between kinds of bodies becomes a spiritual imperative. Passionate love directed toward some bodies and passionate hatred directed toward others become flipsides of the same coin. Affective spirituality may wind up with a formulation for the meaning of life that declares that we know how and why some lives matter because we're certain that other lives do not.

The rest is silence

To understand the implications of the Prioress's performance in this way, however, does not entail an understanding of that performance as a critique of antisemitism. As those implications necessarily involve some demonized racial other, and since Miracles of the Virgin typically place Jews in that role, the extension of Chaucer's critical evaluation of affective spirituality to the tale's antisemitism – in distinction with its more general expression of hatred – could simply be a sort of side effect. Chaucer may not have even recognized this side effect as such, or, if he did, like Wordsworth's later reaction to it, it may not have been of much concern to him.

The transition from the Prioress's performance to Chaucer's performance of the Tale of Sir Thopas may serve as a sort of emblem for this ethically urgent but intractably ambiguous question of authorial purpose.

Near the end of her tale, the Prioress vividly describes the reaction of the abbot and the other monks to the schoolboy's second death:

And whan this abbot hadde this wonder sein,*	seen
His salte teres* trikled doun as rain,	tears
And gruf he fil al plat* upon the grounde,	facedown he fell
And stille he lay as* he had been ybounde.*	as if; bound
The covent* eek* lay on the pavement,	the convent, the other monks; also
Weepinge, and herying* Cristes moder deere.*	praising; mother dear
(7.673–78)	

This communal action, in which everyone present uniformly, passionately, and physically expresses pity toward the murdered boy and, simultaneously, adoration of Mary, constitutes a model for the sort of Christian identity writ large that the tale both imagines and promulgates. Here, the Prioress succinctly dramatizes the consolidation of a racialized Christian identity that serves to unify the community by excluding the demonized other. When in the following stanza the Prioress draws the parallel with "yonge Hugh of Lincoln, slain also/With cursed Jewes.../... a litel while ago" (7.684–86), she insists that this Christian identity, as just represented in the tale, extends to the present reality outside the tale. In this way, she urges her listeners to display the same reaction *to* the tale that she has just dramatized *in* the tale.

It is rather striking, therefore, that the actual reaction to the tale is something like the opposite, or at least quite contrasting. Chaucer describes this reaction at the beginning of the prologue to his Tale of Sir Thopas (and the prologue continues, interestingly, in the Prioress's Tale's rhyme royal stanzas):

Whan said was al this miracle,* every man	i.e., the Prioress's Tale
As sobre was,* that wonder was to see,	as so solemn or grave
Til that our Hoste japen he bigan,*	began to joke
And thanne at erst* he looked upon me,	for the first time
And saide thus, "What man artou?"* quod he.	What sort of man are you?
"Thou lookest as thou woldest finde an hare,	
For ever upon the ground I see thee stare."	
(7.691–97)	

Instead of expressing passionate, weeping pity and Marian adoration or declaiming against the Jews, the other pilgrims are merely silent, absorbed in some sort of serious contemplation, whose nature Chaucer does not explain.

Even the usually loquacious Host is mute until he abruptly determines to dispel the "sobre" mood that has befallen the group. As is characteristic of Chaucer, he presents us with a moment that seems freighted with significance, but he leaves that significance unfathomably underdetermined. If the question of Chaucer's attitude toward the Jews has an answer, it lies buried in this silent response, which he is careful to underscore as also his own response, with the Prioress's Tale leaving him staring at the ground.

Notes

1 For another Chaucer teacher's similar hesitancies about the Prioress's Tale and ultimate recognition of its currency, see the cogent reflections of Winstead 2024.

2 https://www.cnn.com/2018/04/14/politics/kentucky-matt-bevin-teachers-strike/index.html.

3 Or if he wrote some of these tales prior to envisioning the *Canterbury Tales*, he's representing himself as experimenting here.

4 Indeed, in the Prioress's offhand remark about the abbot, who "was an holy man/As monkes been, *or elles oughten be*" (7.642–43), we might detect a disapproving nod toward the sexually voracious monk of the Shipman's Tale, which constitutes another unusual marker of the Prioress's narratorial presence.

7 Dream Visions – The *House of Fame* and the *Legend of Good Women*

Paul Auster's celebrated 1985 postmodern mystery novel *City of Glass* begins with its protagonist, Daniel Quinn, receiving a misdirected phone call from someone looking for a private detective named Paul Auster. Quinn, who happens to be an author of mystery novels, decides to impersonate Auster. Quinn is hired by Peter Stillman, whose father, also named Peter Stillman, is about to be released from a psychiatric hospital. Stillman Sr. had been committed for having raised Stillman Jr. in isolation in a dark room for the first nine years of his life in order to see if his son would in this way develop a perfect 'natural' language. Quinn later seeks out the real Auster when things go awry and winds up meeting with Paul Auster, the author. They have a conversation about writing.

Conventionally, mystery novels themselves function like a perfectly ordered language, in which all the elements of the story, no matter how initially ambiguous, wind up contributing to an ultimate, definite meaning: the solution to the mystery. But in this novel, Stillman Sr.'s unsuccessful search for a perfect language is mirrored by Quinn's unsuccessful attempt to understand and, eventually, locate him. That in turn is mirrored by the character Auster's inability in the end to locate Quinn and by readers' uncertainty over the insights that Quinn does or does not finally achieve. In a series of nested boxes, we follow characters' searches for meaning, which also comprise our own search for meaning, and arrive, like them, at an inconclusive, indeterminate breaking-off point.

As I hope this extremely brief synopsis conveys, this novel, like much postmodern fiction, is characterized by self-reflexiveness – which is to say, by meditations upon itself, its medium, its genre, and its authorship – and by intentional confusion of the fictional world represented in the novel and the author and readers' real world outside of it. Postmodernism in the arts, which developed alongside various schools of thought emerging in the twentieth century, became ubiquitous by the second half of the century. It's evident in fiction such as Auster's, in painting such as Andy Warhol's, and

DOI: 10.4324/9781003273318-8

even in mainstream cinema, as in the 2001 film *Shrek*. It's perhaps surprising, therefore, that many of its characteristic features are also readily evident in the several poetic dream visions that Chaucer wrote in the years prior to his work on the *Canterbury Tales*, some six centuries ago. As we will see, like Auster does in *City of Glass*, in his dream visions Chaucer inserts himself into a fictional world in order to reflect on writing and more generally on the nature of authorship, literature, and language.

Dream visions: the postmodern premodern

Chaucer was by no means unusual in this respect. Many other compositions of his own day and before display features that resemble those of postmodernism. A main reason for this is that postmodernism reacts against some of the conventions of modern fiction that had yet to be decisively established in the late fourteenth century, thereby making the premodern and postmodern seem to have some amount of shared sensibility. These conventions include, for example, a hard fourth wall between the fictionally represented world and the actual world of author and reader, or an insistence on wholly realistic depictions of characters, setting, and action.

In the late medieval era, without the restrictions of such conventions, the genre of the dream vision especially flourished. With roots that go back to the bible if not before, dream visions typically report a dream of their first-person speaker that, as readers are to understand, has some sort of bearing on reality – as, say, a prophesy or coded revelation of some other kind. By their nature, of course, dreams do not have to represent characters, setting, and action realistically, and they also prompt direct consideration of their own meaning and significance, which makes the genre characteristically self-reflexive. At some point, the presumption that the reported dream was an actual one no longer became necessary but could serve just as a framing device, thereby supplying a robust general literary structure for self-reflexive investigations of one thing or another, investigations which often have uncertain resolutions. By the middle of the thirteenth century, the genre reached a highly sophisticated, densely intellectual, and relentlessly self-conscious apogee in the long allegorical French poem the *Romance of the Rose*. Widely read throughout Europe in the decades and centuries that followed, this poem influenced generations of poets who sought to innovate further upon its themes and formal strategies.

For Chaucer, a group of such *Rose*-innovating poets in fourteenth-century France comprised a kind of literary avant-garde. Probably after he himself had translated all or some portion of the *Romance of the Rose*, he began to compose original dream visions that were deeply indebted to writings by these French poets. With these poems – which include the *Book of the Duchess*, the *House of Fame*, the *Parliament of the Fowls*, and the

Legend of Good Women – he was plainly attempting to create English equivalents to their work. This was quite an unusual project in his day, since, among other reasons, the potential audience for such poetry would already have been reading the French originals. Moreover, by the time he wrote the *House of Fame*, he was also responding to what remains in the history of Western literature the most ambitious dream vision ever written, Dante Alighieri's *Divine Comedy* (which, among its ambitions, claims to be a report of a true journey to hell, purgatory, and heaven and not a dream at all).

To some degree, therefore, Chaucer's dream visions are a densely woven fabric of borrowings from and allusions to these and other literary works, which are themselves already similarly intertextual. The result is the sort of variegated pastiche that is another hallmark of postmodern style, as in, for example, the films of Quentin Tarantino. Yet Chaucer's dream visions (or, for that matter, Tarantino films) are not merely derivative. Chaucer infuses the form with an idiosyncratic combination of playfulness, skepticism, and intellectual reach – a combination I've referred to in this book as laconic profundity – to give his dream visions their own specific flavor.

This chapter will explore this quality in two of Chaucer's dream visions: the *House of Fame* and the *Legend of Good Women* (leaving aside, for reasons of scope rather than any literary priority, the *Book of the Duchess* and *Parliament of the Fowls*). In particular, this chapter will consider how these poems' uncanny anticipations of postmodern style harbor meditations that also anticipate some concerns of the skeptical schools of thought that shaped that style, especially the skepticism directed toward language and literature. As illustrated by Auster's *City of Glass*, postmodern literature often involves a search for meaning that turns back on itself, casting doubt on the traditional notion that literature in its most ambitious forms is a uniquely potent linguistic medium for conveying central, universal truths about human life. Simply put, in postmodernism's blurring of the line between fiction and reality, the effect is often not to raise fiction to the level of truth but to reduce truth to the level of fiction.

This sort of skepticism about ultimate truths has not been the sole preserve of postmodern artists but – as I'm sure you're aware – has affected everyday life in the twenty-first century in countless ways. In contrast, such skepticism might seem unlikely for someone in Chaucer's time and place, given what was then the cultural suffusion of Christian doctrine. Yet there were schools of Christian thinking, such as the nominalism formulated by English friar William of Ockham in the early fourteenth century, that have enough overlap with postmodern skepticism to make Chaucer's apparent postmodernism not merely a superficial coincidence. It was certainly possible for someone like Chaucer to question whether literature and language could reach beyond themselves to truth, if not necessarily then also to doubt the existence of truth. These conceptual likenesses, along with the stylistic similarities, make Chaucer's dream visions readily receptive to inquiry from a postmodern perspective.[1]

This chapter will first supply an overview of one aspect of postmodern skepticism – that leveled toward language – that is part of a body of twentieth-century thought referred to as poststructuralism. The chapter will then consider the searches for meaning and reflections on language and literature encompassed by, in turn, the *House of Fame* and the *Legend of Good Women*. In a final, briefer section, the chapter will take up an ethical matter that crisscrosses both poems' searches for meaning and that to some degree punctures their abstract, skeptical inquiries with questions of justice and real-world authorial accountability. This is the matter of a male author's representation of women or, more generally, patriarchy's construction of the female other, which is, of course, still an urgent concern of our day and, as other chapters in this book attest, a ubiquitous topic of reflection in Chaucer's writing.

The linguistic turn: from structuralism to poststructuralism

During the twentieth century, much thinking in the humanities and social sciences turned its attention to language or, more precisely, to the nature and consequences of the centrality of linguistic mediation in culture, society, human consciousness, and academic scholarship's own methods of acquiring knowledge. One of the foundational prompts for this thinking was the work of Swiss linguist Ferdinand de Saussure. Breaking from what had been the typical view of language as consisting of names for things, Saussure argues that language consists instead of sound images (mental impressions of sounds, or *signifiers*) linked to concepts (mental impressions of things, or *signifieds*). This seemingly straightforward reformulation has the dramatic effect of displacing language from the phenomenal world into the mind, where it functions as a self-contained system. Saussure further argues that signifiers and signifieds have no meaning individually in themselves but gain meaning only in relation to each other and to other signifiers and signifieds. Language in general functions like mathematical symbols, in which the numbers 1, 2, 3, etc. have no meaning in themselves (whether as symbols or as ideas) but only in relation to the whole numerical system of which they are a part. As the existence of other numerical systems, such as Roman numerals, confirms, the choice of symbol is arbitrary and meaningless in itself. Any given digit obtains meaning only because it differs from other digits: "1" means "one-ness" only because it's different from "2." Saussure argues that, similarly, words like "cat" have meaning only because they differ from words like "dog." Rather than supplying a mirror of reality, as earlier linguists posited, language thus consists of a self-contained system of differences that in any of its individual terms is empty.

The intellectual movement prompted by Saussure and other linguists became known as structuralism. For those who subscribed to and developed it, structuralism, while it insisted on the substantial emptiness of language – and hence thought – nonetheless leant itself to a science of forms. As its name suggests, meaning for structuralism resides not in what language was earlier thought to refer to but in how it happens to be organized, in the particular structures of signification that characterize a specific time and place. Structuralists believed that they could identify and trace the operation of these structures of signification in various discursive domains, as in political ideologies, religious practices, or literary texts.

Subsequently, the intellectual movement known as poststructuralism, which emerged in the second half of the twentieth century, subjected this very belief to skeptical inquiry. Scrutinizing structuralism's foundational duality of signifier/signified, poststructuralism noticed that in fact there is no duality: signifieds turn out to be just more signifiers. Dictionary definitions, for example, don't actually provide the concept (or signified) that a word (or signifier) denotes. Rather, the words that comprise any given definition lead you to the words of other definitions in a cascading and ultimately circular series. Behind words are just more words, all of which mean nothing in themselves. What constitutes a concept or signified is thus just signifiers pointing at other signifiers *ad infinitum*. Moreover, these constellations of signifiers are far from stable, knowable assemblages, but rather are constantly shifting and inescapably indeterminate in their full extent. Jacques Derrida, perhaps the best-known poststructuralist philosopher, coined the French word *différance*, which combines "differ" and "defer," to convey how meaning resides not in something substantial or positive but only in the *differences* among signifiers, and also how meaning is infinitely *deferred*, lying at some unreachable destination behind the endless chains of signifiers pointing at each other.

For Derrida, the supposition of what he calls (among other names) the *transcendental signified* enables us to communicate with each other, however imperfectly, despite the inherent instability and indeterminacy of language. The transcendental signified is that which we surmise to lie behind the chains of signifiers. It is that which, we assume, all signifiers collectively ultimately point to and, in that way, gives the whole system of signifiers stability and determinacy, enabling us to understand one another through the otherwise volatile medium of language. This signified is *transcendental* because it must transcend or exist outside of the system of language. If it were within the system, it would merely be part of the system's indefinite series of signifiers and so could not serve its stabilizing function. At the same time, while not part of the system, it is paradoxically the system's most essential component, as it is what enables the system to be a system. It is thus simultaneously absent, as it is by necessity not accessible, and seemingly everywhere present, as it is what the system, which we do access, embodies in its totality. Derrida's famous analytical method of *deconstruction* consists of tracing the ways in which the commitments of a text ultimately depend upon a transcendental signified that the text assumes is everywhere present but which is also, simultaneously and necessarily, absent. As Derrida explains, while the transcendental signified has in practice assumed myriad guises – such as Truth, Love, Happiness, Justice, Nature, or Being – its quintessential formulation in Western history has been God. That formulation, of course, readily lends itself to Chaucer's late medieval English Christian culture. Hence with this version of post-structuralism in mind, we may consider how Chaucer in his dream visions arrives at something like a postmodern vision of literature, language, and, more generally, the human condition.

The *House of Fame*

Sources and summary

Perhaps most extremely among Chaucer's dream visions, the *House of Fame* is a veritable junk heap of literary borrowing and allusion. Among its many intertexts are the aforementioned work of his French contemporaries, the *Romance of the Rose*, highly regarded Latin poems by Roman authors such as Virgil and Ovid, religious visions like the biblical Revelations, and fourteenth-century Italian influences, especially Dante's *Divine Comedy*. The last of these, in fact, serves as a sort of overall structuring interlocutor. Chaucer winkingly conveys to his readers that the three-book division of the *House of Fame* mimics that of the *Divine Comedy* by adapting invocations from the latter at key junctures in his poem's progress, along with including several other unmistakable borrowings. Dante's three-book sequence consists of a descent into hell, an ascent up the mountain of purgatory, and a celestial journey through the concentric spheres of heaven. Chaucer supplies, respectively, a 'descent' into a glass temple dedicated to Venus, an ascent into the skies in the clutches of an Eagle (a figure taken from Dante's *Purgatory*), and a journey though the realm of Fame and Rumor, which he describes as situated "in the middes of the waye [at the midmost point]/Bitwixen hevene, erthe, and see [sea]" (714–15). Although the *House of Fame* has been too much shaped by the influence of other sources and the pursuit of its own agenda to be an outright parody of the *Divine Comedy*, much of its postmodern flavor nonetheless derives from its whimsically skeptical response to the latter's lofty claims to provide access to ultimate spiritual truths.

Book 1 begins with the narrator reflecting on the nature of dreams in general and then launching into a report of a specific dream. At the dream's outset, he finds himself "Within a temple ymaad [made] of glas" (120), which he soon determines is a temple dedicated to Venus. He eventually notices a brass tablet, on which is written the story of the *Aeneid*, the renowned epic poem by Virgil. Supposedly following the text of this brass tablet, he begins a rather rapid summary of the story. But when he reaches the affair between the epic's hero, the Trojan refugee Aeneas, and Dido, the Queen of Carthage, and specifically Aeneas's notorious abandonment of Dido, his summary suddenly slows. He dwells upon this episode, supplying Dido with a lengthy first-person speech. For the latter, Chaucer turns for his literary model from Virgil's epic poem to Ovid's very differently oriented *Heroides* (*The Heroines*), which consists of a series of short verse letters written in the voice of women betrayed by men. Just in case readers miss this move, the narrator advises them to "Rede Virgile in Eneidos [the *Aeneid*],/Or the Epistle [the *Heroides*] of Ovyde" (378–79). He then speeds through the rest of the *Aeneid*, exits the temple, and discovers that he's in the middle of a Libyan desert. He spots a golden eagle in the sky, apparently flying directly toward him.

Following an invocation adapted from the *Divine Comedy*, Book 2 picks up right where Book 1 leaves off. The eagle snatches up the narrator in its talons, complains about how heavy he is, and flies him into the clouds. Eventually, the eagle informs him about the reason for this adventure. The god Jupiter apparently feels sorry for the narrator because, while he spends all his free time reading books and writing love poetry, every night he remains cooped up in his lodgings, hermit-like, after a long day of work, and so he hears no "tidinges/Of Love's folk" (644–45), that is, news about lovers. Jupiter has therefore decided to grant him a journey to "the Hous of Fame" (663), where, the eagle claims, he will encounter all such tidings that there are. The eagle goes on to explain how it is that all tidings end up at Fame's house, supplying a humorously pedantic lecture on the nature of spoken language. During this dialogue, the references to the narrator's poetry writing and his day job making "rekeninges" (653) or calculating accounts have the effect of conflating, Paul Auster-like, the fictional first-person narrator with the historically actual Geoffrey Chaucer (whose day job involved such "rekeninges"). And just in case we miss this, the eagle cements the association by calling the narrator "Geffrey" (729). The eagle next encourages the man we now know to be Geoffrey to look down at the earth, across the sky, and up into the heavens, and they talk about why it is that he doesn't want to hear about the names of the stars. They finally arrive at the House of Fame, greeted by the tremendously loud and confused noise of tidings.

Following another invocation adapted from the *Divine Comedy*, at the beginning of Book 3 Geoffrey discovers that Fame's house sits atop a mountain of ice, which he proceeds to climb. The ice is engraved with "famous folkes names" (1137), which are half-melted away on the sun-facing side, while preserved on the other. At the top, he encounters all around Fame's castle a huge press of entertainers of various kinds – harpers, pipers, storytellers, magicians, etc. Entering through the castle gate, he initially finds himself among throngs of noble petitioners for the favor of the sovereign of the place, Lady Fame. Moving into the less crowded interior hall, he sees Lady Fame herself, "A feminine creature" (1365) who first seems very small and then quite gigantic and who is covered in eyes, ears, and tongues. Her shoulders bear the coats of arms of Alexander the Great and Hercules, and around her are seven pillars of various kinds of metal, atop each of which stand famous authors from centuries past (including Lollius, Chaucer's made-up authority for *Troilus and Criseyde*). At this point, a series of groups of petitioners enter the hall, each of whom asks for some sort of fame (good or bad) or no fame at all and to whom Lady Fame arbitrarily, capriciously, and despotically assigns good or bad fame, or no fame at all, regardless of their requests or what they actually deserve.

Someone then approaches Geoffrey and asks if he's come there to acquire fame, and Geoffrey says no but that he was told, rather, that he would find tidings. The unnamed individual escorts Geoffrey outside and points him toward another building, which is unidentified in the poem but which we might call the House of Tidings. This bizarre structure resembles an unfathomably huge, loosely constructed, rapidly spinning wicker basket, with countless tidings pouring into and issuing out of its many openings. Geoffrey's eagle, having been waiting nearby, transports him to this building. Inside, Geoffrey finds himself immersed in a dense crowd of what seem to be embodied tidings or, perhaps, embodied vehicles of tidings. Speech among these beings spreads exponentially and transforms willy-nilly; Geoffrey describes it as "encresing evermo [always increasing]/As fir is wont to quik and go [As fire typically ignites and spreads]/From a sparke spronge amis [from a stray spark]/Til al a cite brent up is [until the whole city is burned]" (2077–80). He observes how individual tidings fuse together in the process of squeezing through crevices and windows to escape. Such conflated tidings then fly to the House of Fame, where Lady Fame gives them a name and duration and sends them on their way, presumably to earth. Geoffrey eagerly circulates among these beings in the House of Tidings, collecting news, until he hears "a gret noise.../In a corner of the halle,/Ther [Where] men of love tidinges tolde" (2141–43). In a chaotic stampede, the crowd gathers in that corner, and the poem suddenly comes to a halt with the notoriously unrealized anticipatory remark, "At the laste I saw a man,/Which that I niste nat ne can [whom I did not and still do not know],/But [Except] he seemed for to be/A man of gret auctoritee [authority]" (2155–58). Whether Chaucer abandoned the poem at this point, had written more that somehow was lost, or intended this to serve as some sort of inconclusive conclusion remains a matter of likely irresolvable debate.

"Fals and sooth compouned"

As attested in the *Middle English Dictionary*, the word *fame* held a considerably broader set of meanings in Chaucer's day in comparison with ours. It encompassed three basic senses: reputation in general, whether good, bad, or neutral; renown or celebrity; and rumor, report, or news. The word thus denoted linguistically mediated information in general as well as positive, negative, accurate, and inaccurate evaluations of that information and the social and psychological consequences of those evaluations. With this range of meanings in mind, the many ways in which the *House of Fame* anticipates poststructuralism are perhaps already evident from the above summary. Many Chaucer scholars (some recent ones include Kirk 2021 and Cawsey 2020) have noticed that, from the poem's beginning through its uncertain ending, it's plainly concerned with the nature and consequences of linguistic mediation in literature and discourse generally, emphasizing throughout the instability, indeterminacy, and capriciousness of that mediation. I'll highlight just a couple of moments in this regard – one from the beginning of the poem and one in Book 3.

The grandest claim that a dream vision can make is that its fictional contents constitute a sort of code that, when properly deciphered, do not just have bearing on the real world of author and reader but also provide access to some central, defining truth – as exemplified, most grandly, by Dante's *Divine Comedy*. Put in poststructuralist terms, a dream vision with these ambitions understands the signifying chains of its contents to reach beyond their fictional frame and ultimately extend to the transcendental signified that gives all human experience meaning. Against this backdrop, it's quite striking, therefore, that the *House of Fame* begins not, like many other dream visions, with some sort of explicit statement or clear implication of this sort of claim about the status of its dream but instead with a whimsically skeptical reflection upon the types and causes of dreams in general.

Geoffrey expresses the hope in the poem's first line that "God turne us every dreem to goode" (1) – that by God's grace all our dreams will benefit us in some fashion – and then goes on to wonder aloud about the many different names given to dreams: "avisioun," "revelacioun," "dreem," "swevene," "fantome," and "oracles" (7–11). While scholars have dutifully sought to determine what these terms exactly did denote, even without that knowledge it's evident that the sort of dreams that they designate varies in respect to their relation to some kind of truth. Geoffrey initially wonders "why the effect folweth of some/And of some it shal never come" (5–6), that is, why some dreams turn out to have some bearing on the real world and others do not. Remarking that he doesn't know the answer and, in fact, doesn't even want to exert the effort to discover it, he nonetheless continues to muse on the general topic, now specifically on dreams' causes. He considers whether dreams reflect (a) some aspect of an individual's physiological constitution; (b) a mental disturbance provoked by an ascetic lifestyle, confinement, or other physical distress; (c) some unusual change in one's normal habits; (d) too much study, melancholy, or anxiety; (e) intense spiritual or romantic/erotic devotion; (f) a vision granted by a spiritual source; or (g) the power of the soul, as the spiritual element of humanity, to have knowledge of the future. Once again, Geoffrey jovially declares that he doesn't know the answer, he's happy to leave the matter to scholars, and he himself has "noon [no] opinioun" (55). He simply hopes, as he first mentioned, that God will make our dreams turn out well.

The effect of this rapid-fire foray into medieval dream theory is one of literary and philosophical disorientation, however light-heartedly expressed. Instead of beginning with a declaration of its truth value, this dream vision begins by destabilizing the general concept of dreams' truth value. With its blizzard of dream types and causes, and its refusal to sort through them, it suggests that certainty about the nature of dreams lies out of human reach. In particular, it implies the impossibility of determining whether a dream's signifying chains ultimately lead to some wholly mundane truth about the body, such as the fact that the dreamer had too much to eat the night before, or to some divinely granted spiritual truth. "My dream," Geoffrey in effect remarks, "either came from God or from spoiled leftovers. Who knows?" He declares that he's unconcerned about this uncertainty, and yet it's not difficult to see that it may have enormous consequences. Obviously, if we believe a dream signifies a spiritual truth when it actually signifies a mundane, corporeal one, or vice versa, the real-word actions we accordingly pursue, or the lack thereof, may be gravely mistaken.

Of course, in Chaucer's day as in our own, most people most of the time just ignored their dreams with few if any consequences. The skeptical inquiry of the poem's opening is thus best understood as directed not toward actual dreams but back at itself, which is to say toward the literary representation of dreams or the genre of the dream vision and in that way toward the truth claims of literature in general. To what sort of truths may the signifying chains of a literary work – in this instance, a work that pretends to be a dream – demonstrably provide access? Are those truths merely mundane, so that, for example, the ultimate meaning of humorous works of literature, such as the *House of Fame*, is just the corporeal experience of pleasure? (Centuries of moralistic condemnation of literature, theater, cinema, comic books, etc. have argued exactly this, of course.) Or do those truths include universal or sacred ones about the human condition? (Centuries of anxious defenses of art forms that also happen to give pleasure have argued exactly this.) For anyone who writes or reads literature – or appreciates any sort of entertainment that makes claims to being an art form – the stakes of this question are high.

To answer the question convincingly, we would need a way of demonstrably and unequivocally tracing the path of a literary work's signifying chains to their ultimate defining signifieds. But the *House of Fame* goes on to illustrate many of the reasons why this project is doomed to fail, at least for anyone who doesn't simply assume that the ultimate truth of a literary work is just there for the taking. In portions of Book 2 and especially Book 3, the poem zeroes in on problems with literature's basic linguistic medium. In the House of Tidings, for example, the narrator observes what might be characterized as the intractable equivocality accompanying the very birth of linguistic mediation. The form of the embodied verbal beings in the House of Tidings serves as a kind of icon of structuralism's supposedly stable signifier/signified duality: the bodies of the beings function as the carriers or signifiers of their associated information or tiding. But with the hypersociality of these beings – a social network run amok, to use a modern analogy – their originally stable signification of information irreversibly devolves into a diffusion of meaning that rapidly multiplies and mutates from being to being, that is, across chains of signifiers. There is no possibility of following these chains backward to the original spark that began this conflagration (to use Chaucer's metaphor), even though that's precisely what we think we're doing when we assign definite meaning to literature.

Shortly after this, the narrator supplies a close-up view of the inevitable indeterminacy of signification:

And somtime saw I tho at ones*	at the same time
A lesing* and a sad sooth sawe*	lie, falsehood; serious, true tiding
That gonne of aventure drawe*	arrived by chance
Out at a windowe for to pace;*	pass
And, whan they metten* in that place,	met
They were acheked bothe two,*	blocked each other's exit
And neither of hem mote* out go	them may
For* other, so they gonne croude*	Because of the; crowded each other
Til ech of hem gan crien loude,*	loudly
"Lat me go first!"—"Nay, but lat me!	
And here I wol ensuren* thee,	promise

With the nones* that thou wolt do so,	On the condition
That I shal never fro thee go,	
But be thyn owne sworen brother!	
We wil medle us ech with other,*	mix ourselves together
That no man, be he never so wrothe*	however irate he becomes
Shal han that oon of two,* but bothe	have just one of us
At ones,* al biside his leve,*	once; regardless of his wishes
Come we amorwe* or on eve,	in the morning
Be we cried* or stille yrouned."*	shouted; quietly whispered
Thus saw I fals and sooth compouned*	blended
Togidre flee for oo* tidinge.	fly as one
(2088–2109)	

Reaching a window in the House of Tidings at the same moment, a signifier pointing at a truth and a signifier pointing at a falsehood (or fiction) jostle each other and then gleefully decide to merge. Hence, from the very initiation of language mediation, truth and fiction here, as in postmodernism, are "compouned." What's more, we know that this blended tiding's next stop is the court of Lady Fame, where it will receive, regardless of the nature of the information it bears, an arbitrary judgment of good or bad, making the social implications of the information just as unreliably connected to truth as its meaning.

What the *House of Fame* tells us, therefore, is that human knowledge and judgment, insofar as they're linguistically mediated, are intractably indeterminate and ungrounded. Oddly, to the extent that this skeptical conclusion itself stands as a universal truth of the human condition, the poem winds up realizing the very ambition of disclosing such truths that it would seem to disavow. And yet this truth – the truth of the impossibility to be sure of truth – is obviously a paradoxically self-cancelling one, pulling the rug out from under its own self-assurance. In this regard, the poem's opening appeal to God, for a late medieval English Christian like Chaucer, serves as the necessary recourse to a transcendental signified that is nowhere in language but which ensures that language – dreams and literature – may "turne…to goode." Neatly bookended with that first line, then, is the poem's terminating anticipation of meeting a man of great authority who doesn't quite make it into the poem. Nothing could better convey the paradoxically absent/present status of the transcendental signified that lies at the end of all signifying chains. This authoritative man seems destined to disclose the ultimate truth toward which the whole poem is leading, and yet he remains forever absent from the poem, leaving its signifying chains extending outward indefinitely – or at least in our hands.

The *Legend of Good Women*

Overview

Taking up the mystery of this man of great authority, some scholars have speculated that Chaucer had originally intended the *House of Fame* to serve as the prologue to a linked collection of narratives, with the initial story told by that authoritative man and subsequent ones told by various other embodied tidings. I find this surmise unlikely, as the 2,158 extant lines of the poem strike me as inevitably headed toward inconclusiveness and because such a bizarre poem of this length would be massively disproportionate to the relatively straightforward function of an introduction. Admittedly, however, Chaucer was clearly drawn to the creative possibilities afforded by framed collections of narratives, and he also had of a habit of leaving projects unfinished. Following his work on the philosophical romance *Troilus and Criseyde*, he began and left incomplete two such collections: the *Canterbury Tales*, of course, and few years before that, the *Legend of Good Women*.

In the Man of Law's comments about Chaucer and his writings in the preamble to his contribution to the *Canterbury Tales*, he says that "Chaucer, though he can but lewedly/On [is largely ignorant about]/metres and on riming craftily," has nonetheless "told of loveres up and doun/Mo [more] than Ovide made of mencioun/In his Episteles [the *Heroides*]" (2.47–48, 53–55). The Man of Law goes on to cite Chaucer's "large volume" called "the Saintes Legende of Cupide" (i.e., "the Legends of Cupid's Saints") and lists its contents: a series of stories about women from Greek and Roman antiquity who are famous for, among other things, having been abused by men. This "large volume" is certainly Chaucer's *Legend of Good Women*, and, as the Man of Law's remarks suggest, Chaucer's basic literary model for this work is Ovid's *Heroides*. Although Chaucer does not use Ovid's device of conveying the women's stories in the form of letters from them to their abusers, each of his narratives centers on a specific abused woman and most allocate some space to her first-person speech. The form that Chaucer does follow is denoted by the term "Legende," which in Chaucer's day meant "saint's life," a biography of one of those individuals officially canonized by the Church as a saint. Such legends were ubiquitous in the Middle Ages, widely available in Latin and the European vernaculars, and read in formal religious contexts as well as informal didactic and recreational ones. Most basically, a legend depicts a saint's exemplary religious devotion, one or more of the saint's miracles, and the saint's suffering and martyrdom. As the Man of Law's title for the "large volume" indicates, for this book's legends, Chaucer substitutes "Cupide" – which is to say, Eros or romantic/erotic love – for God, so that each story depicts a woman's exemplary devotion to and eventual martyrdom for love.

It's impossible to know for certain how far Chaucer got in this project. Medieval manuscripts preserve complete stories for nine women (two combined into a single legend) and most of the story of a tenth. The Man of Law's list includes more stories and yet also fails to mention a couple that do exist. The leave-taking or Retraction to the *Canterbury Tales*, which supplies a retrospect of Chaucer's poetic career, ascribes as many as "five and twenty Ladies" to the *Legend*. Some completed stories may have gotten lost somewhere in the post-mortem transmission of Chaucer's writings, or his ambitions for the project may have been overmatched by the pull of his attention elsewhere (such as to the *Canterbury Tales*) or just by the vicissitudes of life. He clearly devoted substantial effort to the project, drawing on and selectively reshaping an array of learned sources for the legends that survive. Most notably, he completed a complex, poetically lush 579-line prologue, which makes use of the dream vision form to describe the (supposed) circumstances that led to the initiation of the work and to explain the (supposed) rationale behind the generic and topical consistency of the ensuing narratives. He was invested enough in the project to return to this prologue some years later, after he had begun working on the *Canterbury Tales*, to revise it in some significant ways, although leaving in place its substance. (This chapter will keep to what most scholars believe to be the first version, labeled "F" after the manuscript in which appears; what's likely the later and slightly shorter version carries the label "G.")

My above parenthetical qualifications of "supposed" are necessary because, as we'll shortly explore, the dream vision of the prologue is, of course, a fiction and Chaucer's representation of the circumstances and rationale of the project includes some level of irony – although precisely how much and what sort of irony are notoriously ambiguous and thus have been not surprisingly hotly contested by scholars. As this chapter focuses on Chaucer's experiments with the genre of dream vision, the summary and discussion that follow are limited to the *Legend*'s prologue. I do not mean this choice to imply negative judgment about the literary quality of the legends, which over the centuries have received wildly varying levels of appreciation. It merely recognizes that the legends demand consideration with respect to a quite different generic framework, which is beyond the scope of this chapter. If you haven't already done so, I encourage you to read through the legends and form your own opinion.

Sources and summary

Like the *House of Fame*, the Prologue of the *Legend of Good Women* does not possess a single primary source, as does, for example, *Troilus and Criseyde*. Neither does it possess the sort of overall structuring interlocutor such as the *House of Fame* has with Dante's *Divine Comedy*. For this and that passage, Chaucer adapts material from those avant-garde, *Rose*-influenced French poets who were so much of a catalyst for his dream visions generally. Accordingly, the style and tone reflect this influence as well as that of the *Romance of the Rose* directly. But as scholar Michelle Ripplinger (2023) has explored, Chaucer's basic inspiration for the prologue's general idea, if not so much specific details, may have been the medieval tradition of understanding Ovid's *Heroides* as a palinode. This is a work of literature in which an author expresses some sort of regret about an earlier composition and a desire to atone for whatever it is the author regrets. The biography of Ovid as medieval scholars constructed it characterized the *Heroides* as Ovid's recompense for the offense he gave to women in his earlier *Ars amatoria* (*The Art of Love*). While the situation that the *Legend*'s prologue describes (or invents) is original to Chaucer, it likewise represents the ensuing *Heroides*-like legends as recompense for a similar offense.

The prologue begins with its narrator musing on the inescapable mediation of essential knowledge by books and hence his dedication to them, except when it's spring and nice outside: then he proclaims, "Farwel my book and my devocioun!" (39). He proceeds to devote many lines to explaining – in a sometimes-lofty style that draws upon courtly love conventions – how much affection he has for daisies, so much so that he regularly rises before dawn to witness them opening to the sun and then returns in the evening to see them close. He recounts that he spent the entire day in a meadow lounging next to the flower, returning home only after "this flour gan close and goon to reste [closed and went to rest]" (198). He determines to sleep in his garden, has his bed made there, and falls asleep "within an houre or two" (209).

His dream begins by seeming to return him to the very spot next to the daisy where he spent his day, only now he sees approaching "The god of Love [i.e., Cupid] and in his hand [i.e., on his arm] a queene" (213). This queen's appearance resembles a lavishly ornate daisy in the form of a woman. The god of Love is not the frequently depicted mischievous child but rather a stern, spectacularly garbed adult king. Indeed, some of the details of his description associate the god with Chaucer's real-world king, Richard II, while some of the details of the queen's description associate her with Richard's real-world queen, Anne of Bohemia. These connections have led some scholars to believe that the prologue recounts an actual interaction between Chaucer and Richard and Anne, only slightly disguised as a dream. Others suppose that the characters do represent Richard and Anne but the interaction is invented by Chaucer in order to express something to them and their court. While the prologue does have political content that makes plausible some sort of real-world parallel, it's perhaps soundest, given Chaucer's habitual slipperiness, to consider that parallel to have the same vagueness as the movie tagline of "inspired by true events." The characters are carefully drawn fictions that exceed pure invention to some indeterminate degree that Chaucer's contemporaries would likely have noticed.

The narrator remarks upon the approaching god of Love with some foreboding: "al be that [although] men sayn that blind is he,/Algate [Nonethless] me thoughte that he mighte see,/For sternely on me he gan biholde/So that his looking doth myn herte colde [made my heart grow cold]" (237–40). The narrator then launches into a spontaneous hymn in praise of the queen's beauty. He observes nineteen royally dressed women following the couple and, behind them, twenty-thousand (as we later learn) additional women, all of whom, he somehow knows, were "trewe of love" (290). When the group spots the daisy, they halt, and after kneeling by and hailing the flower, they sit in a circle around it. Eventually, the god of Love directs his gaze toward the narrator and demands, "Who kneeleth ther?" (312). When the narrator approaches, the god ratchets up his ire, asking him what he thinks he's doing here so near to his flower and declaring, "It were better worthy [would be better], trewely,/A worm to neighen neer [approach] my flour than thou" (316–18).

The god of Love goes on to explain the offense that he finds in the narrator. The specificity of his charge, like the *House of Fame*'s depiction of "Geffrey," serves as a Paul Auster-like moment, in which real-world author and fictional narrator blend to some indeterminate degree. The god declares that the narrator's translation of the *Romance of the Rose* and his composition of *Troilus and Criseyde* – which is to say, prior works of Chaucer's – have done damage to women and to love. The god concludes, "If that thou live, thou shalt repenten this/So cruelly" (339–40). At this point, the queen intercedes. She tells the god of Love that he shouldn't simply assume the narrator is culpable for his crimes, or at least wholly culpable, and that some of his compositions have furthered love (naming, oddly enough, the *House of Fame*, among others of Chaucer's writings). Interspersed amid these efforts on behalf of the narrator, the queen also supplies general political advice of benefit to any ruler. That some of this advice does not seem especially well suited to Cupid nudges readers to look beyond the boundaries of the fiction, without actually crossing the line, especially since the queen identifies herself in this passage as the legendary Alceste, famous for offering to die in place of her husband.

The queen concludes by suggesting the sort of project that the narrator might pursue in recompense, and the god of Love agrees to put the matter in her hands. The narrator then approaches the queen and attempts to defend himself against the god's accusations. The queen tells him, in effect, to shut up, and she specifies in detail the "penance" that he must perform for his "trespass" (479–80):

Thou shalt whil that thou livest, yeer by yere,
The moste partye* of thy time spende — greater portion
In making of a glorious legende
Of goode wommen, maidenes and wives,
That weren trewe in loving al hir lives,
And telle of false men that hem bitrayen* — betray them
That al hir lif* ne doon nat but assayen* — their whole lives; do nothing but attempt to see
How many wommen they may doon a shame,* — abuse
For in youre world that is now holde a game.* — sport
(481–89)

Giving this project its title ("legend/Of goode women"), she commands him, when he has finally completed it, to "yive it [give it to] the queene/On my behalf, at Eltham, or at Shene" – that is, to the real-world Queen Anne, at the royal residence at Eltham or Sheen. (In the later version of the prologue, Chaucer took out these lines, probably because Anne had died and in his grief Richard had the palace at Sheen destroyed.) The prologue concludes with an exchange between the narrator and the god of Love, in which they praise Alceste's virtues and remark upon her association with the daisy. The god of Love points to the gathered women as those whose stories the narrator must tell and commands him to begin with Cleopatra, Queen of Egypt.

The mediation of truth

While the *House of Fame* is more obviously a meditation on the instability of language per se than the Prologue of the *Legend of Good Women*, the latter nonetheless plainly supplies a pervasively self-reflexive consideration of the meaning and truth value of literature. As with the former poem, we'll examine in this regard the prologue's beginning and a moment near its end.

Knowing how the prologue concludes, in retrospect we might find its opening reflection curiously tangential to its later concerns, as the initial lines do not mention love, the abuse of women, or Chaucer's prior literary efforts. Rather, they raise the question of how anyone knows about the existence of heaven and hell:

A thousand times have I herd men telle
That ther is joye in hevene, and paine in helle,
And I accorde* wel that it is so; — agree
But natheles,* yet woot* I wel also — nevertheless; know
That ther nis noon* dwelling in this contree* — is no one; realm

That either hath in hevene or helle ybe,*	been
Ne may of it noon other wayes witen,*	may know about them in any other way
But* as he hath herd said, or founde it writen,	Except
For by assay* ther may no man it preve.*	direct experience; i.e., is able to demonstrate their truth
But God forbede but men sholde leve*	forbid that men should believe
Wel more thing* than men han seen with eye!	Anything more
Men shal nat wenen* everything a lie	suppose
But if* himself it seeth or elles dooth;*	Except when; sees or does it
For, God woot,* thing is never the lasse sooth,*	knows; something is no less true
Though every wight* ne may it nat ysee.*	person; does not see it

(1–15)

Heaven and hell, of course, were the bookends of medieval Christian cosmology, and certainty in their reality remains fundamental within most Christian communities today. That certainty could not then and in most instances cannot now be eroded without undercutting the whole system of Christian belief and practice, a system which, in Chaucer's place and time, also undergirded society and culture generally. Yet the foundation of this certainty, as the narrator points out, rests wholly upon mediation by human language or, as he later more specifically observes, upon "bookes" (17). We therefore owe to books, the narrator suggests, our understandings of the most essential truths that shape lived human experience. Although the narrator here is ostensibly promoting books *alongside* direct human experience as sources of knowledge, his opening consideration of the reality of heaven and hell betrays his actual prioritization of books *over* experience. His subsequent apparent rejection of books in favor of the direct experience of a springtime meadow actually doubles down on this prioritization, as this section of the prologue, more so than any other, is a tissue of borrowings from other poets and poetic convention generally. As the well-read members of Chaucer's contemporary audience would've readily recognized, the narrator's turn to experience is in fact a deeper immersion in books (Sanok 2001, 33).

While books are still ubiquitous sources of knowledge in our day, they're obviously not as singularly important as they were in Chaucer's bible-centered culture. Nonetheless, it's easy to appreciate how much – and perhaps most – of our foundational grasp of human experience depends upon some form of linguistic mediation. For example, we come by those scientific truths about our bodies and the material world, truths that shape our self-knowledge and determine our actions, most often through some sort of mediation: textbooks, classroom instruction, internet articles, social media postings, etc. We typically have little awareness of this mediation because the certainty of the knowledge seems universally held. When everyone agrees with the meaning and value of linguistically mediated information, its mediation tends to be invisible. In contrast, when there is disagreement (as there has been with gender identity, climate change, and vaccines, for example), mediation may become not just starkly visible but also a site of great conflict. "Where did you learn that from" becomes not just an important question but also, sometimes, an accusation.

Chaucer, with his characteristic laconic profundity, opens the prologue by light-heartedly foregrounding the inescapable necessity of textual mediation in respect to a centrally structuring belief that he could assume his readers were *not* in the habit of questioning. In the rest of the prologue, then, he underscores just how fragile a foundation such textual mediation is, since it turns out to be precisely readers' misunderstanding of his own "bookes" that gets him in trouble. What the remainder of the prologue explores, that is, are the implications of the fact that the meanings of texts – and hence the knowledge that shapes human experience – exist only by way of interpretation, and the business of interpretation is often messy and vexed.

Authorship and the politics of truth

One of the traditional ways of attempting to determine the correct interpretation of a text is to ascertain the meaning that its author intended. This is the method, for example, that some legal scholars and US Supreme Court justices insist upon for the interpreting the meaning of the US Constitution. Among the many complications of this approach, the most obvious is that authors usually aren't available at the moment of our interpretations to resolve any uncertainties about their intentions. Rather archly, therefore, Chaucer dramatizes an act of interpretation that occurs when an author *is* so available, when that author is literally standing directly before his interpreters. And the basic implication of this dramatization is evident: an author's intentions, even when they seem readily obtainable, don't in fact matter in determining a text's meaning. But what then does matter?[2]

The narrator's translation of the *Romance of the Rose*, the god of Love states, "is an heresye agains my lawe/And makest wise folk from me withdrawe./And of Criseyde," he continues, "thou has said as thee liste [whatever you wanted]/That maketh men to women lasse triste [men trust women less]/That been as trewe as ever was any steel" (330–34). The god is upset because, he insists, the narrator's writings have led to his losing control over "wise folk" and the men who before had trusted women in amorous relationships. What matters here is not whatever meaning an author intended but the effect a text has on its readers. Or, more precisely, what matters is the effect a figure of authority and power declares a text has had on readers over whom that figure claims jurisdiction. For such a figure – a type whom scholar Serena Howe-Warnky (2021) labels an "ideological reader" – the meaning of a text resides in its perceived sociopolitical impact, and that meaning is to be judged by whoever is in charge. This view on interpretation should be familiar to us, as it remains the basis of, say, the removal from school libraries of books that those who hold political sway deem ideologically objectionable. Or, more positively and to include myself in a group of those in charge, it's also more or less the rationale behind literature professors' development of a curriculum that emphasizes social justice. In both cases, authors' intentions are largely irrelevant: what matters most are texts' social and political effects.

When the queen intercedes, she brings intention back into the picture, but only in a highly attenuated fashion. For the queen, intention relates not so much to meaning as to the simple act of creation. The narrator, the queen suggests, either did not or did not want to translate the *Romance of the Rose* or compose *Troilus of Criseyde*, or, at worst, he didn't understand what he was doing or already recognizes his misdeed. To his credit, the queen then adds, the narrator has written other works that have had the sort of effects of which she and the god of Love approve. She therefore believes that the narrator may not be culpable for the sociopolitical effects of these two texts, although the implication remains that those sociopolitical effects are what matter most. The blame for those effects just lies elsewhere.

Of course, we can be sure that contrary to the queen's suppositions, Chaucer in fact willingly and knowingly created these texts. We understand that her defense of the narrator carries an irony of which she's not aware, and this irony turns our attention back toward the question of what matters in interpretation. If the queen is wrong, and we know with certainty that she is, does that then make Chaucer culpable for the sociopolitical effects of his texts, regardless of his intent? When the narrator is given an opportunity to speak for himself, he appears to answer, no, intent *is* what matters. He asserts that he "Nought have agilt [is not guilty] ne doon to love trespass [nor have trespassed against love]" (463) because "a trewe lovere ought me nat to blame [should not blame me]/Though that I speke a fals lover som shame" (466–67). He continues,

Algates,* God woot,* it was myn entente	In any event; knows
To forthren* trouthe in love and it cherice,*	further, advance; cherish
And to be war fro* falsnesse and fro vice	to warn others away from
By swich ensample;* this was my meninge.*	such examples of falseness; meaning

(471–74)

His intended aim, he clarifies, was to encourage fidelity in love by depicting – for readers who strive for such "trouthe," whether for themselves or their partners – how lovers can be unfaithful. Therefore, assuming that the god of Love supports fidelity, he, like all true lovers, shouldn't condemn the narrator for what he has written, regardless of whatever might have been the texts' actual sociopolitical effects.

This self-defense, although perhaps not utterly factually wrong like the queen's advocacy, is nonetheless just as self-evidently ironic. Even on its own terms, it leaves plenty of room for doubt. Are stories about infidelity and "vice" actually an effective means for encouraging fidelity? Such stories are as ubiquitous today, of course, as they were in Chaucer's time (as in, for example, the famous story of Guinevere and Lancelot). Surely, they weren't any more impactful in this respect then than they are now. Moreover, why shouldn't someone faithful in and deeply devoted to love object to literary representations of infidelity, since that someone might reasonably suppose that such representations cast a poor light on love relationships generally – precisely as the god of Love charges? In other words, inasmuch as the narrator's intended meaning also involves an intended effect (to bolster love by encouraging fidelity), the god of Love's condemnation of the narrator's writings on the basis of what he believes to be their actual effects would seem to hold.

We may safely assume that these fallacies would not have been lost on Chaucer. More importantly, we may be just as certain that Chaucer can't possibly have understood the meaning of these particular works to be encompassed by the simple, straightforward aim the narrator supplies. Obviously, Chaucer was acutely aware that the respective meanings of the generically complex, thematically ambitious, and literarily erudite *Romance of the Rose* and *Troilus and Criseyde* cannot be reduced to the function of warning lovers about "falsnesse" and "vice." That Chaucer puts into his own mouth such a gross oversimplification of these works (which, if voiced by someone else, he may well have found insulting) is a classic instance of his puckish irony. In effect, Chaucer in this way acknowledges that his narrator's self-defense offers no real challenge to the god of Love's accusations and that to the contrary of what the narrator states, the authorially intended meaning of works such as the *Romance of the Rose* and *Troilus and Criseyde*, if it's even recoverable, cannot be reduced to such soundbites.

Across history, I would guess that most authors of sophisticated imaginative literature would similarly insist that the meaning of their writings does not lend itself to simple paraphrase. Indeed, their resistance in this regard is an expression of their very claim to sophistication, which is to say, to literature as an art form. A rather grand argument for the value of literary *autonomy* – the independence of an author's artistic vision from any prescribed ideological function – thus potentially emerges by way of the ironic undercutting of the narrator's feeble self-defense. This argument does not quite amount to the view of art-for-art's sake, which is a product of the modern era, but it does seem to trend in that direction. Then and now, however, this sort of argument, as appealing as it may be to authors, only exacerbates the problem of interpretation. It produces the paradox of insisting on the priority of what an author means over how readers respond, even while it moves out of reach certain recovery of what an author means.

Not surprisingly, therefore, the queen – whether or not she perceives the narrator's irony – has zero patience for the narrator's reasoning. She tersely dismisses his entire speech with the command "Lat be thyn arguinge," and, rather imperiously, she continues, "For Love ne wol nat countrepleted be [be contradicted]/In right ne wrong, and lerne that of me!/Thou hast thy grace, and hold thee right therto [hang onto it]" (475–78). It doesn't matter whether the god of Love's interpretation of the two works is correct or incorrect ("right ne wrong"). The view that the god and queen share – that the perceived sociopolitical effects of literature are what matters – remains unchanged. Since in this view it's the god's authority and power that are ultimately at stake, his judgment of those effects necessarily holds sway. In fact, the narrator has dug himself into a deeper hole by admitting, contrary to the queen's suppositions, that he knowingly, willingly, and unapologetically wrote the two works. In effect, she's warning him to keep quiet lest he lose the "grace" or diminishment of the god's ire that she has secured for him.

The "penance" (495) of literary labor that the queen then commands him to perform involves the composition of stories that all have the same basic form and meaning, which she has presumably prescribed on the basis of their likely sociopolitical effects. In response to his plea to value *his* intent (both the superficial one and its ironic undercarriage), she assigns him the task of realizing in literature *her* intent. Notably, this task largely consists of providing, in comparison with *Troilus and Criseyde*, enormously simplified stories of erotic betrayal, with the sexes of betrayer and betrayed swapped. As such, the project actually seems to match the oversimplified intentions explicitly voiced in the narrator's self-defense and might even cause some "wise folk" – in this instance, real women made wary by the repeated stories of male abuse – to "withdrawe" from the pursuit of love, just as the god of Love fears about the other writings. Once again, then, we are confronted by an irony: that of the queen prescribing as "penance" very much something like the sort of literary objectives that she has just refused to acknowledge. And, once again, we may fairly suppose that this irony is Chaucer's way of highlighting the inadequacy of such a narrow conception of literary meaning and function.

The scholar Lynn Arner (2013), understanding the implications of Chaucer's irony in this fashion and likewise detecting in it an advocacy for literary autonomy, sees this strategy as itself political. She argues that it enables Chaucer to evade ethical responsibility for the ideological baggage necessarily carried by his writings, which in practice served to perpetuate the ideology of the wealthy, powerful men who ruled England in his day. And surely Arner is correct to be suspicious of claims that envision literature as somehow wholly insulated from the ideologies that it necessarily absorbs and reproduces. Yet to understand the *Legend of Good Women* as straightforwardly devoted to such a claim requires us to see it as staging, from beginning to end, a principled rejection of the very project that on the surface it seems to be pursuing – to be saying to us, in effect, "what I'm doing is not worth doing." Many other scholars have shared this general view if not Arner's associated political argument, seeing the *Legend*'s stories, for example, as a parody of bad literature. Still others have pointed out that Chaucer's manifest dedication to the work – evident in its sheer length and his determination to revise the prologue – is difficult to reconcile with a basic purpose of self-devaluation. If that were the purpose, it would seem that Chaucer would have stopped saying "what I'm doing is not worth doing" sooner rather than later.

Perhaps, therefore, the ironies of the prologue do not constitute an evasion of responsibility for ideological baggage but instead call attention to the inevitability of that baggage and highlight how literature will be held accountable for its sociopolitical effects regardless of what other values it may possess. If the *House of Fame* teaches us that the meaning of a text ultimately lies within a transcendental signified that the text does not ever quite reach, the Prologue of the *Legend of Good Women* suggests that in practice some real-world man of great authority will occupy the position of that transcendental signified. The prologue in fact depicts a sort of competition between two such men: the god of Love or, more generally, the judgment of those in charge, and the author. Or, more precisely, the competition is among the god, the queen, and the author, with the queen representing both those in charge and those readers adversely affected by the misogynistic strains of the ruling ideology. The ironies of the prologue suggest that while the god of Love and/or the queen may seem to win, the competition actually continues. Chaucer quite literally has the final word, albeit that word might be one that the queen demanded he write.

More generally, in the context of the prologue's opening meditation on heaven and hell, these ironies suggest the consequences of human knowledge being immersed in, and human experience being shaped by, linguistic mediation. They imply that ongoing, sometimes volatile, unpredictable competitions for interpretive hegemony, as illustrated by the competition among god-queen-Chaucer, are what in any time and place constitute the meaning of those texts by which we know ourselves and our world. They suggest that what we take to be truth – whether the truth of *Troilus and Criseyde* or of heaven and hell – is always in some way political, always subject to the interpretive determinations of some god of Love. Yet it's also never *only* political, since that god of Love is merely just one among other competitors for the necessarily empty chair of the actual man of great authority.

Defamed women

In Book 1 of the *House of Fame*, near the end of her first-person speech, Dido decries,

O, wailaway* that I was born!	alas
For thurgh you is my name lorn*	name, i.e., reputation, lost
And alle mine actes* red and songe*	actions; told and sung
Over al this lond, on every tonge.*	tongue
O wikke* Fame, for ther nis*	wicked; is
Nothing so swifte, lo, as she is!	
O, sooth is* everything is wist*	i.e., the fact is that; known
Though it be kevered* with the mist.	covered over
Eek,* though I mighte duren ever,*	Also; live forever
That I have doon,* recovere I never*	done; i.e., I will never recover, i.e., contain the news
That I ne shal be said,* allas,	i.e., That it will always be said that I was
Yshamed be thurgh Eneas.* (345–56)	disgraced by Aeneas

The immediate target of Dido's reproach here is "Eneas," who, as Virgil depicts in the *Aeneid*, has abandoned their relationship in order to realize his epic destiny of founding what would become the Roman Empire. But in this passage, her sorrow specifically concerns how everywhere and down through history she will be known for this abandonment and their preceding sexual relationship. Her target therefore widens to encompass Fame itself, the personification of the linguistic mediation of information, whom she charges with causing all her "actes" to be "red and songe/Over al this lond, on every tonge."

In the passage's larger context, moreover – in which Chaucer is ostentatiously pirouetting between the famous accounts of Dido by Virgil and Ovid – there are plainly additional targets. Virgil and Ovid, as we later encounter in the poem's third book, are two of the most privileged poets in

Fame's court. Hence they, along with a host of lesser authors, are the very agents of linguistic mediation most culpable for representing Dido in this fashion. By the same token, with the very poem that we are reading, "Geffrey" himself joins this crowd, since, however ironic, self-reflexive, and sympathetic to Dido his adaptation of Virgil and Ovid may be, it nonetheless perpetuates her "fame" for the same reasons. Thus, when Dido says "thurgh you is my name lorn," some part of the "you" whom she is blaming is the very poet who is ventriloquizing her voice, which is to say, Chaucer here points an accusatory finger back at himself.

As the Prologue of the *Legend of Good Women* teaches us, all linguistically mediated truth is to some degree political, since the stabilization of linguistic meaning involves judgments by those who hold power. In patriarchal cultures, this typically entails that the linguistic representations of women that are granted most authority are those that perpetuate patriarchy. As countless feminist scholars have demonstrated, patriarchal control of the discourse of what women are, what they should strive to be, and to what they are susceptible has ensured the reproduction of male dominance, and in no small part by women understanding themselves in terms of this discourse. Among the most prominent vehicles of this discourse have been works of imaginative literature, as we tend to consume their compelling stories and vivid characterizations without noticing the ideological ingredients we are thereby ingesting.

In this regard, what the *House of Fame* calls attention to is the fact that men of great authority – those who occupy the position of transcendental signified and so stabilize the truth of texts – have indeed usually been *men*. And when the Prologue of the *Legend of Good Women* imagines that position as occupied by Queen Alceste, it suggests that even a woman of great authority, within a patriarchal culture, cannot escape the patriarchal representations of the female sex that have shaped her own self-understanding. For what the queen prescribes is a series of stories that feature women very much akin to the *House of Fame*'s Dido: stories of women famous or infamous for being the sexualized victims of men's abuse. These representations of women, like that of Dido (who in fact makes a repeat appearance in the *Legend*), have been fashioned for suitability to the gaze of a male reader, one who condemns the abuser even while appreciating the beauty and pathos of the suffering, sexually objectified victim (Desmond 1994, 150).

In this respect, the prologue's ironies function like Dido's complaint about "wikke Fame." By calling attention to the limitations of the project that the queen assigns even while embarking upon it, these ironies point an accusing finger back at Chaucer as an agent of the patriarchal representation of women. In this way, Chaucer registers his entrapment within the discursive confines of the patriarchal literary tradition. As scholar Irina Dumitrescu has incisively explained,

> When the narrator fulfills his task of describing the suffering women of the *Legend*, he becomes author of their woes and complicit in the aestheticization of female pain. Worse, because pity so often occasions desire in the *Legend*, by depicting women's sorrows he makes them into objects of predatory lust...The more adroitly the narrator carries out his assignment, the more he resembles the men who victimize the *Legend*'s heroines.
>
> (2017, 109)

Dumitrescu goes on to consider that the "narrator may have no way out of his dilemma. Writing of unfaithful women such as Criseyde leads to his condemnation; writing of good ones implicates him in their abuse" (2017, 121). In short, the discursive resources of Chaucer's patriarchal culture provided no readily available alternative to those female representations, whether good or bad, that perpetuate patriarchy. Today, we obviously have a much broader repertoire of female representations available for literary and other use. Yet a quick survey of the most prominent of such representations – whether in books, film, television, comics, video games, etc. – will disclose that our progress in this regard has not been as great as the elapsed time of six centuries might lead us to expect.

It would certainly be anachronistic – and, most likely, to give Chaucer too much credit – to understand his recognition of his entrapment within patriarchal discourse as motivated by what we would now call feminism. More confidently, we may suppose that the problem of female representation served for him as a convenient site for exploring more general problems of literary representation and, even more broadly, the consequences of linguistic mediation for human life. With his keen eye for the obsessions and limitations of the literary traditions that he inherited, the problem of female representation would have readily materialized as a concern that would give his writings focus and interest even while allowing him to explore a range of other issues. Not surprisingly, therefore, as other chapters of this book attest, he repeatedly returned to this problem across his entire career, including in his two works of greatest ambition. The problem lies, as the Prologue of the *Legend of Good Women* acknowledges, at the center of *Troilus and Criseyde*, and it haunts most corners of the *Canterbury Tales*, reaching a sort of culmination, as Chapter 4 discusses, with the Wife of Bath's query, "Who paintede the leaoun?"

That the proto-postmodernism of the *House of Fame* and the Prologue of the *Legend of Good Women* winds up fixated on this problem has higher stakes, moreover, than whatever it may suggest about the nature of Chaucer's writing. In particular, it bears on the fraught relation between postmodernism and ethics. Because of postmodernism's insistence on an inescapable political dimension to truth claims, and on how all such claims cannot be disentangled from the contexts of their making, it has been accused of being ethically empty. Postmodernism's understanding of truth's contingency, that is, has led some to charge it with making all truth claims equal. In this view, for postmodernism it must necessarily hold that there is no essential difference between, say, the claim that individuals of all sexes should have equal opportunities and the claim that cis men rightly deserve the privilege that they have held in most societies. In fact, this is a crude caricature of any thoughtful form of postmodernism, as Derrida's dedication of much of his lengthy career to ethical questions attests. Even from the proto-postmodernism of the *House of Fame* and the *Legend of Good Women*, we can see how recognition of the inherent indeterminacy of linguistic mediation does not in itself preclude questions of justice. In these works, Chaucer's exploration of this indeterminacy, whatever may have motivated its particular thematic focus, exposes the intricacies of the discursive operations of patriarchal injustice. As we have seen, for example, these works disclose the processes by which even an author's good intentions and depictions of men's crimes against women may remain trapped within an ideology ruled by men of great authority. These sorts of entrapments are, as you well know, still with us today, and we'll find our way beyond them only if we recognize how thoroughly enmeshed in them we may be.

Notes

1 Seaman 2007 similarly approaches the dream visions in this fashion.
2 For a cogent account of Chaucer's reflections on intention across his writings, including in the *Legend of Good Women*, see Barrington 2021.

8 *Troilus and Criseyde*

In 1378, Chaucer made a second trip to Italy, doing so, as in his first Italian voyage of 1372–73, as a member of a negotiating team pursuing his king's political, military, and economic interests. Although Chaucer left behind no personal record of his activities there, they almost certainly also included some pursuit of his own interests, specifically those in Italian literature. For not coincidentally, the following decade witnessed a great expansion in the amount and sophistication of his writing, much of which has inspirations in Italian writings from earlier in the century. Chaucer in particular came under the spell of Giovanni Boccaccio (d. 1375), to whose works he would repeatedly return as models of, and sometimes direct sources for, quite ambitious literary compositions that had little precedent in English literature. As I note in Chapter 2, among these compositions is an initial version of what became the Knight's Tale, the sprawling, imposing inaugurating performance of the *Canterbury Tales*. But by far the most ambitious of these efforts is *Troilus and Criseyde*, which Chaucer wrote in the mid-to-late 1380s as a free (and, as usual, unacknowledged) adaptation of Boccaccio's mid-fourteenth-century *Il Filostrato* (*The One Made Prostrate by Love*). The consensus critical appraisal of this effort is evident in the common supposition that if he hadn't later gotten around to writing the *Canterbury Tales* (itself perhaps modeled on Boccaccio's *Decameron*), he would still be almost as well known as the author of *Troilus and Criseyde*.

The story of the ancient war between Trojans and Greeks that forms the setting for *Troilus and Criseyde* was certainly familiar to Chaucer before his encounter with Boccaccio's poem. Indeed, as conveyed in the opening lines of *Sir Gawain and the Green Knight*, a Middle English poem written by a (still unknown) contemporary of Chaucer's, the then-semi-official origin myth of human civilization on the island of Great Britain went back to the Trojan War. Purportedly, a great-grandson of the Trojan refugee Aeneas, named Brutus, found his way to the island and became its first king. As the Trojan War therefore had broad political and historical significance in medieval England, we can readily imagine Chaucer's intrigue

DOI: 10.4324/9781003273318-9

when he first read through the *Filostrato*. Here, Chaucer found an epic-sized poem that decenters the usual political, military, and historical concerns of epic poetry, pushing them to margins in favor of a love story. And this love story, he discovered, is neither a happy one ending in marriage nor, as with the story of Lancelot, Guinevere, and Arthur, a love triangle that ends in disaster for everyone. It's rather a tale of a couple's romantic and erotic fulfillment followed by their relationship's tragic dissolution. He encountered a story of ambiguous moral import that capriciously blends comedic, heroic, and erotic styles, tones, and subject matters. Most importantly, he discovered a poem that has at the heart of its plot and themes the complex decision-making process of a female character.

The question of female agency

Strictly speaking, the principal protagonist of both Boccaccio's *Filostrato* and Chaucer's *Troilus and Criseyde* is Troilo/Troilus. The prostrated lover of the title of Boccaccio's work refers to Troilo (and to Boccaccio himself, as his proem makes plain), while Chaucer's poem begins by stating that its "purpos" is "The double sorwe of Troilus to tellen" (1.5, 1), and it ends with Troilus looking back on that double sorrow. Yet throughout much of their middle portions, both poems focus on Criseida/Criseyde, and Chaucer especially devotes extensive space to the twists and turns of Criseyde's internal dialogue. In the history of the genre of courtly romance that provides the conventional backbone for both works, accounts of what's going on inside the head of the female object of male desire are infrequent and usually brief and formulaic. Cued by the *Filostrato*, Chaucer was inspired to make such an account a central concern and the most memorable feature of an 8,239-line poem.

Specifically, Chaucer's version of the story charts in detail the intricate internal processes of Criseyde's acceptance of Troilus's romantic interest, her struggle with the political and military circumstances that subsequently threaten their relationship, and her eventual abandonment of that relationship. That grim conclusion to the story would've been no surprise to anyone. Chaucer would've already known it from the sources that Boccaccio drew upon, and he clearly expects his readers to be familiar with it, as the doubleness of the sorrow that he announces in his first line refers to Troilus's initially unrequited love and his later suffering following Criseyde's abandonment. With that abandonment as the plot's ultimate destination, Boccaccio does not escape turning Criseida into a misogynist example of female treachery and his poem as a whole into a warning to men about the instability of female carnal desire (at least in my reading of the *Filostrato*). And insofar as the public reception of *Troilus and Criseyde* that Chaucer depicts in his later Prologue to the *Legend of Good Women* corresponds to anything real or even likely, Chaucer's poem is vulnerable to a similar interpretation. Yet, as discussed in the preceding chapter, Chaucer's very staging of this interpretation in that prologue suggests that he had different or at least much broader artistic aims.

My suspicion is that Chaucer found the *Filostrato*'s implied answer to the question of why Criseida abandons Troilo – because that's just typical of women – inadequate to the actual heft of the story that Boccaccio rendered. In response, he created his own version of the story that pursues an expansive exploration of the question, one that traverses philosophical, psychological, theological, ideological, and sociopolitical terrains (among others). The question in this way becomes Chaucer's vehicle for far-reaching reflection in all those dimensions. Nonetheless, the urgency of the specific question of Criseyde's abandonment never dissipates under all this added thematic weight, even if the poem ultimately fails to arrive at a definite explanation (unsurprisingly, for Chaucer). For reasons such as these, *Troilus and Criseyde* has been critically celebrated as "perhaps the most profound love poem in English" (Aers 1986, 94).

The most pivotal moment within Chaucer's exploration of Criseyde's decision-making is not, however, her abandonment but rather when she seems to agree to have sex with Troilus for the first time. My "seems" here recognizes the ambiguity in Chaucer's rendering of the scene and the ongoing debate about the existence and nature of Criseyde's consent as well as about consent in general, then and now, in fiction and in real life. In many ways, the complications within the concept and practice of consent encapsulate the poem's extensive consideration of female agency within a patriarchal society. At once internal and external, psychological and social, consent presumes an individual self who freely chooses, and hence it necessarily depends upon philosophical, theological, and ideological frameworks that underwrite notions such as selfhood and free choice. Criseyde's sexual consent, like the abandonment to which it is the necessary precursor – or a foreshadowing – is thus both a vehicle of capacious thematic reflection and a specific crux of urgently important and yet deeply ambiguous interpretation. If *Troilus and Criseyde* is indeed a candidate for "most profound love poem in English," it achieves that stature because it is also, as another scholar quips, "Chaucer's masterpiece on consent" (Somerset 2021, 36).

As these opening paragraphs perhaps suggest, it would not be difficult to devote an entire book like this one just to *Troilus and Criseyde*. To keep within the bounds of a single chapter, following the consideration of genre and sources and full summary of the poem, much of the chapter's discussion will focus on the moment of Criseyde's possible consent, exploring some of the reasons for its ambiguity and pursuing a few of its larger implications. I've chosen this moment not just for its evident importance in Chaucer's artistic aims but also for its obvious relevance to our own time.

For among the many continuing impacts of the #MeToo movement has been recognition of the ways in which sexist, patriarchal societies have constructed the notion of female consent in the interest of male dominance. We now have greater appreciation for how seemingly individual, freely chosen actions are performed in complex relation to larger ideological structures and social pressures – so that while we may with confidence embrace the formula of "no means no," it's by no means clear that "yes" simply or always means "yes." In the courtly romance conventions that inform the *Filostrato* and *Troilus and Criseyde*, the noble lady's initial "no" to her knightly suitor traditionally means "try harder and someday you might succeed." In different ways and to different effects, Boccaccio and Chaucer explode this convention by having the lady say "yes." And in Chaucer's version, the ways in which that "yes" is both pivotal and murky, and the implications thereof, both inform and are informed by our present-day grappling with the concept and practice of consent.

Genre(s) and sources

Chaucer's Knight's Tale – which features a love triangle set in ancient times, even before the Trojan War – has been called "a chivalric romance of a philosophical complexion" (*Riverside Chaucer*, 827). This description also ably describes *Troilus and Criseyde*'s most prominent generic affiliation. "Chivalric" refers to the cultural protocols of the social and political elite of Chaucer's own day, which he projects backward onto the ruling class of Troy. "Romance," among its many characteristics, involves narratives that explore in a fantasy setting (here, the faraway past) real-world norms of gender and sexuality as they manifest in romantic relationships and, usually, martial conflict between men. What I've referred to above as the conventions of courtly romance – as in the language that a knight was expected to use when pleading for a noble lady's affection and in the sort of responses expected from her – brings these two generic elements together, as those conventions constituted the discursive substance of the cultural protocols specifically pertaining to norms of gender and sexuality. As this discourse of culturally refined erotic negotiation evolved across the European Middle Ages, life inevitably imitated art. Courtly romance came to have great social and cultural potency in the real world, despite however exaggerated, artificial, or fantastical its characters, settings, and plots. For this reason, in the hands of writers such as Chaucer and Boccaccio, it served as a ready platform for dissecting the beliefs, behaviors, and ideologies of the ruling class.

Boccaccio pursues such dissection in part by incorporating many other and sometimes conflicting generic affiliations. Chaucer follows Boccaccio and indeed goes beyond him in this respect. As scholar Barry Windeatt (2023) has enumerated, these generic affiliations include epic, history, tragedy, drama and debate, lyric, fabliau, and allegory. Such affiliations are in practice loose frameworks of conventions that encourage some literary features while discouraging others. While there are palpable differences among them, they have many overlaps, and it's not unusual for them to comingle in the same work. Nevertheless, their copresence can sometimes be startling. For example, fabliaux – brief, comic tales usually involving trickery and coarse sexuality – would seem to be starkly at odds with the earnest idealism that typically characterizes chivalric romance. One of Chaucer's most fortuitous insights was to recognize the literary potential of the reverberating contradictions between exactly these two genres, which he puts to use, for example, in the *Canterbury Tales* sequence of Knight's Tale–Miller's Tale, as discussed in Chapter 2. In *Troilus and Criseyde*, alongside the generic presence of, say, epic and tragedy, the thematic implications of those reverberating contradictions feel enormous. For tricking someone into sex, even if it ever could be funny, carries dark and weighty significance against the backdrop of the story's epic sweep and tragic outcome.

One effect of this intensive multiplication of generic affiliations is that the poem implicitly and sometimes explicitly turns back on itself to engage in critical scrutiny of its own literary resources. As Windeatt remarks, the poem's "sense of intertextuality, of an inclusiveness of genres, tends to a mutual, interrelating critique between genres: by being included together, they ultimately react and comment upon each other" (2023, 146). Part of the way that the poem achieves this, as the term "intertextuality" suggests, is through the incorporation of allusions to and ideas and passages from a wide array of sources beyond the *Filostrato*. As Stephen Barney observes in the introduction to his Norton Critical Edition of *Troilus and Criseyde*, only about one third of the poem's lines are directly indebted to the *Filostrato* (2006, x). Conveniently, Barney prints a translation of Boccaccio's Italian alongside Chaucer's Middle English, so that readers can evaluate for themselves the nature and scope of Chaucer's engagement with his primary source. It's evident, for example, that when Chaucer departs from the *Filostrato*, he sometimes deepens the story's seriousness, as when he incorporates material from the *Consolation of Philosophy*, a Latin philosophical treatise by sixth-century Roman author Boethius – a major contributor to the poem's "philosophical complexion." Other times, he restores some of the story's epic outlook and historical significance that Boccaccio had pushed to the margins, often by drawing on sources that Boccaccio himself used. Still elsewhere, he amplifies the poem's rendering of courtly love conventions, as well as its ironic and comedic elements, by way of the *Romance of the Rose*, a widely known thirteenth-century allegorical French poem. And so on.

From this multiplicity and diversity of sources, it's easy to imagine Chaucer working on *Troilus and Criseyde* with an open copy of the

Filostrato on his lap and a desk covered by numerous other books. However fanciful this may be, the resulting poem is unmistakably as much about those books – and sometimes their mutually irreconcilable claims to truth and authority – as about the love between Troilus and Criseyde. Notoriously, Chaucer explicitly claims to be following a single source throughout: not Boccaccio but the Roman "auctour called Lollius" (1.394) – an "auctour" who doesn't in fact exist. Surely, among its many other functions, this blatant misdirection serves as Chaucer's puckish device, at least for his most knowing readers, for calling attention to the actual source gymnastics he performs, along with the sheer scope of his own invention.

Summary

Book 1

Chaucer divides the poem into five books.[1] Book 1 begins with a direct address to readers, in which the narrator, after calling for aid from Tisiphone, a Fury from Greek myth, explains the nature of the ensuing poem and asks for readers' prayers. He then summarizes the events leading up to the main story, in which the Trojan prophesier Calchas, who is Criseyde's father, defects to the Greeks upon foreseeing the Trojan defeat, leaving Criseyde behind. Criseyde, in her vulnerable plight, asks for and receives protection from Hector, eldest prince of Troy, Troilus's brother, and the city's greatest warrior. The narrator briefly mentions the ongoing military conflict and then moves on to Troilus's 'love at first sight' moment. This occurs at a citywide religious/social event, which Troilus attends with "His yonge knightes" (1.184). Troilus mocks those who express romantic devotion to specific women. This attitude incenses the god of Love (i.e., Cupid), who promptly shoots him with an arrow from his bow. Troilus is immediately and unshakably smitten with Criseyde. He pretends to continue to mock love and leaves without speaking to her.

At home, he suffers immensely from his feelings of love, which he believes he must keep secret. He vents his turmoil earnestly but also more or less precisely according to the discursive and behavioral conventions expected of courtly lovers. These include refined poetic expressions of his pain and devotion, as well as actual physiological malaise, deriving from loss of sleep and appetite, which are symptoms of intense love melancholy (though he still manages to kill a lot of Greeks during this time, as the narrator notes). Helpless before this suffering, he prays for his own death. Pandarus, Troilus's friend and coincidentally also Criseyde's uncle, makes a surprise visit. Seeing Troilus in this plight, he eventually wheedles out of him the reason. After some teasing about Troilus's earlier mockery of love, he pledges to help him win Criseyde's affection. Troilus makes clear that he wishes for an entirely honorable relationship, desiring nothing "That toucheth [involves] harm or any vileinye [dishonor]" (1.1033). Pandarus laughs, says something that amounts to an ambiguous "of course," and goes on his way.

Book 2

Book 2 begins with the narrator asking for help from a different Greek demigod – the Muse of history, Clio – after which he picks up the thread of the narrative. Pandarus goes to visit his niece the day after his promise to help Troilus. A long, bantering conversation between them ensues (much of which has no parallel in the *Filostrato*), in which Pandarus craftily props up Troilus as a praiseworthy young man before springing the news of his romantic interest in her. In that moment, he drops his playful tone, telling Criseyde he will no longer see her if the news angers her. He insists that if she doesn't show favor to Troilus, she will be responsible for his death, and in fact he himself will die as well. "If that ye doon us bothe dien [cause us both to die]/Thus giltelees [guiltless], thanne have ye fisshed faire [i.e., made a fine catch]" (2.327–28), he sardonically comments, and he continues to pressure her in this and other ways. At this point, readers receive an initial glimpse into Criseyde's mind, as the narrator tells us that she says to herself, "I shal feelen what he meneth" (2.387): she knows that she's being manipulated, and she's trying to determine exactly how and why. Soon after, she bursts into tears and declares that her "beste frend" (2.412), Pandarus, has betrayed her. Pandarus doubles down on the charge that she'll cause his and Troilus's death and gets up to go, and here we receive a longer peek into Criseyde's mind. Genuinely afraid that what Pandarus threatens might occur, she determines "ful slyly for to playe" (3.462). She'll take up Pandarus's entreaty but with care, alertness, and clear limits. She agrees to show loving kindness to Troilus but no more than that. Pandarus then relays what seems to be a wholly fabricated story (given what we know from Book 1) of how he discovered Troilus's love for her.

At this juncture, the narrator shifts fully into reporting Criseyde's thoughts, doing so at length as she mulls over the situation. By coincidence, Troilus, rather battered from fighting the Greeks, rides by her house. Seeing him now, without him noticing her (so temporally free from the direct pressure of the male gaze) and in light of the knowledge of his romantic interest, she becomes aware of her incipient desire for him. She asks herself, "Who yaf me drinke?" (2.651); that is, "why do I feel suddenly intoxicated [metaphorically, overcome with desire]?" But that awareness does not, by itself, sway her. She continues to ponder her precarious situation and that of women generally and registers her appreciation for the relative independence that she has had as a widow. Without coming to a clear decision, she goes to join her three nieces in her garden.

One of these women, Antigone, entertains the group by singing a hymn in praise of love, and, though Criseyde is careful to hide her feelings, the song deeply moves her. At night, she dreams that an eagle rips out her heart and replaces it with his own, but, strikingly, she "nought agroos ne nothing smerte" (2.930); that is, she felt neither fear nor pain.

In the remainder of Book 2, the narrator recounts the evolving relationship between Troilus and Criseyde by way of tracking Pandarus's crafty orchestration of it. Pandarus reports to Troilus his conversation with Criseyde, and he urges Troilus to write to her and guides the letter's composition. Arriving at Criseyde's house early the next day, Pandarus makes up an excuse to talk to her privately, tells her he is there to deliver a letter from Troilus, and reiterates Troilus's nearness to death from love melancholy. Criseyde refuses to take the letter, expressing outrage at what she understands as an affront to her "estat" (2.1134), a word with a range of meanings in Chaucer's day, here likely denoting the moral propriety of an upper-class widow in Trojan society. Pandarus calls her foolish and says, "Refuse nought [Do not refuse it]" (2.1154). To enforce his command, he "hente hire faste [seized her tightly]/And in hir bosom the lettre down he thraste [stuffed the letter down her cleavage]" (2.1154–55). He dares her to throw it away and thereby potentially draw attention. She smiles but says she will not write back, and they go to dine, laughing. Criseyde sneaks off and reads the letter carefully, finding in it "no lak [fault]" (2.1178). After she returns, Pandarus again talks to her privately, urging her to respond to Troilus and offering his help. She agrees to write back and composes a letter that states that she will not be his lover but "as his suster [sister], him to plese,/She wolde fain [would gladly] to doon his herte an ese [ease his heart]" (2.1224–25). When she returns, Pandarus conveys his approval of what he believes to be her erotic concession. He then calls her attention to the window, where Troilus happens to be riding by as what we know this time to be part of Pandarus's machinations. Again Criseyde, to herself, recognizes her growing desire for Troilus. Pandarus, sensing an opportunity, proposes that she and Troilus meet, which she rejects.

Pandarus takes his leave and goes directly to Troilus, giving him Criseyde's letter, which, providing Troilus some hope, increases his desire and hence also his suffering. In an addition to the story's plot with no parallel in the *Filostrato*, Pandarus then contrives an elaborate plan for a private meeting between Troilus and Criseyde. Taking advantage of Criseyde's political precarity, he fabricates a tale about how a Trojan named Poliphete, who before had taken legal action against Criseyde, is once again bringing charges against her. For help in the matter, he approaches Troilus's older brother Deiphebus, who readily agrees and, subtly steered by Pandarus, determines to invite both Criseyde and Troilus to his home to develop a plan for Criseyde's defense. Pandarus goes to Criseyde, repeats the false story about Poliphete, and explains how he has sought Deiphebus's help, making no mention of Troilus. Meanwhile, Troilus – who has been in on the plan from the start – goes to Deiphebus's house a day early. Coached by Pandarus to say to Deiphebus that he is ill and must go to bed, Troilus does exactly that but remarks to Pandarus beforehand that he will not need to pretend he is sick. When the guests arrive the next morning, conversation soon turns to the ailing Troilus. Book 2 then concludes with a sequence of events, all orchestrated by Pandarus's deceptions, that eventuates in Criseyde approaching Troilus's room "arm in arm" (2.1725) with Pandarus.

Book 3

Book 3 begins with an invocation to Venus that also becomes a meditation on the scope and nature of her power over humanity. We then return to the situation at the end of Book 2. Criseyde – with Pandarus leading her by the hem of her dress – asks Troilus for his continued protection, as she still believes in the false pretext of her visit. Troilus "wex sodeinliche reed" (3.82), that is, he blushes in "shame" (3.89), and when he regains his composure, recites his devotion to Criseyde. Pandarus urges her to grant Troilus "routhe" (8.122) or pity. Criseyde, under the heavy pressure of her prince's and uncle's demands, remains nonetheless keenly aware of what's at stake, knowing that 'pity' can be a euphemism for sexual yielding. She accordingly demands a clarification, asking Troilus directly to tell her "the fin of his entente" (8.125), that is, his ultimate objective. He replies, in effect, that he only wishes that she will allow him to serve her, secretly, as one who loves her, and that she show kindness and – implicitly – be faithful to him in response. Pandarus says, if he were a god, he'd kill her on the spot if she refused such a request. Criseyde carefully provides an affirmative response in which she twice insists on the preservation of her honor. She further declares, although Troilus is "A kinges sone [son] .../Ye shal namore han sovereinetee [have no more sovereignty]/Of [Over] me in love than right in that cas is [i.e., is appropriate]" (3.170–72). She takes him in her arms and kisses him. The meeting ends when Pandarus hears others approach.

After Criseyde leaves, Pandarus and Troilus engage in a conversation that supplies a sort of editorializing commentary on the situation so far. Pandarus recognizes that his actions might be considered like those of a pimp and as having betrayed his niece, raising the topic as a way to insist on both his good intentions toward Troilus and the necessity for secrecy. Troilus affirms his commitment to secrecy and declares that Pandarus is no pimp, offering (quite uncomfortably to most readers) to do the same for him, whether his choice be one of his own sisters or Helen of Troy herself.

In the days that follow, contact between Troilus and Criseyde is necessarily limited by the requirements of discretion, and so Pandarus contrives a plan to bring them together at his house for an entire night. He invites Criseyde to dinner on a near-moonless evening that threatens rain. She hesitates because of the inclement weather but also because she suspects he's up to something. She asks him directly whether Troilus will be there. He says no, Troilus is "out of towne" (3.570), and even if he were not, she can trust him (Pandarus) to be discreet. Criseyde agrees to come. The narrator coyly remarks at this point that his source doesn't indicate whether or not Criseyde believes Pandarus. In fact, this entire scene is Chaucer's invention, and hence he is calling attention to the ambiguity.

Criseyde comes to dinner with her retinue, and, indeed, heavy rainfall breaks out, preventing their departure. Pandarus slyly organizes the sleeping arrangements according to his premeditated plan. He goes to Troilus, who has been hidden away in a private room all this time, and leads him to where Criseyde is sleeping. Pandarus wakens her, informs her that he has snuck into her room via a "secree trappe dore" (3.759), and tells her not to call out. He says – lying – that Troilus has just arrived at the house, unseen, in severe distress after having heard that Criseyde has been unfaithful to him by loving a man named Horaste. Alarmed, Criseyde laments the fragility of happiness and the insidiousness of jealously and says she will clear up everything "tomorwe and [if] I him see" (3.809). Pandarus replies that waiting until tomorrow will surely kill Troilus. Criseyde offers one of her rings for Pandarus to bring to Troilus as a token of her fidelity until she sees him in the morning. Again, Pandarus insists that waiting will ensure Troilus's death from a broken heart. Criseyde wavers. The narrator says that the "accident" or happenstance seemed to her "so lik a sooth at prime face" (3.918–19), that is, that she felt it had the appearance of being true, suggesting an uncertain mixture of belief and suspicion, innocence and knowingness. She tells Pandarus that she is "At dulcarnoun" (3.931), a geometric allusion meaning that she is stymied. She puts the matter into her uncle's hands, saying that she will at least arise from bed, but Pandarus tells her to stay where she is.

Troilus comes in and kneels at her bedside. Pandarus withdraws to the fireplace and pretends to read a book. Criseyde passionately, tearfully affirms her complete fidelity to Troilus and laments the power of jealousy. Shaken by her anguish, Troilus is overcome with remorse over the deceptions that have led to this point, and he faints. Leaping into action (and seizing the opportunity), Pandarus lifts the prostrate Troilus, puts him into Criseyde's bed, and strips him down to his undershirt, imploring Criseyde to help bring Troilus back from the brink. Troilus awakens to her kisses. He and she reconcile, and Pandarus again withdraws to the fireplace and, eventually, goes to sleep. In the famous ensuing 'consummation scene,' which we'll consider below, Troilus and Criseyde have sex.

From this point through the end of Book 3, the poem mostly celebrates their love and happiness, expressing this in various ways and from different points of view. For us of course, this celebration is necessarily haunted by the foreknowledge that the story ends with abandonment. And we are reminded, too, of the sordid element of Pandarus's machinations, and the ambiguity of Criseyde's responses to them, when Pandarus comes to Criseyde's bedside the next morning. He teases her with sexually suggestive insinuations about her time with Troilus, and she responds by explicitly naming his manipulative deception: "God helpe me so, ye caused al this fare [to happen]," she declares, "for alle youre wordes white [i.e., supposedly sincere language]./O whoso seeth you knoweth you ful lite [little]" (3.1566–68). She then covers her face with her bedsheet and blushes "for shame al reed [red]" (3.1570). Pandarus, far from being apologetic, reaches under the bedsheet, pretends to offer her his head to cut off, thrusts his hand "sodeinly" (3.1574) under her neck, and kisses her. The narrator discreetly says that he's skipping over the rest of their interaction. We learn just that Criseyde forgives her uncle and, after they amuse themselves, she goes home. The narrator concludes, "And Pandarus hath fully his entente" (3.1582); that is, Pandarus has accomplished everything he intended.

Book 4

Book 4 begins grimly with the narrator complaining about the cruel whims of Fortune, here personified as a woman, who will cast Troilus from her wheel and raise up the Greek warrior Diomede. The narrator seems to express real regret over having to move on to "how Criseyde Troilus forsook –/Or," he qualifies, "at the leeste how that she was unkinde" (4.15–16). He declares that if his source authors are lying about her, they are the ones who should be disgraced. He seems to have come to consider Criseyde a real person, not a fictional character whose story Chaucer has chosen to repeat (and rework), and he's worried that she may have been falsely maligned.

Leaving the love story aside for a moment, Book 4 returns to the military struggle, describing a battle in which the Trojan warrior and nobleman Antenor is captured by the Greeks. A truce is established to consider prisoner exchanges, and Calchas, hearing of this, requests that the Greeks include Criseyde in their negotiations for whom to bring out of Troy. They determine to exchange Antenor for her and King Thoas. Priam, the Trojan king, calls a meeting of parliament to consider the offer. Troilus attends but sits silently in anguish. Hector, ignorant of his brother's love affair, nonetheless opposes the deal on principle, saying, "Sires, she nis no [isn't a] prisoner .../.../We usen here no [It is not our custom a] womman for to selle" (34.179–83). But the majority insist that obtaining the militarily valuable Antenor for the militarily superfluous Criseyde is an excellent bargain. (The narrator points out the irony that Antenor "was after traitour to the town," an agent of Troy's later destruction, and so wasn't so valuable after all.) Troilus quickly retreats to his home and agonizes over the situation, reflecting sorrowfully and philosophically on fortune and love and repeatedly wishing for his own death.

Having also been present at the meeting of parliament, Pandarus rushes to Troilus's house (notably, he doesn't consider first going to Criseyde), joins in Troilus's complaints about fortune, and then, in an attempt to be consoling, says in effect that there are many fish in the sea. Troilus responds with outrage. He declares his love for Criseyde to be unshakable and once more wishes for his own death. Pandarus seems to realize his error, thinks for a moment, and then offers practical advice. "Go ravisshe hire" (4.530), he suggests, with "ravisshe" meaning here "abduct." This term applies because the action of parliament presumes its jurisdiction over Criseyde's body and hence its right to send her to the Greeks regardless of her wishes (despite her being a free citizen of Troy and no prisoner, as Hector pointed out). Pandarus thus proposes that Troilus take the law into his own hands. Troilus considers this possibility thoughtfully. He eventually rejects it for various political reasons but mostly because of the inevitable damage it would do to Criseyde's honor, which he has pledged to protect. Pandarus offers several counterarguments, most prominently the possibility that Criseyde herself would urge her own abduction, and persuades Troilus to let him speak with Criseyde about the matter.

Meanwhile, Criseyde, having heard the news, becomes profoundly distressed, expressing her feelings philosophically, as Troilus did, and likewise affirming her steadfast commitment to their love and wishing for her own death. Pandarus arrives, and she directs her distress toward him. Eventually he convinces her to meet with Troilus to determine how best to respond to the situation. The scene then shifts to Troilus, who has fallen back into utter despair. Praying in a temple, he gives voice to a complicated meditation on free will – or, rather, the lack thereof – which Chaucer has closely adapted from Boethius's *Consolation of Philosophy*, notably ending the meditation before Boethius's concluding affirmation of free will. Pandarus appears and, rejecting Troilus's fatalism, tells him that he has arranged a meeting with Criseyde in which they may determine their own destiny.

The lovers meet. Overwhelmed with sorrow, they cannot speak. Criseyde lapses into a deathlike faint, and Troilus, believing her dead, prepares to kill himself with his own sword. Criseyde revives just in time to prevent what would have been, she avers, a double suicide. Criseyde then says it's foolish of them to waste time on lamentation when the purpose of their meeting is "To finde boote of wo [remedy for our woe]" (3.1259).

She proposes a solution: yes, they'll be separated, but what's to prevent their reunion sometime soon after her departure? "For, dredeles [without doubt, certainly], within a wike [week] or two/I shal been here" (4.1278–79), she says, and later she reduces the time apart to "ten dayes" (4.1328). She provides several seemingly plausible explanations for how this may come about. At the conclusion of her speech, the narrator briefly intrudes to insist that Criseyde here is wholly sincere, paradoxically reminding us of her future abandonment while declaring her intentions to be entirely innocent.

Troilus initially accepts Criseyde's plan but then voices a series of doubts, including that, once away from him, she may redirect her affections toward "a lusty [handsome] knight/Among the Grekes" (3.1485–86). He proposes instead Pandarus's suggestion, albeit in a more consensual formulation: that they "stele away and been togidre so" (4.1507). Criseyde, after declaring her steadfast fidelity to Troilus and promise to return, rejects this proposal. She offers several reasons, which amount to the near certainty of their future unhappiness should they take that course. Troilus accepts her decision and at her urging pledges fidelity to her. She proclaims that her love for him is based, not on his outward accomplishments and status, but on his "moral vertu, grounded upon trouthe" (4.1672).

Book 5

As Book 5's task is to supply the tragic ending of the story, the narrator begins with an address to the Fates of Greek mythology. He also mentions for the first time the relatively long length of the love affair: about three years have passed since Cupid first struck Troilus with an arrow. He then picks up the story on the morning of Criseyde's transfer to the Greeks. Diomede is in charge of the Greek party, and Troilus rides along with the Trojans. In agony, Troilus silently urges himself to take matters into his own hands, seize Criseyde, kill Diomede, and ride away. All that prevents him is his fear that Criseyde might be killed in the chaos of the action. He takes leave of her, approaching close enough to whisper a reminder of her promise to return. Diomede observes this and quickly deduces the situation. Viewing her as a prize to be won from a Trojan prince, he determines to take advantage of Criseyde's precarious situation. Uncannily echoing the same courtly rhetoric used earlier by Troilus, he promises to help her in any way she requires, mentions his sudden love for her, and concludes, "But mighte me so fair a grace falle/That ye me for youre servant wolde calle,/So lowely ne so trewely you serve/Nil noon of hem [Will none of them, i.e., others] as I shal til I sterve [die]" (5.172–75). Criseyde, distracted by her distress, does not really listen to him, although she seems to catch the idea that he'll be an ally in the enemy camp, and so she accepts his offer of "frendshipe" (5.185).

The narrator dwells on Troilus's torment as he awaits Criseyde's return. Troilus has terrible dreams; he expects to die. Pandarus tells him to buck up – that ten days is not very long. He proposes that they visit their friend King Sarpedon to help shorten the wait. They go, and everyone there is having a good time, except, of course, Troilus, who, in despair, immerses himself in memories of Criseyde. He wants to leave; Pandarus makes him stay for a week. After they return, Troilus takes Pandarus with him to look at Criseyde's empty home. He proceeds to revisit the many places in Troy that hold memories of Criseyde. He goes to the city gates out of which Criseyde rode. He ascends to the top of the city walls and, seeing the Greek encampment, thinks, "Lo, yonder is my owne lady free [noble]" (5.669).

We then return to Criseyde and her internal dialogue. She has become acutely aware of her highly precarious situation within a military encampment "With wommen fewe among the Grekes stronge" (5.688). She recognizes now the sheer improbability of her plan to return and despairingly expects that Troilus will believe her unfaithful when that plan fails. She looks at the walls of Troy and, like Troilus, sorrowfully recalls their time together. She regrets her overruling of his proposal that they "stele away" (5.740) and resolves that she will somehow discover a way to escape to Troy and subsequently leave with Troilus to "wher as him lest [wherever he wishes]" (5.753), no matter what the consequences. The narrator here intrudes to remind us that in fact she does not proceed with this plan. He then shifts to Diomede, who is mulling over "How he may best, with shortest taryinge [delay],/Into his net Criseydes herte bringe;/.../To fisshen hire he laide out hook and line" (5.774–77). Well aware of her love for Troilus, Diomede relishes the challenge of turning her affections toward him.

The narrator again intervenes, providing readers with brief and much belated character portraits of Diomede, Criseyde, and Troilus. Criseyde's includes the notorious observation that while "Tendre-herted," she is also "sliding of corage" (5.825), an ambiguous phrase meaning something like "indecisive" or, more pejoratively, "wavering of heart." Returning to the story, the narrator tells us that it is now the tenth day after Criseyde's departure. Diomede comes to Criseyde and Calchas's tent to press his suit. He tells her that if she loves someone in Troy, she should know that all the inhabitants of the city are doomed and so she would be better off loving a Greek and in particular himself. Once more, he adopts the same conventions of courtly love speech that Troilus had used. Criseyde turns him away but quite equivocally. She says she understands Troy's dire straits but is not willing to concede their defeat. Lying, she says she loved her Trojan husband and no one else and is not interested in loving another. If the Greeks are victorious, she admits, her views might shift, and in that eventuality, if she were to "han routhe [pity, affection]" (5.1000) for any Greek, it would be him. Seemingly to herself, she prays to see Troy once again. Diomede takes her glove and leaves.

That night, lying in bed, Criseyde mulls over the conversation with Diomede, considering Troy's and her own exceptionally vulnerable conditions – the "peril of the town,/And that she was allone and hadde neede/Of frendes help" (5.1025–27). She decides, at last, that she will not attempt to return. When Diomede arrives at her tent in the morning, the narrator becomes suddenly more reserved in his report of their interaction, quickly summarizing what his sources say about Criseyde's yielding to him, uncertainly remarking that "Men sayn – I noot [I do not know] – that she yaf [gave] him hir herte" (5.1050). He then provides Criseyde's own speech of lamentation over her actions – her expectations that throughout history she will be infamous for her betrayal, that "bookes" (5.1060) will advertise her disgrace, and that "wommen most" (5.1063) will hate her because of the shame she brings to her sex. Yet because she can "see ther is no better way,/And that too late is now for me to rewe [feel regret]," she finally resolves, "To Diomede, algate [at any rate],/I wol be trewe" (5.1069–71). The narrator continues to direct uncertainty and hesitation toward the very story he's relating, again as if Criseyde is a historically actual individual. He states that it's not clear how long it took Criseyde to give up on her love for Troilus and turn to Diomede. He says it's not his intention to chide "this sely womman …/Ferther than the storye wol devise" (5.1093–94), with "sely" having a range of possible meanings, from "innocent" to "gullible" to "foolish." He says he would like to excuse her, given her expressions of remorse.

The scene shifts back to Troilus. The narrator describes the several phases of his awaiting Criseyde's return, desperate with both hope and anxiety. Pandarus joins and encourages him but privately suspects the truth. Several days pass. At last, Troilus concludes that she will not return and is overcome with physically debilitating suicidal melancholy and jealous rage. He dreams that he encounters Criseyde in a forest, kissing a happily sleeping boar. He takes this as a certain token of her betrayal and says as much to Pandarus, who tells him he's being foolish to base such certainty on a dream. Pandarus has Troilus write to Criseyde. The narrator supplies the lengthy letter verbatim, which in the fervent language of courtly love expresses Troilus's continued devotion, his intense suffering, and – delicately – a reminder of her broken promise. In contrast, the narrator provides just a brief summary of Criseyde's reply, in which she reiterates her promise to return but expresses uncertainty about when that will be. Troilus's suffering increases, and he sends for his sister Cassandra, a prophetess, to interpret his dream about the boar. Her long, historically and mythographically erudite explanation culminates in the precise identification of the boar as Diomede. Outraged, Troilus calls her a lying "sorceresse" (5.1520) and leaps out of bed, his energy restored.

The narrator recounts how the tide of war turns against Troy, in particular with Hector's death at the hands of Achilles. Meanwhile, Troilus alternates between complete despair and continued hope in Criseyde's return, which prompts him to write to her often. Criseyde at last replies, and the narrator this time supplies her full letter verbatim. It is not long and is perhaps best described as evasive. She continues to affirm that she plans to return but cannot say when and how and expresses vague anxiety about other eyes seeing the letter. She suggests that he should bear up better under difficult circumstances and even insinuates that it is he who has been leading her on, but then dismisses that, reasserting her belief in his devotion. She concludes by apologizing for the letter's brevity. Troilus is puzzled and made suspicious by the letter but continues to hold out hope. Not long after, the accuracy of Cassandra's dream interpretation is proven when Deiphebus returns from battle with Diomede's tunic, which, Troilus notices, carries a brooch that he had given Criseyde. He goes home, sends for Pandarus, complains fervently of his mistreatment, and vows to seek his own death on the battlefield. Pandarus, unusually terse, declares that he hates Criseyde and pledges to do whatever he can to help Troilus. Troilus does indeed return to the battlefield, seeking out Diomede in particular, but, although they often meet, neither kills the other.

Nearing the end of the story, the narrator once more expresses discomfort with its culmination in Criseyde's betrayal. He asks women readers not to be angry with him, as "hire gilt" has been firmly established by "other bookes" (5.1776), and he expresses a wish to write instead about legendary women famous for their fidelity, such as Penelope and Alceste. In fact, he continues, seemingly anticipating Chaucer's later *Legend of Good Women*, his intention has been to supply a warning to the many *women* who are betrayed by men through their "grete wit and subtiltee [craftiness]" (5.1782). He then supplies *Troilus and Criseyde*'s famous envoy. In this farewell address from author to poem, he expresses a hope someday to write a "comdeye" (5.1787), in contrast to the present "tragedye" (5.1786), and boastfully places himself in the company of the classical literary giants "Virgile, Ovide, Omer [Homer], Lucan, and Stace [Statius]" (5.1792) by humbling depicting his poem as kissing their footprints. He goes on to express anxiety about whether his poem will be properly understood, given that English's many dialects and its lack of a written standard will likely result in its being miscopied by scribes who don't reproduce his own dialect precisely.

All this direct authorial self-commentary – on Chaucer's literary accomplishment, his future plans, and the present poem's potential vulnerability to its means of dissemination – would seem to signal the work's termination. Instead, the narrator returns to the story. He reports that Achilles kills Troilus and describes how Troilus's soul ascends to the "eighthe spere"

(5.1809) – that is, in the geocentric model of the universe, the sphere of fixed stars that contains the inner spheres of the planets. Looking down from this transcendent position, Troilus feels not love but contempt for the material world that he has left behind and the physical passions to which humans are subject. He laughs disdainfully at those who weep for him on earth. This attitude toward all that has occurred, the narrator says, is the end to which Troilus's story has led. The narrator then addresses youthful readers of the poem and exhorts them to think, not of the mutable material world, but of God, and not of romantic love, but of love of Christ. He devotes a stanza to casting Christian aspersions on "payens" or the ancient pagans and their "goddes" (5.1849–50) and follows with a stanza in which he directs the poem to his friends John Gower (a poet) and Ralph Strode (a philosopher and lawyer). Finally, he concludes with a stanza-long prayer to the Christian Trinity and Virgin Mary.

Consent within patriarchy

I hope that the above summary makes plain not only the centrality of Criseyde's decision-making in the poem's plot and themes but also the relentlessly patriarchal environment in which she makes those decisions. Criseyde lives in a world in which men control political power and economic resources and in which women – even wealthy, socially elevated women like Criseyde – are ultimately subject to men's decisions about them. Her world is one in which women are ubiquitously sexually objectified and preyed upon and where men compete with one another to 'conquer' women sexually and as part of this competition weaponize the language of love and commitment and the woman's presumed obligation to return a man's earnestly expressed romantic interest. Sadly, albeit women today obviously have opportunities and alternatives not available to Criseyde, her world continues to resemble our own in these respects, as #MeToo has acutely reminded us.

Whether anyone's decisions are truly freely made is a philosophical and theological question that *Troilus and Criseyde* explicitly considers, most prominently with Troilus's meditation on the topic in Book 4. But with the character of Criseyde, the poem throughout its length also explores, albeit more tacitly, the narrower question of how freely made – that is, how unconstrained or uncoerced – are the decisions of women living within a patriarchy. Criseyde makes several narratively pivotal decisions, all of which bear on this question. But the most crucial – the one that unequivocally establishes her relationship with Troilus and hence her presumed culpability for her later abandonment – is her apparent consent to sex with him at the virtual center of the story's plot.

Modern feminist studies of female consent will help us appreciate the complications and stakes of this moment as well as its significance for the real world of the twenty-first century. Adrienne Rich, in an influential essay that she first published in 1980, supplies the notion of *compulsory heterosexuality*. She argues that patriarchal societies devote tremendous social, cultural, political, and economic resources toward maintaining a status quo in which women's normative destiny is to be men's sexual possession. Rejecting the widespread belief, even among feminists, that heterosexuality is simply a fact of nature, she painstakingly assembles evidence from across history and from many different cultures that demonstrates that whatever its biological underpinnings, heterosexuality has always also been in practice a political institution that in patriarchal societies has been a primary guarantor of female subjection. As she famously remarks, "the institution of heterosexuality itself" constitutes "a beachhead of male dominance" (1980, 633). For Rich, women's supposed choice to participate in this institution is no choice at all, as it is rather what society has made compulsory. Most women, Rich argues, have incorporated this social dictate into their self-understanding and so understand themselves as willing participants even while sometimes expressing profound dissatisfaction with their experiences. Those women who resist the institution face an array of coercions to keep them in line, with physical violence the all-to-common tactic of last resort, and hence with some level of threat thereof pervading much interaction between men and women. Plainly, these arguments are no less current notwithstanding the many decades that have elapsed since Rich's essay. Countless illustrations of them remain pervasive, such as Donald Trump's notorious 2016 remarks about women in a taped conversation with television personality Billy Bush: "Grab 'em by the pussy. You can do anything."

Feminist legal scholar Catharine MacKinnon has considered the nature of female sexual consent in light of Rich's arguments. Quite obviously, consent to anything is not true consent if the situation involves coercion by the threat of violence. It's a legal truism that, say, bank tellers are not complicit in the crime of robbery if, with a gun pointed to their head, they agree to open a safe. On this basis, MacKinnon queries whether authentic female consent is a meaningful concept when the institution of heterosexuality in general has incorporated the threat of male coercive violence as part of its constitutive fabric. As she points out, "The law of rape presents consent as free exercise of sexual choice under conditions of equality of power without exposing the underlying structure of constraint and disparity" (1989, 175). That "underlying structure of constraint and disparity" includes the still-widespread norms of sexual interaction in which a man 'makes a move' – initiates a sexual encounter, however welcome or not

– and the targeted woman is tasked with responding in some fashion. Often in these interactions, the woman chooses neither the situation of the encounter nor the available set of options for an acceptable response. And most likely, she brings to the situation some awareness, whether from her own experience or knowledge of that of others, that negative responses have been regularly overturned by some form of violent coercion (again as #MeToo has reminded us). Hence, even when force is absent, its potential remains present. Consequently, the degree of the woman's willingness is a murky question. As MacKinnon writes,

> If sexuality is relational, specifically if it is a power relation of gender, consent is a communication under conditions of inequality. It transpires somewhere between what the woman actually wanted, what she was able to express about what she wanted, and what the man comprehended she wanted.
>
> (1989, 182)

Or, more succinctly, "If sex is *normally* something men *do* to women, the issue is less whether there was force than whether consent is a meaningful concept" (1989, 178, emphases added).

To be sure, Rich's and MacKinnon's arguments and the implications thereof have been controversial, not just for those who predictably would be resistant to them but also for some of those who are sympathetic with their overall projects. Yet it seems difficult to contest that, at the very least, their arguments apply to some degree in some situations. Thus, insofar as the fictional situation of Criseyde represents a kind of thought exercise about the nature of female consent within a patriarchy, we may think through her situation in Rich's and MacKinnon's terms as a way of gaining insight into the concerns of Chaucer's poem and, conversely, into the theories with which we examine it.

The sheer breadth and depth of Pandarus's manipulations of Criseyde, especially those that culminate in the sexual encounter that he literally hosts, should be evident from the above summary. In his role as Troilus's enthusiastic sexual procurer, Pandarus is a virtual personification of the norm of male sexual aggression, one who doesn't hesitate, when it seems to him called for, to signal a coercive threat of violence, as when in Book 2 he stuffs Troilus's letter down Criseyde's cleavage. Yet alongside Pandarus's almost caricatured embodiment of this norm, Chaucer is careful to include more systemic – and hence more insidious – sources of coercion. For example, he highlights the structural precarity of any woman living in a society in which men have ultimate control over women's bodies by calling attention from the outset to Criseyde's political vulnerability and thus dependence on men. Criseyde, bereft of both husband and father, requires protection, which she receives from Hector, which is to say from the Trojan royal family and thus also from Troilus. In this regard, Pandarus's later invention of Poliphete's threat to her (which is also Chaucer's invention) is simply the readiest stratagem to get Criseyde and Troilus into the same room. Such aggressions are plainly understood, by both her and her royal protectors, to be an almost inevitable inducement of her structural precarity.

Even more insidious – because not clearly marked as a problem and at times manifestly celebrated – are the conventions of courtly love that, as discussed above, provided the cultural norms for upper-class male sexual initiation both in the romance literary tradition and to some degree in actual late medieval European society. In these conventions, the woman from the start supposedly has total power over the man. She provokes his desire, over which he has no control. He experiences intense suffering from that desire, emotional as well as physical, which threatens his very life. To survive, he has no choice except to beg her for 'mercy' or 'pity' – to urge her to consent to show some ambiguous and likely euphemistic 'favor' toward him, in exchange for which he pledges to do anything she demands. The insidiousness of these conventions is obvious: they make the woman responsible for the man's sexual aggression toward her, and they recast the agency of her consent as an instrument of potential violence against the man.

As antiquated as it may seem, this widespread and often idealized medieval framing of female consent is not at all a mere relic of the past. That it persists in modified forms to the present is evident in the way that MacKinnon, in her analysis of female consent in our own day, captures it so perfectly. "Fundamentally," she writes,

> desirability to men is supposed a woman's form of power because she can both arouse it and deny its fulfillment. To woman is attributed both the cause of man's initiative and the denial of his satisfaction. This rationalizes [the man's] force.
>
> (1989, 175)

In effect, MacKinnon suggests, the actual protocols at work in male sexual initiation, the ones that in practice enforce compulsory heterosexuality, are turned upside-down in the normative understanding of that initiation. What in fact disempowers women is refigured as their empowerment and hence also as men's justification for their forceful 'resistance' to that power. As a consequence, MacKinnon continues, "Consent in this model becomes more a metaphysical quality of a woman's being than a choice she makes and communicates. Exercise of women's so-called power presupposes more fundamental social powerlessness" (1989, 175).

Criseyde's consent?

Let's now examine *Troilus and Criseyde*'s most pivotal moment of consent – if consent is what it is – in this light. In the lead-up to their sexual encounter, Criseyde has repeatedly verbalized her desire not to have a sexual relationship with Troilus and, that evening specifically, not even to meet with him. She insists to Pandarus, when he sneaks into her room and awakens her, that she will see Troilus only the next morning. (Pandarus, as we know, has falsely told her that Troilus has only just arrived, and he is at that very moment concealing Troilus right behind him.) What finally pushes Criseyde into paralyzing confusion ("dulcarnoun") is Pandarus's repeated, vehement assertions that Troilus's life is in jeopardy. Criseyde – by being pronounced the cause of Troilus's desire, suffering, and jealously, and also the sole holder of the power of his salvation – becomes convinced that she is performing a kind of violence against him, which is to say against a member of the royal family upon which she depends for protection. A few moments later, as a result of Pandarus's quick thinking, she finds herself in bed with this man, who is unconscious, stripped nearly naked, and possibly because of her about to die, as Pandarus says and she now believes. Pandarus prods her to pull "out the thorn/That stiketh in his herte" (3.1104–5). She complies, eventually succeeding at reviving Troilus with her kisses, at which point Pandarus steps away with the candle, leaving them in bed in the dark.

At Criseyde's urging, Troilus, lying, explains the cause of his supposed jealousy, which is to say, the false pretenses that have placed him in bed with her. She forgives him for the jealousy that he never actually possessed and then also asks for his forgiveness for any "smerte" (5.1182) or pain that she has caused him. This tipping of the balance of power seems to supply the cue for which Troilus was waiting, as he suddenly swerves from passivity to aggression. The narrator tells us that Troilus is "sodeinly avised" or determined, and "He hire in armes faste to him hente" (5.1186–87): he seizes Criseyde tightly in his arms. Pandarus, going to sleep somewhere close by, mutters dryly, "If ye be wise,/Swouneth nought now" (5.1189–90); that is, now is no time to faint, Troilus. To underscore the scene's male predation, the narrator provides the editorializing metaphor, "What mighte or may the sely larke [innocent or vulnerable skylark] saye/Whan that the sperhawk [sparrowhawk] hath him in his foot?" (3.1191–92). He then moves on to the moment of consent (which, like this entire scene, is original to Chaucer):

Criseyde, which that felte hire thus ytake* –	felt herself taken
As writen clerkes in hir bookes olde[2] –	
Right as an aspes leef* she gan to quake,*	aspen leaf; began to tremble

Whan she him felte hire* in his armes folde.	felt herself
But Troilus, al hool* of cares colde,*	healed; cold distress[3]
Gan thanken tho* the blisful goddes sevene.*	then; the seven planetary gods
Thus sondry paines* bringen folk to hevene.	various pains or `distresses
This Troilus in armes gan hire straine,*	began to bind or constrain her
And saide, "O sweete, as ever mote I gon,*	may I thrive
Now be ye caught. Now is ther but we twaine.*	two
Now yeldeth* you, for other boote is noon."*	yield, surrender; there is no other remedy
To that Criseyde answerde thus anon,*	immediately
"Ne hadde I er* now, my sweete herte deere,	Had I not before
Been yolde,* ywis,* I were now nought here."	Been yielded, surrendered; in fact

(3.1198–1211)

No few Chaucer scholars have queried the nature and indeed the existence of the consent depicted in these lines.[4] The passage repeatedly emphasizes that Troilus makes use of physical force, including twice noting, from Criseyde's point of view, how she "felte" constrained. Troilus's verbal expression of desire for sex is not so much a request as the demand of someone who has physically overwhelmed his target ("Now be ye caught"). It's akin to when a victorious knight puts the point of his sword against the throat of his fallen opponent and declares, "Now yeldeth you." As this analogy underscores, the verb *yield*, which both Troilus and Criseyde use, is not precisely equivalent to *consent*, despite their overlapping sets of meanings, with degree of coercion one of the factors that separate them. Significantly, when Criseyde finally speaks, she quite strikingly formulates her verbal yielding in the past tense and passive mood. She does not yield to Troilus here, but instead, she says, she has *already been yielded*, and, if that condition did not hold, she would not be where she is now.

Readers may understandably be prompted to wonder exactly who it was who yielded her and when that yielding occurred. From the preceding discussion of Rich's and MacKinnon's arguments and the many ways that Criseyde's situation exemplifies them, one ready (if complicated) answer presents itself. Ultimately, her yielding had always already been accomplished by the collective coercive force of the structural imperatives of patriarchal society and its concomitant compulsory heterosexuality, with their accompanying threats and actual acts of violence, as focalized most immediately in her uncle's manipulations. From this perspective, Criseyde's choice here, as argued by Rich and MacKinnon about women's plight more generally, is no choice at all.

To be sure, in the scenes that follow, Criseyde appears truly to love Troilus. She is at times blissfully happy and seems to enjoy their sexual relationship. And well before this pivotal moment, the narrator unambiguously indicates that the desire between them is not wholly one-sided. Criseyde, albeit only to herself, recognizes her attraction to Troilus, even while seeking to put limits on their relationship. To acknowledge these elements of mutuality and joy, however, is simply to recognize that patriarchal social structures do not necessarily preclude some measure of female desire, happiness, and satisfaction. That these may not endure is a source of sadness but not the tragedy that the poem ultimately records. When examined through the lens of Rich's and MacKinnon's arguments, that tragedy is not merely the fall from the happy state at the midpoint of the story, not simply the inevitable turning of fortune's wheel, as some of the poem's own commentary and medieval literary theory in general would have it. Rather, the tragedy is that the same condition, as verbalized by Criseyde to Troilus, of having always already been yielded will necessarily continue to hold when she is handed over to the Greeks.

As becomes evident in her exchange for Antenor, Criseyde had always already been yielded to the political authority of the Trojan parliament, among other patriarchal structures. In the Greek camp, the flag has changed but the condition remains the same, and thus she finds herself always already yielded to whatever patriarchal political authority reigns there. That authority is most immediately embodied for her by Diomede, the man who leads the party that brings her into the camp. He, just like Troilus, combines the promise of political protection with courtly attraction to her. For this reason, Diomede's 'seduction' of Criseyde, as again numerous Chaucer scholars have noted, uncannily seems to reenact (albeit more rapidly) Troilus's and Pandarus's seduction of Books 1–3, and, in fact, Diomede is in a sense a conflation of those two characters. Criseyde's 'abandonment' of Troilus is therefore an inevitable consequence of the changing of the flags. For Criseyde, this 'seduction'/'abandonment' is a reiteration of a basic structural condition that she cannot escape, a repetition of the same. Hence, the tragedy compassed by the poem is the tragic condition of women within patriarchy generally, which becomes doubly tragic with the knowledge that, as Criseyde realizes in Book 5, women will be blamed for their choices that are not in fact choices. Or the tragedy is that for a brief moment in the second half of Book 3, Criseyde and Troilus believe that they can rise above this tragic condition.

Free will

This understanding of *Troilus and Criseyde* might conceivably inspire an activist feminist response, a call to overturn the continued tragic condition of women in today's patriarchal societies. Yet at the same time, it has some rather bleak potential implications. Pursued further, its logical trajectory may lead to the conclusion that it's not just Criseyde's supposed consent to Troilus and then to Diomede that is an illusion but also any agency whatsoever that she – or any other human being – seems to possess. The grim insinuation of the poem may be that Criseyde's plight exemplifies not just that of women but also the general principle that human life consists merely of mechanistically playing out the cards that we are dealt and that we are more deluded the more we believe that any of our actions matter. The scenes of Criseyde's consent focalize this more general question of human agency, or, to use the term that Chaucer would readily recognize, the question of free will.

The determination of whether or not there is authentic consent in these scenes, as well as in any given situation, obviously depends upon the assumption that there do exist situations in which humans make freely chosen decisions about their own destiny. If all our choices are somehow coerced, the question of whether or not we 'consent' is nonsensical. This very concern is the topic of Troilus's long Book 4 speech on free will. Here, the coercion in question is that of God's Providence, or the still-debated problem of how to reconcile God's certain foreknowledge of everything that will happen with the notion that it is our choices that make things happen that wouldn't otherwise. Through the ages, philosophers, theologians, and other thinkers – including Boethius, Chaucer's source for this passage – have offered various and competing arguments for this reconciliation. In lieu of attempting to summarize these arguments, I'll just suggest that for me and many others, they all require some amount of a leap of faith, which is to say, they all leave room for doubt. By concluding Troilus's meditation before the argument that Boethius goes on to propose, Chaucer gives that doubt the last word. In this way, he has situated Criseyde's plight – her coercion by the structures of patriarchal society – within an encompassing cosmos in which the structures of divine creation are irresistibly and inevitably determining of human action. Although the absolute beneficence usually also attributed to God makes the term *coercion* feel perhaps too hostile of a descriptor for this determination, the effect is the same: human choice is no choice at all. We are all Criseyde.

In our more secular historical era, of course, the potential erasure of free will by God's Providence is not as widespread a concern. Nonetheless, modernity has formulated its own versions of the problem. Alongside specifically feminist accounts of coercion, such as Rich's and MacKinnon's, modern theorists have developed general models of human action and selfhood that in effect replace the role of God's Providence with social, political, economic, and cultural forces, which operate together to ensure that human individuals reproduce the very structures that constrain them.

Michel Foucault, for example, in his famous 1975 book *Discipline and Punish*, depicts a world in which what we believe to be our selfhood, our interior agency of self-determination, has been in fact produced by the exterior force of what he calls *discipline*, to which we are subject from birth to death, in hospitals, schools, places of employment, etc. To crudely paraphrase his complex argument: from the moment we are born, we are in myriad ways ceaselessly told what to do and say, and thus when we believe we are making free choices, we are actually just doing what we are told – even when, perhaps especially when, we think we are not.

This view may seem counterintuitive in respect to our everyday experiences of making choices – say, to have a second cup of coffee, as I've just done. Yet every such choice has a constellation of motivations, the sources for which ultimately lie outside of me and connect to social and economic institutions, cultural norms, etc. Those external forces in turn function as constraints on the kinds of motivations that I may have in the first place and the sort of actions I may take. If we were magically supplied with a comprehensive view of everything implicated in even such mundane decisions, we might be surprised by how little freedom seems left in our supposedly free choices. If everything that we are has been somehow imposed upon us, from our DNA to our knowledge to the objects of our desire, in what meaningful way can we affirm that we possess uncoerced agency?

As with the problem of Providence and free will, this secular version of the question of human agency has received many answers, whose very number and complexity suggest that the question is not an easy one to solve. For this chapter's purposes, we may understand *Troilus and Criseyde* as Chaucer's attempt to tackle a fourteenth-century version of this question by way of exploring the greater significance of Criseyde's plight. As much as that plight vividly illustrates the coercions of patriarchal society that Rich and MacKinnon analyze so well, Chaucer's inquiry does not stop there. It continues on to face up to what may be the more general implications of Rich's and MacKinnon's arguments, in which not just women but all human beings, even those who hold great political power, are intractably subject to coercive forces.

Belief, culpability, and Criseyde

What it means to face up to these implications becomes especially evident in Criseyde's internal struggle over her course of action not long after arriving in the Greek camp. Having imagined before – self-deludingly, she now realizes – a range of actions that she might take to return to Troy, she's now acutely aware of the forces that constrain her. Specifically, she knows now that her "fader" (5.694) will never permit her to go, that the Greek guards will likely catch her and condemn her as "a spye" (5.703) if she tries to escape, and that if she does somehow evade them, a "wreeche" (5.705) or predatory man, encountering her without male protection on her way to Troy, would likely rape and/or murder her. Nevertheless, for the moment, she resolves to flee to Troy, "bitide what bitide" (5.750), that is, come what may.

She doesn't flee, of course, although throughout the conversation that she has with Diomede on the very day she promised to return, she seems to be arranging matters to serve either choice. By stating her willingness to talk to him the next day and expressing her lack of interest in love and yet also her awareness that circumstances may alter that, she puts him off in a way that will facilitate her flight (as he won't expect and hence try to prevent it, and her promise to see him then won't matter) as well as her remaining in the camp (as her vague encouragement keeps him a needed ally). Nevertheless, her circumstances do not allow her to keep both options open for long. Criseyde goes to bed that evening, the narrator tells us,

> Returning* in hir soule ay up and down — Revolving, i.e., meditating upon
> The wordes of this sodein* Diomede, — unexpected
> His grete estat,* and peril of the town,* — high social status; i.e., Troy
> And that she was allone and hadde neede
> Of frendes help; and thus bigan to breede
> The cause why – the soothe for to telle –
> That she took fully purpos for to dwelle.* — remain
> (5.1023–29)

Is this choice freely made? Even without the lens of Rich's and MacKinnon's arguments, we may readily spot numerous coercions, many of them identified by Criseyde herself, and so we might answer negatively. She will not be granted permission to leave by anyone with the authority to do so. The consequences attending her then illicit flight would be, she surmises, horrific and probably fatal, and we have no reason to doubt her estimation of their likelihood. Her situation may be justly compared with that of the bank teller with a gun to their head.

Nonetheless, Criseyde herself seems to believe that she is in fact choosing. She has carefully thought through the pros and cons and the relative probability of various outcomes and then "took fully purpos" – made up her mind. If Criseyde here exemplifies not just women's plight but that of humanity generally, then Chaucer's explanation for our stubborn sense of free will, despite our dwelling in a cosmos that denies that in its very structure, is that we *choose to believe* that we do have agency, even when fully aware of the forces that are determining our choices. Our selfhood – our sense of an interiority not reducible to exterior forces – is the "soule" that we necessarily become aware of when we choose, like Criseyde does here, to meditate upon choices that aren't really choices. If this is a delusion, it's paradoxically a freely chosen one and one that we share with each other.

As a necessary consequence of so believing our choices are free, we must accept that we may be held responsible for them, even when in fact we could not do otherwise, or, as Criseyde puts it a bit later, "see ther is no bettre way" (5.1069). The belief in free will makes moral accountability possible and hence also principles of justice. It's what enables us to make moral and legal distinctions between the respective actions of bank teller and bank robber, both of which are otherwise integral to the crime of theft. This consequence, too, Criseyde exemplifies. While she bemoans the infamy and hatred her choice will bring her and, most of all, the pain to Troilus that it will cause, she does not suggest that the former is undeserved and the latter is unintended. Again paradoxically, the very injustice of blaming Criseyde for what is, in effect, her own victimization at the hands of patriarchal forces is inseparable from the belief that makes justice per se comprehensible – the belief in free will that Criseyde enacts and hence models for us.

Ideals and the meaning of life

As *Troilus and Criseyde* further suggests, these paradoxes incur dreadful costs. The example of Criseyde indicates that insofar as women's subjection to patriarchy epitomizes humanity's more general subjection to universal coercive forces, the paradox of women's culpability for their own victimization makes women a kind of scapegoat for the problem of free will. In addition, and even more generally, in her reimagination of coercion as choice, Criseyde illustrates how that paradox may entail obliteration of the kinds of ideals that for many human beings make life worth living.

This topic – in simple terms, the value, purpose, or meaning of life – is one that concerns Chaucer over the course of his writing career. In this book's Introduction, I define the topic as an inquiry into the relations between our basic material existence, our physical life, and those nonmaterial ideas, ideals, and values that shape our experience of that existence – our grasp of what we're living for, the principles that underlie the struggles of our material existence. *Troilus and Criseyde* plainly examines one such ideal that has been perennially supplied as an answer to this inquiry, which is, in its most cliché phrasing, true love. According to *Troilus and Criseyde*, this ideal consists of the belief that two people may mutually, freely, and wholly agree to commit themselves to one another romantically and erotically and thereby achieve a permanent, life-affirming depth of intimacy and satisfaction and accompanying self-knowledge that transcends whatever coercions led to and extend from that moment of commitment. This, at least, is what both Criseyde and Troilus seem to believe they have achieved in the second half of Book 3. In a happier sort of paradox, something authentic seems to be born from the delusions that enable it, and this authenticity then makes those delusions bearable, if not necessarily also justifiable.

When Criseyde makes the decision to believe that she is freely choosing Diomede over Troilus, she at the very least destroys the supposed permanence of this ideal of love. More darkly, the decision may also suggest that her earlier choice to commit to Troilus was in the final analysis not fundamentally different from this later one, and thus the ideal's core notion of an authenticity that transcends delusion was itself a delusion. For Troilus, his eventual acknowledgment of the first, lesser consequence is by itself more than he can bear. He doesn't really even entertain the darker consequence. Rather, he insists that his now one-sided commitment remains permanent, and – by repeatedly throwing himself into battle – he finally enacts the belief that he has avowed since he was struck by Cupid's arrow: that life without the fulfilment of true love is not worth living. In contrast, precisely because Criseyde can bear the weight of the darker consequence, she also carries the weight of the blame for the ideal's collapse back into the delusion from which it arose.

Intriguingly, as much as this makes her yet again a scapegoat, it also models for us a way to keep living in a world in which our belief that we have agency, and so have something to live for, is constantly threatened by evidence importing otherwise. To be sure, Pandarus and Diomede also constitute such a model, and in fact Criseyde's differences from them are what convey the affirmative qualities of her model. For Pandarus and Diomede, belief in human agency rests upon the assumption that domination of others, often by way of deluding them, is the reality of human existence, the ultimate purpose of human life in the physical world. This view is one that Chaucer considers in various ways across his writings, very often as a foil to a view that emphasizes, like Troilus's does, the ascendance of some kind of transcendent purpose. In contrast to both of these alternatives, with Criseyde Chaucer paints a portrait of how we may sincerely continue to act *as if* we have agency, and *as if* there continue to be ideals worth living for, while knowingly playing the cards that we're dealt in a game stacked against us. Or, in other words, if Troilus illustrates the consequences of maintaining good faith in a fallen ideal, and Pandarus and Diomede illustrate the bad faith practice of weaponizing that ideal, then Criseyde illustrates how life may be lived by embracing the paradox that one's recognition of an ideal as fallen does not preclude one's acting ingenuously as if it hasn't.

The sheer perplexities of this paradox as it emerges in Book 5 perhaps help to explain why in the final stanzas of the poem Chaucer seems to reject everything that has come before. The poem's pagan characters, its focus on earthly, romantic love, its depiction of a woman's betrayal: toward all of this he directs, in what seems unmistakably his own, authorial voice, regret and even some contempt. As many scholars have felt, it's difficult to believe that the sheer categorical comprehensiveness of this rejection is entirely sincere. If it were, the proper response would seem to be for Chaucer to destroy the poem rather than, as he is instead doing in this very moment, place the finishing touches upon it. At the same time, it seems impossible to suppose that the heartfelt Christian piety that he expresses in his own voice in these stanzas is anything but sincere. Even if he (and his deeply Christian culture) were capable of what would be, if these lines are facetious, unmitigated blasphemy, such oblique, poisonous irony would be unfathomably out of step with the project at hand, not to mention likely illegible to any of his contemporary readers.

Instead, then, we may better understand the self-cancelling palinode that ends the poem as Chaucer's own adaptation of Criseyde's paradoxical model for living in the world. The palinode declares that the ideal of freely chosen love seemingly realized in Book 3 is a delusion, and it gives voice to the superior ideal of the freely chosen love of God, the ideal upon which everything in Chaucer's Christian culture depended. But then Chaucer's manifest decision to retain the entirety of the lengthy poem that precedes this ending Christian negation of it – and boastfully to envision himself among past poetic greats for writing it – expresses his choice nonetheless to continue to believe, if not exactly in the love exemplified in Book 3, at least in the value of creating a literary monument to those who did so believe.

"Here taketh the makere of this book his leve" – the Retraction of the *Canterbury Tales*

Chaucer leaves to his readers to decide whether he can really have his cake and eat it too in this way. And over the course of more than six centuries, readers have, in one form or another, debated this question in respect to this moment and several other, similar ones across his writings. Indeed, he hauls out this strategy one last time in the so-called Retraction of the *Canterbury Tales*, which, as its actual rubric quoted above indicates, terminates that work. In this instance, in an authorial voice of deep Christian piety, Chaucer rejects and begs forgiveness for almost all of his prior writings. He proceeds to itemize these, which include among others most of the *Canterbury Tales* ("thilke [those] that souen into [are conducive of] sinne" [17]), "the book of Troilus" (14), and the dream visions. Obviously, since all these writings survive (except for the mysterious "book of the Leoun" [18]), this rejection did not entail his actual destruction of them. Rather, we might suspiciously point out, this supposed retraction also ably serves, if ironically so, as a self-congratulating advertisement of the many accomplishments of his writing career. Similar to how *Troilus and Criseyde* concludes with a paradoxically self-rejecting, self-congratulating palinode, this later boastful retraction, Chaucer's final palinode, occupies the place of honor at its respective work's end. Chaucer bids farewell with an ambiguously profound wink, one that is perhaps morally dubious, spiritually questionable, and/or puckishly vain. Nonetheless, having arrived at the end of this present book, if you are in any way grateful that it enabled him to preserve writings that he seems to believe he had reason to destroy, then I have done my job.

Notes

1 My run-through of the five books is indebted to Jenni Nuttall's (2012) detailed summary of and informative commentary on the entire poem.
2 That is, Chaucer, lying, indicates that this scene comes from his sources.
3 That is, his death-like fainting but also more generally the distress from the formerly 'chilly' reception from Criseyde.
4 This chapter has especially benefited from the discussions of Aers 1979; Fradenburg 1992; Cannon 2000; Robertson 2001; Slayton 2019; and Somerset 2021.

Essential Resources

Resources I've used throughout

- Correale, Robert M., and Mary Hamel, editors. *Sources and Analogues of the Canterbury Tales*. Vols. 1 and 2. D. S. Brewer, 2002, 2005.
- Douay-Rheims bible online (English translation of the Latin Vulgate). https://www.drbo.org/.
- Middle English Dictionary Online. http://quod.lib.umich.edu/m/med/.
- *The Riverside Chaucer*. Edited by Larry D. Benson, 3rd ed., Houghton Mifflin Company, 1987.

Other exceptionally useful resources

- Annotated Online Chaucer bibliography. https://chaucer.lib.utsa.edu/items/search.
- Harvard's Geoffrey Chaucer Website. https://chaucer.fas.harvard.edu/.
- New Chaucer Society compilation of online resources. https://newchaucersociety.org/page/resources.
- The Open Access Companion to the *Canterbury Tales*. https://opencanterburytales.dsl.lsu.edu/.

DOI: 10.4324/9781003273318-10

Works Cited

Aers, David. 1979. "Criseyde: Woman in Medieval Society." *The Chaucer Review* 13 (3): 177–200.

Aers, David. 1986. *Chaucer*. Brighton: Harvester Press.

Agamben, Giorgio. 1998. *Homo Sacer: Sovereign Power and Bare Life*. Translated by Daniel Heller-Roazen. Stanford: Stanford University Press.

Althusser, Louis. 2001. *Lenin and Philosophy and Other Essays*. Translated by Ben Brewster. New York: Monthly Review Press.

Anzaldúa, Gloria. 1987. *Borderlands/La Frontera: The New Mestiza*. San Francisco: Aunt Lute Books.

Arendt, Hannah. 1965. *On Revolution*. London: Penguin Books.

Arner, Lynn. 2013. *Chaucer, Gower, and the Vernacular Rising: Poetry and the Problem of the Populace After 1381*. University Park: Pennsylvania State University Press.

Attridge, Derek. 2015. *The Work of Literature*. Oxford: Oxford University Press.

Baechle, Sarah, and Carissa M. Harris. 2021. "The Ethical Challenge of Chaucerian Scholarship in the Twenty-First Century." *The Chaucer Review* 56 (4): 311–21.

Barrington, Candace. 2021. "Entente." In *A New Companion to Critical Thinking on Chaucer*, edited by Stephanie L. Batkie, Matthew W. Irvin, and Lynn Shutters, 43–58. Leeds: Arc Humanities Press.

Bhabha, Homi K. 1994. *The Location of Culture*. London: Routledge.

Bloom, Harold. 1994. *The Western Canon: The Books and School of the Ages*. New York: Harcourt Brace & Company.

Butler, Judith. 1990. *Gender Trouble: Feminism and the Subversion of Identity*. New York: Routledge.

Cannon, Christopher. 2000. "Chaucer and Rape: Uncertainty's Certainties." *Studies in the Age of Chaucer* 22: 67–92.

Cawsey, Kathy. 2020. *Images of Language in Middle English Vernacular Writings*. Woodbridge, Suffolk: D.S. Brewer.

Chaucer, Geoffrey. 2000. *The Canterbury Tales: Complete*. Edited by Larry D. Benson. Boston: Houghton Mifflin.

Chaucer, Geoffrey. 2006. *Troilus and Criseyde*. Edited by Stephen A. Barney. New York: W. W. Norton.

Chaucer, Geoffrey. 2024. *The Oxford Chaucer*. Vols. 1 and 2. Edited by Christopher Cannon and James Simpson. Oxford: Oxford University Press.

Colley, John. 2021. "Chaucer's 'Ebrayk Josephus' and *The House of Fame*." *Studies in the Age of Chaucer* 43: 45–74.

Collins, Suzanne. 2008. *The Hunger Games*. New York: Scholastic Press.

Coole, Diana, and Samantha Frost. 2010. "Introducing the New Materialisms." In *New Materialisms: Ontology, Agency, and Politics*, edited by Diana Coole and Samantha Frost, 1–43. Durham: Duke University Press.

Corber, Robert J., and Stephen Valocchi. 2003. "Introduction." In *Queer Studies: An Interdiciplinary Reader*, edited by Robert J. Corber and Stephen Valocchi, 1–16. Malden: Wiley-Blackwell.

Crane, Susan. 1994. *Gender and Romance in Chaucer's Canterbury Tales*. Princeton: Princeton University Press.

Crocker, Holly A. 2024. "Reconsidering the Subject." *Studies in the Age of Chaucer* 46: 211–20.

Derrida, Jacques. 1976. *Of Grammatology*. Translated by Gayatri Chakravorty Spivak. Baltimore: Johns Hopkins University Press.

Desmond, Marilynn. 1994. *Reading Dido: Gender, Textuality, and the Medieval Aeneid*. Minneapolis: University of Minnesota Press.

Dinshaw, Carolyn. 1989. *Chaucer's Sexual Poetics*. Madison: University of Wisconsin Press.

Dinshaw, Carolyn. 1995. "Chaucer's Queer Touches/A Queer Touches Chaucer." *Exemplaria* 7 (1): 75–92.

Dumitrescu, Irina. 2017. "Beautiful Suffering and the Culpable Narrator in Chaucer's *Legend of Good Women*." *The Chaucer Review* 52 (1): 106–23.

Foucault, Michel. 1977. *Discipline and Punish: The Birth of the Prison*. Translated by Alan Sheridan. New York: Pantheon Books.

Fradenburg, Louise O. 1992. "'Our Owen Wo to Drynke': Loss, Gender, and Chivalry in *Troilus and Criseyde*." In *Chaucer's Troilus and Criseyde: "Subgit to Alle Poesye": Essays in Criticism*, edited by R. A. Shoaf, 86–106. Binghamton: Medieval & Renaissance Texts & Studies.

Gates, Henry Louis, Jr. 1992. *Loose Canons: Notes on the Culture Wars*. Oxford: Oxford University Press.

Girard, René. 1965. *Deceit, Desire, and the Novel: Self and Other in Literary Structure*. Translated by Yvonne Freccero. Baltimore: Johns Hopkins Press.

Hansen, Elaine Tuttle. 1992. *Chaucer and the Fictions of Gender*. Berkeley: University of California Press.

Harris, Carissa M. 2018. *Obscene Pedagogies: Transgressive Talk and Sexual Education in Late Medieval Britain*. Ithaca: Cornell University Press.

Harris, Carissa M. 2024. "Rape and Justice in the *Wife of Bath's Tale*." In *Open Access Companion to the Canterbury Tales*. https://opencanterburytales.dsl.lsu.edu/wobt1/.

Heng, Geraldine. 2003. *Empire of Magic: Medieval Romance and the Politics of Cultural Fantasy*. New York: Columbia University Press.

Heng, Geraldine. 2018. *The Invention of Race in the European Middle Ages*. Cambridge, UK: Cambridge University Press.

Heng, Geraldine. 2019. *England and the Jews: How Religion and Violence Created the First Racial State in the West*. Cambridge, UK: Cambridge University Press.

Hines, Jessica. 2022. "'The Pitous Pite Deserveth': Justice, Violence, and Pity in the Prioress's Tale and 'The Jew and the Pagan.'" *Exemplaria* 34 (2): 130–47.

Howe-Warnky, Serena. 2021. "'Charitable and Trewe': Multiplicity, Prudence, and Pity in the Prologue of Chaucer's *Legend of Good Women*." *The Chaucer Review* 56 (3): 258–79.

Innocent III, Pope. 1978. *De Miseria Condicionis Humane*. Edited by Robert E. Lewis. Athens: University of Georgia Press.

Irigaray, Luce. 1985. *This Sex Which Is Not One*. Translated by Catherine Porter and Carolyn Burke. Ithaca: Cornell University Press.

Johnson, Hannah, and Heather Blurton. 2017. *The Critics and the Prioress: Antisemitism, Criticism, and Chaucer's Prioress's Tale*. Ann Arbor: University of Michigan Press.

Kirk, Jordan. 2021. *Medieval Nonsense: Signifying Nothing in Fourteenth-Century England*. New York: Fordham University Press.

Lampert-Weissig, Lisa. 2021. "The Wasps' Nest: Antisemitism, Conspiracy Theory, and the Prioress's Tale." *Studies in the Age of Chaucer* 43: 111–49.

Lavezzo, Kathy. 2017. "Protest, Complaint, and Uprising in the *Miller's* Tale." In *Open Access Companion to the Canterbury Tale*. https://opencanterburytales.dsl.lsu.edu/milt1/.

Levine, Caroline. 2015. *Forms: Whole, Rhythm, Hierarchy, Network*. Princeton: Princeton University Press.

Lipton, Emma. 2019. "Contracts, Activist Feminism, and the *Wife of Bath's Tale*." *The Chaucer Review* 54 (3): 335–51.

Lochrie, Karma. 2005. *Heterosyncrasies: Female Sexuality When Normal Wasn't*. Minneapollis: University of Minnesota Press.

MacKinnon, Catharine A. 1989. *Toward a Feminist Theory of the State*. Cambridge, MA: Harvard University Press.

Mann, Jill. 1973. *Chaucer and Medieval Estates Satire: The Literature of Social Classes and the General Prologue to the Canterbury Tales*. Cambridge, UK: Cambridge University Press.

Mattison, J. R. 2024. "The *Prioress's Tale* and *La France Juive*: Chaucer in Nineteenth-Century French Antisemitism." *The Chaucer Review*, 59 (3): 316–40.

McRuer, Robert. 2002. "Compulsory Able-Bodiedness and Queer/Disabled Existence." In *Disability Studies: Enabling the Humanities*, edited by Sharon L. Snyder, Brenda Jo Brueggemann, and Rosemarie Garland-Thomson, 88–99. New York: Modern Language Association of America.

Meyer-Lee, Robert J. 2013. "Abandon the Fragments." *Studies in the Age of Chaucer* 35: 47–83.

Meyer-Lee, Robert J. 2023. *The Problem of Literary Value*. Manchester: Manchester University Press.

Miles, Laura Saetveit, and Diane Watt. 2020. "Introduction: Women's Literary Culture and the Medieval English Canon: Gender and Genre." *Studies in the Age of Chaucer* 42: 285–93.

Minnis, Alastair. 2003. "Chaucer and the Queering Eunuch." *New Medieval Literatures* 6: 107–28.

Minnis, Alastair. 2008. *Fallible Authors: Chaucer's Pardoner and Wife of Bath*. Philadelphia: University of Pennsylvania Press.

Minnis, Alastair. 2016. *From Eden to Eternity: Creations of Paradise in the Later Middle Ages*. Philadelphia: University of Pennsylvania Press.

Mukherjee, Ankhi. 2014. *What Is a Classic? Postcolonial Rewriting and Invention of the Canon*. Stanford: Stanford University Press.

Norako, Leila K. 2024. "Reading the *Prioress's Tale* as Recovery Romance, or The Tale of a Prioress, a Sniper, and the Cross-Temporal Weaponization of Empathy." *The Chaucer Review* 59 (3): 367–86.

Nuttall, Jenni. 2012. *Troilus and Criseyde: A Reader's Guide*. Cambridge, UK: Cambridge University Press.

Open Access Companion to the Canterbury Tales, edited by Candace Barrington, Brantley L. Bryant, Richard H. Godden, Daniel T. Kline, and Myra Seaman. https://opencanterburytales.dsl.lsu.edu/.

Orlemanski, Julie. 2019. *Symptomatic Subjects: Bodies, Medicine, and Causation in the Literature of Late Medieval England.* Philadelphia: University of Pennsylvania Press.

Otaño Gracia, Nahir I. 2020. "Borders and the Global North Atlantic: Chaucer, Pilgrimage, and Crusade." *English Language Notes* 58 (2): 35–49.

Page, Judith W. 2000. "'Nor yet Redeemed from Scorn': Wordsworth and the Jews." *Journal of English and Germanic Philology* 99: 537–54.

Patterson, Lee. 1991. *Chaucer and the Subject of History.* Madison: University of Wisconsin Press.

Pearsall, Derek. 1985. *The Canterbury Tales.* London: Routledge.

Pramaggiore, Maria. 2013. "Queer Theory." In *Oxford Bibliographies* in Cinema and Media Studies. https://www.oxfordbibliographies.com/view/document/obo-9780199791286/obo-9780199791286-0185.xml.

Rich, Adrienne. 1980. "Compulsory Heterosexuality and Lesbian Existence." *Signs* 5 (4): 631–60.

Ripplinger, Michelle. 2023. "Chaucer's Proleptic Palinode." *Studies in the Age of Chaucer* 45: 139–69.

Robertson, Elizabeth. 2001. "Public Bodies and Psychic Domains: Rape, Consent, and Female Subjectivity in Geoffrey Chaucer's *Troilus and Criseyde.*" In *Representing Rape in Medieval and Early Modern Literature*, edited by Elizabeth Robertson and Christine M. Rose, 281–310. New York: Palgrave.

Robertson, Kellie. 2008. "Medieval Things: Materiality, Historicism, and the Premodern Object." *Literature Compass* 5 (6): 1060–80.

Robertson, Kellie. 2017. *Nature Speaks: Medieval Literature and Aristotelian Philosophy.* Philadelphia: University of Pennsylvania Press.

Roger, Euan. 2022. "Appendix 2. Transcriptions and Translations." *Chaucer Review* 57 (4): 440–49.

Roger, Euan, and Sebastian Sobecki. 2022. "Geoffrey Chaucer, Cecily Chaumpaigne, and the Statute of Laborers: New Records and Old Evidence Reconsidered." *The Chaucer Review* 57 (4): 407–37.

Sanok, Catherine. 2001. "Reading Hagiographically: The *Legend of Good Women* and its Feminine Audience." *Exemplaria* 13 (2): 323–54.

Schibanoff, Susan. 1996. "Worlds Apart: Orientalism, Antifeminism, and Heresy in Chaucer's Man of Law's Tale." *Exemplaria: A Journal of Theory in Medieval and Renaissance Studies* 8 (1): 59–96.

Schirmer, Elizabeth. 2022. "Borderlands Chaucer." *New Chaucer Studies: Pedagogy and Profession* 3 (1): 8–18.

Schwebel, Leah. 2024. *Tropes of Engagement: Chaucer's Italian Poetics of Intertextuality.* Toronto: University of Toronto Press.

Seaman, Myra. 2007. "Teaching Chaucer's Postmodern Dream Visions." In *Approaches to Teaching Chaucer's Troilus and Criseyde and the Shorter Poems*, edited by Tison Pugh and Angela Jane Weisl, 97–100. New York: Modern Language Association of America.

Sedgwick, Eve Kosofsky. 1985. *Between Men: English Literature and Male Homosocial Desire.* New York: Columbia University Press.

Slayton, Kendra. 2019. "Tied in 'Lusty Leese': Gender and Determinism in *Troilus and Criseyde.*" *The Chaucer Review* 54 (1): 67–90.

Smith, Zadie. 2021. *The Wife of Willesden.* London: Penguin.

Solberg, Emma Margaret. 2021. "Response to '#MeToo, Medieval Literature, and Trauma-Informed Pedagogy.'" *New Chaucer Studies: Pedagogy and Profession* 2 (2): 134–53.

Somerset, Fiona. 2021. "Consent/Assent." In *A New Companion to Critical Thinking on Chaucer*, edited by Stephanie L. Batkie, Matthew W. Irvin, and Lynn Shutters, 27–41. Leeds: Arc Humanities Press.

Spector, Stephen. 1991. "Empathy and Enmity in the Prioress's Tale." In *The Olde Daunce: Love, Friendship, Sex, and Marriage in the Medieval World*, edited by Robert R. Edwards and Stephen Spector, 211–28. Albany: State University of New York Press.

Stanbury, Sarah. 2004. "Ecochaucer: Green Ethics and Medieval Nature." *The Chaucer Review* 39 (1): 1–16.

Steel, Karl. 2019. *How Not to Make a Human: Pets, Feral Children, Worms, Sky Burial, Oysters*. Minneapolis: University of Minnesota Press.

Steiner, Emily. 2017. "The *Prioress's Tale*: Relating to the Past, Imagining the Past." In *Open Access Companion to the Canterbury Tales*. https://opencanterburytales.dsl.lsu.edu/prt1/.

Swanson, R. N. 2007. *Indulgences in Late Medieval England: Passports to Paradise?* Cambridge, UK: Cambridge University Press.

Turner, Marion. 2019. *Chaucer: A European Life*. Princeton: Princeton University Press.

Turner, Marion. 2023. *The Wife of Bath: A Biography*. Princeton: Princeton University Press.

Walter, Katie L. 2018. *Middle English Mouths: Late Medieval Medical, Religious and Literary Traditions*. Cambridge, UK: Cambridge University Press.

Whitaker, Cord J. 2017. "Race and Racism in the Man of Law's Tale." In *Open Access Companion to the Canterbury Tales*. https://opencanterburytales.dsl.lsu.edu/mlt1/.

White, Hugh. 2000. *Nature, Sex, and Goodness in a Medieval Literary Tradition*. Oxford: Oxford University Press.

Wilson, Anna. 2024. "Whiteness, Innocence, and Childhood in the *Prioress's Tale* and Its Devotional Milieu." *The Chaucer Review* 59 (3): 387–408.

Windeatt, Barry. 2023. *Oxford Guides to Chaucer: Troilus and Criseyde*. 2nd ed. Oxford: Oxford University Press.

Winstead, Karen. 2024. "Thinking About (and With) the *Prioress's Tale*: From Medieval Alterity to Modern Hate Narrative." *The Chaucer Review* 59 (3): 409–24.

Wright, Sarah Breckenridge. 2020. *Mobility and Identity in Chaucer's Canterbury Tales*. Woodbridge, Suffolk: D.S. Brewer.

Index

Pages followed by "n" refer to notes.

Printed in Dunstable, United Kingdom

76357601R00134